Wai-yee Ng

Water Symbolism in John

An Eschatological Interpretation

PETER LANG
New York • Washington, D.C./Baltimore • Boston • Bern
Frankfurt am Main • Berlin • Brussels • Vienna • Oxford

Library of Congress Cataloging-in-Publication Data

Ng, Wai-yee.
Water symbolism in John: an eschatological interpretation / Wai-yee Ng.
p. cm. — (Studies in biblical literature; vol. 15)
Includes bibliographical references and index.
1. Bible. N.T. John—Criticism, interpretation, etc. 2. Water in the Bible.
3. Symbolism in the Bible. 4. Eschatology—Biblical teaching. 5. Bible.
N.T. John IV—Criticism, interpretation, etc. I. Title. II. Series.
BS2615.6.W33N4 226.5'064—DC21 99-18184
ISBN 0-8204-4453-7
ISSN 1089-0645

Die Deutsche Bibliothek-CIP-Einheitsaufnahme

Ng, Wai-yee:
Water symbolism in John: an eschatological interpretation / Wai-yee Ng.
–New York; Washington, D.C./Baltimore; Boston; Bern;
Frankfurt am Main; Berlin; Brussels; Vienna; Oxford: Lang.
(Studies in biblical literature; Vol. 15)
ISBN 0-8204-4453-7

The paper in this book meets the guidelines for permanence and durability
of the Committee on Production Guidelines for Book Longevity
of the Council of Library Resources.

Printed in the United States of America

Water Symbolism in John

Studies in Biblical Literature

Hemchand Gossai
General Editor

Vol. 15

PETER LANG
New York • Washington, D.C./Baltimore • Boston • Bern
Frankfurt am Main • Berlin • Brussels • Vienna • Oxford

ACKNOWLEDGMENTS

I am grateful to friends and colleagues at China Graduate School of Theology who have helped me in completing this work, in particular, Dr. Ronald Fung who so genuinely encouraged me to publish my dissertation, and Miss Pauline Yip who worked closely with me as a copy editor.

Gratitude is also due those at Westminster Theological Seminary, including, Dr. Moisés Silva, the friendly adviser of my research, and Miss Grace Mullen, Achivist of Montgomery Library, whose help was always gracious and dependable.

Special thanks to Dr. Mary Tse, my dear friend of many years, for being helpful to the extent of placing my interest above her own, and to my church for their prayer support. This book is dedicated to the memory of Rev. Ching-ping Seto whom I respected dearly—he died in the year I began this work.

TABLE OF CONTENTS

EDITOR'S PREFACE

More than ever the horizons in biblical literature are being expanded beyond that which is immediately imagined; important new methodological, theological, and hermeneutical directions are being explored, often resulting in significant contributions to the world of biblical scholarship. It is an exciting time for the academy as engagement in biblical studies continues to be heightened.

This series seeks to make available to scholars and institutions, scholarship of a high order, and which will make a significant contribution to the ongoing biblical discourse. This series includes established and innovative directions, covering general and particular areas in biblical study. For every volume considered for this series, we explore the question as to whether the study will push the horizons of biblical scholarship. The answer must be *yes* for inclusion.

In this volume Wai-yee Ng explores in considerable detail the water symbolism in the Gospel of John. The author argues that it is in the Gospel of John that water is used most extensively as a symbol in the New Testament. In addition to the many eschatological scenarios, Wai-yee Ng also explores a variety of other situations in which water plays an essential symbolic role. The author uses a methodological approach which might be described as a composite, recognizing literary, historical and theological components. Scholars will undoubtedly find in this volume a wealth of important information. The horizon has been expanded.

ABBREVIATIONS

AB	The Anchor Bible
AnBib	Analecta biblica
ATR	*Anglican Theological Review*
BA	*Biblical Archaeologist*
BAGD	W. Bauer, W. F. Arndt, F. W. Gingrich, and F. W. Danker, *Greek English Lexicon of the NT*
BETL	Bibliotheca ephemeridum theologicarum lovaniensium
Bib	*Biblica*
BJRL	*Bulletin of the John Rylands University Library of Manchester*
BR	*Biblical Research*
BSac	*Bibliotheca Sacra*
BT	*The Bible Translator*
BTB	*Biblical Theology Bulletin*
BZ	*Biblische Zeitschrift*
CBQ	*Catholic Biblical Quarterly*
ETL	*Ephemerides theologicae lovanienses*
EvQ	*Evangelical Quarterly*
ExpTim	*Expository Times*
FFNT	Foundations and Facets: New Testament
HeyJ	*Heythrop Journal*
HTR	*Harvard Theological Review*
IBS	*Irish Biblical Studies*
ICC	International Critical Commentary
Int	*Interpretation*
JBL	*Journal of Biblical Literature*
JETS	*Journal of the Evangelical Theological Society*
JJS	*Journal of Jewish Studies*
JSNT	*Journal for the Study of the New Testament*
JSNTSup	*JSNT* Supplement Series
JSOT	*Journal for the Study of the Old Testament*

JTS	*Journal of Theological Studies*
MTZ	*Münchener theologische Zeitschrift*
Neot	*Neotestamentica*
NICNT	New International Commentary on the New Testament
NICOT	New International Commentary on the Old Testament
NovT	*Novum Testamentum*
NovTSup	*Novt* Supplements
NTS	*New Testament Studies*
OED	*Oxford English Dictionary*
RB	*Revue biblique*
ResQ	*Restoration Quarterly*
RevExp	*Review and Expositor*
RevThom	*Revue thomiste*
RTR	*Reformed Theological Review*
SBLDS	SBL Dissertation Series
SBLMS	SBL Monograph Series
SBLSP	SBL Seminar Papers
SBT	Studies in Biblical Theology
SE	*Studia Evangelica* 1, 2, 3 (=*TU* 73 [1959], 87 [1964], 88 [1964])
SJT	*Scottish Journal of Theology*
SNTSMS	Society for New Testament Studies Monograph Series
SR	*Studies in Religion/Sciences religieuses*
ST	*Studia Theologica*
TDNT	G. Kittel and G. Friedrich (eds.), *Theological Dictionary of the New Testament*
TLZ	*Theologische Literaturzeitung*
TrinJ	*Trinity Journal*
TRu	*Theologische Rundschau*
TS	*Theological Studies*
TynBul	*Tyndale Bulletin*
TZ	*Theologische Zeitschrift*
VT	*Vetus Testamentum*
WBC	Word Biblical Commentary
WTJ	*Westminster Theological Journal*
WUNT	Wissenschaftliche Untersuchungen zum Neuen Testament
ZNW	*Zeitschrift für die neutestamentliche Wissenschaft*

INTRODUCTION

The eschatological reference of the Gospel of John has a meager appearance in comparison with that of the First Epistle of John.[1] However, while the latter has not attracted attention, the former has been "a storm center of scholarship," as noted by R. Kysar.[2] The storm began, it seems, with R. Bultmann's bringing into focus the apparent "conflict" between the present and the future eschatological sayings in the Gospel of John. Subsequent discussions have largely been attempts to account for this conflict. Bultmann's influence on the discussion has proven immense, as there is now hardly any substantial work on the subject that does not reflect some of Bultmann's original concern.

Bultmann's original concern was, basically, to investigate the gospel's literary inconsistencies historically. In Bultmann's work, as J. Ashton points out, "there is a roundedness that makes it unusually difficult of access, exemplifying as it does the so-called 'hermeneutical circle.'"[3] Ashton tries to "cut into the circle" by dealing first with Bultmann's literary questions.[4] My opinion, however, is that the circle does not begin with his work on literary questions but with his presupposition of the history of religions. Among Bultmann's various concerns, his concern for the historical remains fundamental. The historical development of the New Testament forms the basis upon which he investigates both the literary and the theological. His impact upon the study of Johannine eschatology is not only that the present and future sayings in John are now viewed as a conflict, but that a historical approach is always used in looking for an explanation. Writings on Johannine

---

1 I have earlier worked on the eschatology of First John; Wai-yee Ng, "Johannine Eschatology as Demonstrated in First John" (unpublished thesis, Westminster Theological Seminary, 1988).

2 R. Kysar, *The Fourth Evangelist and His Gospel: An Examination of Contemporary Scholarship* (Minneapolis: Augsburg Publishing House, 1975), 207.

3 J. Ashton, *Understanding the Fourth Gospel* (Oxford: Clarendon, 1991), 45.

4 Ibid., 45–50.

eschatology are, therefore, filled with theories of a historical nature: redaction, assimilation, and stories of a Johannine community. The objective has mainly been to nail down historically an origin of the particularity of Johannine eschatology. Solutions proposed may differ greatly from Bultmann's, but the program has remained basically the same.[5]

Is it not regrettable that such a program monopolizes so much of the discussion on the subject, and that we have been led to reconstruct the setting rather than comprehend Johannine eschatology itself? In this present work, instead of establishing yet another historical solution, we will take a fresh look at the literary presentation of eschatology in John, and, subsequently, its theological implications. It is not hard to see that John's eschatology is expressed in a much richer way than just the mention of future events such as judgment, resurrection and parousia. Symbolism is typical of John. Christology in John is filled with the symbolic such as the bread of life, the light of the world and the door. Likewise eschatology in John has to be studied in terms of the symbols used, such as, the water, the bread, a place in the Father's house. To miss the symbols is to miss the forest for the trees, no matter how well we analyze the inconsistencies found in John's eschatological sayings.

Here we want to work on the symbol of water in John, one that stands out as being most extensively used throughout the gospel. There is John's water baptism mentioned in chapter one, Jesus' changing of water into wine narrated in chapter two, his teaching on rebirth out of water and spirit reported in chapter three, his offering living water to the Samaritan woman recounted in chapter four, and so on. Eschatological significance can no doubt be found in some of these incidents. Jesus himself somewhat decodes this symbol in John 4:14b, "The water I give him will become in him a spring of water welling up to eternal life." Then the writer of the gospel further decodes it in 7:39, "By this he meant the spirit, whom those who believed in him were later to receive."[6] Besides these more obvious uses of the water symbol in reference to eschatology, our investigation here will

---

5 A summary of these explanations can be found in J. D. Thompson's dissertation, "An Analysis of Present and Future in the Eschatology of the Fourth Gospel, and An Examination of the Relationship between the Two" (dissertation, Emory University, 1967).

6 These passages will be interpreted later on in this work.

locate other such uses in the gospel. It will be shown that water symbolism in John as a whole bears a significant role in shaping the eschatological message of the gospel.

I am taking a composite approach in this interpretation, recognizing the literary, the historical, as well as the theological character of Johannine water symbolism. While the three, essentially speaking, should not be treated disjointedly, they will be given emphasis in three different chapters in this book. In chapter two I will survey the literary development of water symbolism throughout the gospel narrative, making exegetical notes on individual occurrences of the symbol and giving special attention to their eschatological reference. Chapter three will contain a historical study of the water symbol as used in John 4:1–42, selected here for focus because of its clear eschatological reference. I will attempt to exegete the two dialogues in the passage and reconstruct meanings of the water symbol in its historical context. In chapter four there will be a canonical treatment of the water motif, prefaced with a discussion on John's use of the Old Testament. This will expound the theological meaning of Johannine water symbolism as a whole, and hence shed light on its eschatological significance. In my expectation such a composite method will uncover the full sense of Johannine eschatology much better than traditional historical criticism.

My methodology will be further described and justified in chapter one, in which I will clarify my own definition of symbolism by first exploring the views of others. It will be seen that discussion on the subject has been difficult because of the diversity in understanding among scholars. I will, however, attempt to classify their presumed definitions of what a symbol is. From there I will locate and elaborate my own presuppositions, and those presuppositions will form the basis of the rest of my work.

CHAPTER ONE

WHAT IS MEANT BY JOHANNINE SYMBOLISM

The Gospel of John is known to be rich in the use of symbolic language. The allusive and elusive style of the gospel may be attributed partly to this use. However, what is symbolism after all? How can we define symbolism in John? Is it just a literary device, or does it involve something else? In this initial chapter we will clarify our understanding of John's "symbolism," before we proceed with John's "water" symbolism. By doing so we will set up a working definition and a methodology for the rest of this work.

A survey of scholarship is necessary here because the few scholars who have approached the topic do so from vastly different standpoints. My interaction with them will clarify my own position.

Various Expressions That Can Be Called Symbolic

Symbolism is not just one rhetorical method employed by the Evangelist, but can be associated with a number of literary skills. There is, as has been said, "a thriving variety of symbolism throughout the gospel."[1]

Metaphorical Symbolism

The first to be enumerated here should be the metaphorical kind of symbolism. This includes the standard metaphors in John such as the living water, the bread of life, and the true vine. As a literary device it is among the most noticeable ones in John. C. H. Dodd calls it the "explicit" use of symbolism, differentiating it from the synoptic parables which are to be understood in a different sense.[2] The "three core symbols" highlighted by

---

1 R. W. Paschal, Jr., "Sacramental Symbolism and Physical Imagery in the Gospel of John," *TynBul* 32 (1981): 156.

2 C. H. Dodd, *The Interpretation of the Fourth Gospel* (Cambridge: Cambridge University Press, 1953; repr., 1988), 134–35.

R. A. Culpepper, light, water, and bread, are all of this kind.[3] J. Leal classifies it as "simbolismo alegórico."[4]

In this usage, things spoken of ("vehicle") are daily things easily perceived in life, and things referred to ("tenor") are realities not so easily perceived.[5] Such realities are "revealed" by Jesus, so to speak, and this kind of symbols, as recounted in the text, were used by Jesus himself.[6] Many of these symbols are used with the 'Εγώ εἰμι formula and represent Jesus' christological claims: "I am the bread of life" (6:35), " . . . the light of the world" (8:12), ". . . the gate for the sheep" (10:7), ". . . the good shepherd" (10:11,14), ". . . the resurrection and the life" (11:25), ". . . the way and the truth and the life" (14:6), and ". . . the true vine" (15:1). So J. Painter calls them "evocative symbols."[7] G. W. MacRae calls them "christological symbols."[8]

Symbols and metaphors are related on a continuum as literary devices, but symbols have a broader application and a more expansive nature. Two recent writers on the subject note the following. First, a symbol may be more than a literary device. It "points toward something other than itself and in some way presents and represents that to which it points," L. P. Jones observes.[9] So, Jesus as the good-shepherd-Christ is indeed a good shepherd! Then, while metaphors are always verbally expressed, symbols

---

3 A. Culpepper, *Anatomy of the Fourth Gospel: A Study in Literary Design*, FFNT (Philadelphia: Fortress, 1983), 190–98.

4 J. Leal, S. J., "El simbolismo histórico del iv evangelio," *Estudios bíblicos* 19 (1960): 338.

5 "Tenor" and "vehicle" are terms coined by literary critics. See N. Friedman, *Form and Meaning in Fiction* (Athens: The University of Georgia Press, 1975), 289.

6 Discussions on the theme of "revelation" in the Gospel of John were recently revived by a literary scholar, Gail R. O'Day, who tried to supersede R. Bultmann and E. Käsemann by emphasizing the "how" of revelation. I agree with O'Day that the Johannine language is to be studied as literature for better understanding, but my focus here is on symbolism, whereas O'Day singles out "irony" as the specific literary mode of revelation. See G. R. O'Day, "Narrative Mode and Theological Claim: A Study in the Fourth Gospel," *JBL* 105 (1986): 657–66.

7 J. Painter, "John 9 and the Interpretation of the Fourth Gospel," *JSNT* 28 (1986): 46.

8 G. W. MacRae, S. J., "Theology and Irony in the Fourth Gospel," in *The Word in the World: Essays in Honor of F. L. Moriarity, S.J.*, ed. R. J. Clifford and G. W. MacRae (Cambridge, MA: Weston College Press, 1973), 93.

9 L. P. Jones, *The Symbol of Water in the Gospel of John*, JSNTSup 145 (Sheffield: Sheffield Academic Press, 1997), 14.

may be made or used in ways other than the literary. Thus, before functioning symbolically in the statement "I am the bread of life" (6:15), C. R. Koester observes, "Bread initially functions symbolically in actions like breaking five loaves" (6:11–13).[10] It can well be demonstrated in John that recurrence is what we may expect of a symbol, and, as Jones adds, "as it recurs, a symbol typically expands in meaning and that to which it points becomes more clearly defined."[11] It may be to this effect that Leal classifies it as "allegorical symbolism."

Narrative Symbolism

Another obvious use of symbolism can be found in the accounts of miracles in John, characteristically called σημεῖα. Recognition of these accounts as being symbolic is almost unanimous.[12] Leal, who classifies them as "historical symbolism," considers it "most characteristic of the Fourth Gospel."[13] Literary scholars take interest in them for their narrative nature. R. Kieffer, for example, studies them as "stage pictures."[14] Dodd is often credited as the one who first discovered the interrelation of narratives and discourses in John to be indicative of a "symbolic understanding."[15]

---

10 C. R. Koester, *Symbolism in the Fourth Gospel: Meaning, Mystery, Community* (Minneapolis: Fortress, 1995), 6–7.

11 Jones, *Symbol of Water*, 14.

12 Culpepper, *Anatomy*, 188; Dodd, *Interpretation*, 141; W. F. Howard, "Symbolism and Allegory," in *The Fourth Gospel in Recent Criticism and Interpretation*, rev. ed. C. K. Barrett (London: Epworth, 1955), 185; H. A. A. Kennedy, *Philo's Contribution to Religion* (London: Hodder & Stoughton, 1919), 46; Leal, "Symbolismo histórico," 339; R. Kieffer, "Different Levels in Johannine Imagery," in *Aspects on the Johannine Literature: Papers Presented at a Conference of Scandinavian New Testament Exegetes at Uppsala*, ed. L. Hartman and B. Olsson, Coniectanea Biblica, New Testament Series 18 (Uppsala: Almqvist & Wiksell, 1987), 74–84; MacRae, "Theology and Irony," 92–93; Painter, "John 9," 42; Paschal, "Sacramental Symbolism," 154; S. M. Schneiders, "History and Symbolism in the Fourth Gospel," in *L'Évangile de Jean: Source, rédaction, théologie*, ed. M. de Jonge, BETL 44 (Leuven: Leuven University Press, 1977), 371–76; S. M. Schneiders, "Symbolism and the Sacramental Principle in the Fourth Gospel," in *Segni e sacramenti nel Vangelo di Giovanni*, ed. P.-R. Tragan, Studia Anselmiana 66 (Rome: Editrice Anselmiana, 1977), 221–35.

13 Leal, "Simbolismo histórico," 339.

14 Kieffer, "Johannine Imagery," 80–82.

15 Dodd, *Interpretation*, 133–34. As an example, see how Paschal takes his word for granted ("Sacramental Symbolism," 154, n. 10).

Actually, as early as 1919, and before Dodd, H. A. A. Kennedy pointed out this symbolic element in John, namely, "the Evangelist's description of the typical miracles which he selects as 'signs'" and "his deliberate association of these with elaborate discussions which aim at a spiritual interpretation of them."[16]

What exactly is a symbolic understanding, or a spiritual interpretation, or how should these "signs" be decoded? There is no unified answer among scholars, for their conceptions of what a symbol is are all very different. Recent literary scholars, however, try to be precise about the meaning of "signs," and they seem to be in agreement with two points.

First, the English term "sign" in its modern sense is misleading. Whereas signs may stand arbitrarily for something other than themselves, symbols bear inherent analogical relationship to the symbolized. Thus a symbol may be universally understood, but a sign functions only among those who have learned its meaning. Symbols "evoke" their meanings, opening up minds for understanding, but signs "delimit" meanings, asking only for identification. Culpepper articulates, "the use of symbols as signs diminishes their revelatory power."[17] The following quotation from S. M. Schneiders summarizes the point.

> But whatever the reason for John's choice of σημεῖα, there is growing consensus among scholars in the semantic disciplines that "sign" and "symbol" are very different realities and that using the two terms interchangeably leads to substantial confusion. The Johannine σημεῖα are, in contemporary terms, not signs but symbols.[18]

Secondly, the narratives themselves are symbolic, not just the σημεῖα. Painter, exegeting John 9, comments that "the full symbolic interpretation is to be perceived in the completed narrative, not in the miracle story as it was in the signs source, and only in a limited way in the primary interpretation of the story."[19] Recent literary scholars have thus gone further than Dodd in making the narratives in the gospel significant for symbolic interpretation. The motivation behind this is a new principle spelt out by G. R. O'Day, namely, revelation is given not only in terms of "Dass" or

16 Kennedy, *Philo*, 46.
17 Culpepper, *Anatomy*, 182.
18 Schneiders, "Sacramental Principle," 223.
19 Painter, "John 9," 42.

"Was," but "Wie" as well, which is the narrative mode.[20] Or, in the words of W. A. Meeks, the reader's experience is "grounded in the stylistic structure of the whole document."[21] Along this same lines there is D. A. Lee's dissertation, written in 1991, "The Symbolic Narratives of the Fourth Gospel."[22] In this work a literary form, "symbolic narrative," is identified as the common pattern for six of the narratives in the gospel. The σημεῖα, along with other foundational images, are found to be "central symbols" of these narrative structures.

Double Meaning

Symbolism may sound elusive to historico-grammatical exegetes, but it would be unsound to totally ignore the use of "double meaning" in John. So D. W. Wead, who opposes the symbolic understanding of σημεῖα in John, works extensively on Johannine double meaning.[23] Wead acknowledges the double meaning of only certain words: ἄνωθεν (3:3), ὑψόω (3:14; 8:28; 12:32, 34), ἀμνὸς τοῦ θεοῦ(1:29, 36), ἀκολουθέω (1:37, 38; 6:2; 8:12), and his approach is one of semantics and historical lexicology. He pursues the alternative meanings of ἄνωθεν, the etymology of the Semitic root of ὑψόω, the sense of the Aramaic equivalent of ἀμνὸς, the figurative use of ἀκολουθέω and νύξ and so on. Evidences are exclusively historical and the conception of double meaning restrictive. Even so he has to name the secondary meaning "symbolic meaning," and he admits that we cannot deny the existence of the symbolic uses of the gospel.[24]

According to Wead, symbolic meaning occurs only "lexically" with the Evangelist's choice of words, but can we limit the case so easily? Should we overlook the double or multiple sense of ambiguous sayings and expressions? Most scholars would admit more double meaning in John than Wead does, and C. K. Barrett has, as commended, "the farthest reaching

20 O'Day, "Narrative Mode," 661–63.

21 W. A. Meeks, "Man from Heaven in Johannine Sectarianism," *JBL* 91 (1972): 69.

22 D. A. Lee-Pollard, "The Symbolic Narratives of the Fourth Gospel: The Interplay of Form and Meaning" (unpublished thesis, University of Sydney, 1991), later published in 1994 under the name D. A. Lee.

23 D. W. Wead, *The Literary Devices in John's Gospel*, Theologischen Dissertationen 4 (Basel: Friedrich Reinhardt Kommissionsverlag, 1970).

24 Ibid., 45. See also his article, "The Johannine Double Meaning," *ResQ* 13 (1970): 119–20.

influence" in searching for double meaning in John.[25] Interpretation remains controversial, of course. For example, some suggest a double meaning of καταλαμβάνω in 1:5, meaning both "to understand" and "to master."[26] Others, however, insist on only one meaning, "to receive" or "to understand."[27]

We should also locate double meaning in the Evangelist's frequent use of ambiguous sayings. For example:

> The bride belongs to the bridegroom. The friend who attends the bridegroom waits and listens for him, and is full of joy when he hears the bridegroom's voice (3:29).
>
> You are right when you say you have no husband (4:17).
>
> I have food to eat that you know nothing about (4:32).
>
> I tell you the truth, unless a kernel of wheat falls to the ground and dies, it remains only a single seed. But if it dies, it produces many seeds (12:24).
>
> Unless I wash you, you have no part with me. . . . A person who has had a bath needs only to wash his feet; his whole body is clean (13:8–10).

Such ambiguous sayings, characteristic of the Gospel of John, can be found in both narratives and speeches. Kennedy considers them part of the symbolic element of the gospel and calls them "mysterious sayings."[28] Yet the implicit meaning of these sayings is quite often explained in the text. Note the respective explanations for the above citations:

> That joy is mine, and is now complete (3:29).
>
> You have had five husbands, and the man you now have is not your husband (4:18).
>
> My food is to do the will of him who sent me and to finish his work (4:34).
>
> The man who loves his life will lose it, while the man who hates his life in this world will keep it for eternal life (12:25).
>
> You are clean, though not every one of you (13:10).

In this usage the Evangelist seems concerned about making ambiguous meanings clear. The last citation clearly indicates this. Jesus decoded briefly, "You are clean." Then he said something ambiguous again, "though not

---

25 E. Richards, "Expressions of Double Meaning and Their Function in the Gospel of John," *NTS* 31 (1985): 96–97, referring to C. K. Barrett, *The Gospel According to St. John*, 2d ed. (Philadelphia: Westminster Press, 1978).

26 Richards, "Double Meaning," 104.

27 R. Schnackenburg, *The Gospel According to St John*, 3 vols., vols. 1–2 trans. K. Smith et al. (New York: Seabury, 1980), vol. 3 trans. D. Smith and G. A. Kon (New York: Crossroad, 1982), 1:246–47.

28 Kennedy, *Philo*, 46.

every one of you." Immediately, the Evangelist explained, "For he knew who was going to betray him, and that was why he said not every one was clean" (13:11). His intention to clarify is quite clear. We may argue from here that although symbolism is by nature allusive or elusive, it is not meant to conceal, but to reveal.[29]

Misunderstanding and Irony

A more complex element of ambiguous meaning would be irony. If normally the author tends to clarify, in the case of an irony, he refrains from commenting. We find excellent examples of this in chapter seven, where there are rhetorical questions raised against Jesus' identity as Messiah. "How did this man get such learning without having studied?" (7:15) "Have the authorities really concluded that he is the Christ?" (7:26) "How can the Christ come from Galilee?" (7:41) "Has any of the rulers or of the Pharisees believed in him?" (7:48) These questions revolve around the rhetorical question, "Is he the Christ," to which the Evangelist gives no answer. But why does the Evangelist tolerate so many uncorrected objections? It is a literary effect that he makes. The questions stand for a series of contradictions between what appears to be and what really is. The victim of the irony is left confident of the former and unaware of the latter, as the author leaves the truth unspecified.[30] So, here, it is the literary effect that is meant for, rather than the ambiguity. Wead makes this comment:

> To those not expecting irony it will seem that the author is allowing the objection to stand. . . . It becomes apparent that the author is relying upon the audience to complete the argument from information that they have gained from other sources. John is relying on the fact that the audience shares his superior knowledge of the full implication of the events.[31]

The use of irony in John is more extensive than just this, and the discovery of it has made a long history. Martin Luther is noted for first

---

29 As X. Léon-Dufour says, "That is the final aim of all authentic symbolism, to open the way to communication." See Léon-Dufour, "Towards a Symbolic Reading of the Fourth Gospel," *NTS* 27 (1981): 442.

30 Cf. Culpepper, *Anatomy*, 166–67, citing D. C. Muecke, *Irony*, The Critical Idiom 13 (London: Methuen & Co., 1970), 35.

31 D. W. Wead, "Johannine Irony as a Key to the Author-Audience Relationship in John's Gospel," in *American Academy of Religion Biblical Literature: 1974*, comp. F. O. Francis (Missoula, MT: Scholars Press, 1974), 39.

spotting an irony in Pilate's question, "What is truth?"[32] (18:38). As literary analysis became popular in this century, the Fourth Evangelist has increasingly been acknowledged a "master of irony."[33] As recently as 1983, however, Culpepper noted that there had not been a monograph or a definitive article written on the subject.[34] Wead (1970) and MacRae (1973) were pioneers.[35] Then came P. D. Duke's work on "Irony in the Fourth Gospel," which Culpepper commended as "a best treatment."[36] Culpepper himself also contributes an insightful discussion.[37]

There is no consensus as to how irony is used as or related to symbolism. Culpepper treats the two as separate but related categories.[38] E. Richards equates irony with symbolic ambiguity.[39] MacRae considers all Johannine symbols "thematic irony," perceiving in irony a Johannine worldview, saying, "It is in irony that John expresses his own insight into the meaning of Christ for the world."[40] Duke also holds the same view.[41] Along the same line, O'Day considers irony the main narrative mode, which conveys theology.[42] So there are several scholars who sees irony as inclusive of all symbols. This view, however, expands the use of the term so much

---

32 O'Day, "Narrative Mode," 663, citing W. Büchner, "Über den Begriff der Eironeia," *Hermes: Zeitschrift für klassische Philologie-Einzelschriften* 76 (1941): 358.

33 Dodd, *Interpretation*, 357; and W. A. Meeks, "The Divine Agent and His Counterfeit in Philo and the Fourth Gospel," in *Aspects of Religious Propaganda in Judaism and Early Christianity*, ed. E. S. Fiorenza (Notre Dame, IN: University of Notre Dame Press, 1976), 59.

34 Culpepper, *Anatomy*, 166.

35 D. W. Wead, "Irony," chap. in *Literary Devices*, 47–68; MacRae, "Theology and Irony," 83–96. The two scholars differ in their views regarding the origin of Johannine irony. Wead identifies it strictly with Sophoclean irony ("Johannine Irony," 33–36), but MacRae specifies that it should not be identified with Sophoclean irony ("Theology and Irony," 85–86).

36 P. D. Duke, "Irony in the Fourth Gospel: The Shape and Function of a Literary Device" (Ph.D. diss., Southern Baptist Theological Seminary, 1982); later published as *Irony in the Fourth Gospel* (Atlanta: John Knox Press, 1985).

37 Culpepper, *Anatomy*, 152–65.

38 Culpepper puts "misunderstanding," "irony" and "symbolism" together under the section "Implicit Commentary," assuming a parallel relationship (ibid., 180–81).

39 Richards, "Double Meaning," 97.

40 MacRae, "Theology and Irony," 92–94; 89.

41 Duke, *Irony*, 111, quoted in Lee-Pollard, "Symbolic Narratives," 31.

42 O'Day, "Narrative Mode," 663–68.

that "it becomes almost meaningless," as Lee rightly points out.[43] We should, I think, reckon the pervasiveness of symbolism in John and note that irony is just one of the various literary devices that carry it. Both symbolism and irony involve ambiguity.

Closely related to irony is the Johannine "misunderstanding," also an interest of modern literary scholars. Symbolism is by nature ambiguous, and ambiguity causes misunderstanding, and unresolved misunderstanding becomes irony. Some of the double meaning sayings cited in the previous section appear actually in the form of misunderstanding. Whereas irony in John occurs mostly in conflicts, misunderstanding is used in dialogues between Jesus and his audience. There is an observable sequence of "ambiguity," "misunderstanding," and "clarification" in the formation of Johannine misunderstandings. The form critics have long been trying to isolate such patterned units in the text.[44] There is disagreement as to how the form is defined. Bultmann limits the form to conceptual misunderstandings, which have to do with the confusion of the heavenly and the earthly.[45] H. Leroy, who wrote an extensive work on the subject in 1968, limits the form to the ambiguity of vocabularies used in the Johannine community.[46] Culpepper considers both of them "too rigid" and expects Johannine misunderstandings to be "more artistically" developed.[47] As a result he comes up with a list of eighteen misunderstandings, whereas Leroy admits only eleven. J. C. Fenton treats misunderstandings and ironies separately and notes twelve major examples of misunderstandings between

---

43 Lee-Pollard, "Symbolic Narratives," 31.

44 J. H. Bernard, *A Critical and Exegetical Commentary on the Gospel According to St. John*, 2 vols., ICC, ed. A. H. McNeile (New York: Charles Scribner's Sons, 1929), 1:cxi; Barrett, *John*, 208; J. C. Fenton, *The Gospel According to John* (Oxford: Clarendon Press, 1970), 19; Culpepper, *Anatomy*, 152.

45 R. Bultmann, *The Gospel of John: A Commentary*, ed. G. R. Beasley-Murray, trans. R. W. N. Hoare and J. K. Riches (Philadelphia: Westminster Press, 1971), 135, n. 1. See also C. H. Dodd who also finds the closest parallels in the Shepherd of Hermas and the Hermetic literature, *Historical Tradition in the Fourth Gospel* (Cambridge: Cambridge University Press, 1963), 321, quoted in Culpepper, *Anatomy*, 152–53.

46 H. Leroy, *Rätsel und Missverständnis: Ein Beitrag zur Formgeschichte des Johannesevangeliums*, Bonn Biblische Beitrage 30 (Bonn: Peter Hanstein, 1968), 157–60.

47 Culpepper, *Anatomy*, 152–54.

chapters 12 and 16 of the gospel.[48] D. A. Carson does not see misunderstanding as merely a literary device. Instead, he considers "understanding, misunderstanding and not understanding" a pervasive theme of the gospel and locates a total of sixty-four passages connected with the theme, ironies included.[49] Here, we should see that misunderstanding and irony are continuous in purpose if not in form. The underlying significance of the theme has to do with redemptive events, and, as Carson points out, "the solution to the misunderstanding in many cases awaits the occurrence of a major redemptive event . . . which is past from the perspective of the readers," namely, that of Jesus.[50]

Sacramental Symbolism

This is by far the most controversial: the presence of sacramental symbolism in John. R. E. Brown remarks in his lucid account of the issue: "On no other point of Johannine thought is there such sharp division among scholars as there is on the question of sacramentalism."[51] On the one end O. Cullmann and others find numerous sacramental references in John.[52] On the other end Bultmann and others find very few of them, considering them only later redactions.[53] Brown takes a middle way, saying that there are explicit sacramental references such as 6:51–58, and that there are also implicit or "symbolic" references which ought to be supported by evidences of authorial intention and early Church usage.[54] There is also the anti-sacramental view that John contains a polemic against sacramentalists.[55]

How can one justify a reading of the sacraments in the seemingly non-sacramental John? My observation is that the controversy arises not only from the historical issue of John's sacramental view but also from the literary

---

48 Fenton, *John*, 18–19; he also gives a list of 14 ironies in the gospel (ibid., 20).

49 D. A. Carson, "Understanding Misunderstandings in the Fourth Gospel," *TynBul* 33 (1982): 59–91.

50 Ibid., 79.

51 R. E. Brown, *The Gospel According to John*, 2 vols., AB, vols. 29 & 29A (Garden City, NY: Doubleday, 1966–70), 1:cxi–cxiv.

52 O. Cullmann, *Early Christian Worship* (London: SCM, 1953), 59–117; P. Niewalda, *Sakramentssymbolik im Johannesevangelium?* (Limburg: Lahn, 1958).

53 Bultmann, *John*, 11. Cf. Kysar, *The Fourth Evangelist*, 249–59.

54 Brown, *John*, 1:cxii–cxiii.

55 J. D. G. Dunn, "John VI—A Eucharistic Discourse?" *NTS* 17 (1970–71): 330.

problem of symbolism. If John had not been written in what we call a symbolic style, there would not have been such a controversy. I can almost say that the root of this debate lies in the fact that there is no conclusive definition for symbolism. If one rules out the use of symbolism in John, for instance, one would reckon only the explicit references, such as 6:51–58. Bultmann analyzes the text "mythologically" rather than symbolically, and so he admits very few sacramental references.[56] On the contrary, according to Cullmann, history in John is "not a mythological garment" to be stripped off but a "symbolic" reference to salvation history.[57] That opens up a lot of sacramental references in the narratives.[58] Brown safeguards himself from eisegesis by looking for contextual evidences, but he also looks for "symbolic" references "scattered in scenes throughout the ministry."[59] He believes that the Evangelist could not, but teach his sacramental theology through symbolism, because he has to "remain faithful to the literary form of Gospel" and at the same time "show the sacramental undertones of the words and works of Jesus."[60] We should note that although both Cullmann and Brown hold sacramentalist views, their ideas of symbolism are not quite the same. Cullmann understands symbolism in terms of salvation history, but Brown is thinking more of the Evangelist's implicitness of language and the fuller meaning of Jesus' words and works.

We should note that in this discussion the sacraments themselves are referents, and scholars look for symbols that refer to them, including symbolic sayings and narratives in which materials such as water and wine often feature. Cullmann, in his search for Johannine sacramentalism, works not only on words but on episodes as well. This perception comes close to

---

56 Bultmann, *John*, 138, 234–37.

57 Cullmann, *Early Christian Worship*, 56.

58 Examples include the initial mention of the Baptist, 1:6–8, 19–34; the marriage at Cana, 2:1–11; the cleansing of the temple, 2:12–22; the conversation with the woman, 4:1–30, and the mention of the food, 4:31–34; the healing at Bethesda, 5:1–19; the healing of the blind, 9:1–39; the washing of the disciples' feet, 13:1–20; and the farewell discourses, including that on the vine 15:1–8. See Cullmann, "The Gospel According to St. John and Early Christian Worship," chap. in *Early Christian Worship*, 37–119.

59 Brown, *John*, 1:cxiii–cxiv.

60 Ibid., cxiv.

what literary scholars call "narrative symbols" or "symbolic narratives."[61] That is, the narratives in John not only give us σημεῖα but also sacramental references.[62] In connection with this referential relationship, R. W. Paschal raises a meaningful question: does John really refer to sacraments in his symbolic language or does he actually use sacraments in reference to something else? Paschal himself suggests that they are "primarily symbols used in reference to another object, in this case the meaning of the mission of Jesus and its results for believers."[63] Paschal's suggestion is worth considering.

Representational Symbolism

To further our discussion on sacramental symbolism, we must quote from Schneiders (1977) and Painter (1979). Schneiders's initial view is a literary view. "If," she says, "a text is essentially symbolic, then there is no literal meaning of that text apart from the symbolic meaning. . . . a non-symbolic interpretation of a symbolic text is not a literal interpretation. It is an inadequate interpretation."[64] Her definition of symbolism springs from a literary understanding of the portrait of the historical Jesus in John, which she calls "a literary icon."[65] However, when she talks about sacramentalism, she takes an audaciously theological approach. The symbol becomes "an epiphany of present reality" which has to do with incarnation.[66] She proposes a "sacramental principle" which ties history and symbolism together and applies it to various aspects of the Johannine narrative. Thus, for example, the disciples were "Jesus' symbolic and thus real presence"; the Fourth Gospel is "a prototypal exercise of the symbolic witnessing by word of the Church"; and "the Beloved Disciple who writes 'these things'" is also a symbol, a symbol of "the Church herself"![67] There is a fusion of literary and theological interests in her conception. She expands the sacramental

---

61 Painter, "John 9," 42; D. A. Lee, *The Symbolic Narratives of the Fourth Gospel: The Interplay of Form and Meaning*, JSNTSup 95 (Sheffield: JSOT, 1994), 11–12.

62 Cf. previous section on "Narrative Symbolism."

63 Paschal, "Sacramental Symbolism," 154–55.

64 Schneiders, "History and Symbolism," 372.

65 She uses the artistic symbol as an analogy, citing Van Gogh's self-portrait as an example (ibid., 374–75).

66 Schneiders, "Sacramental Principle," 224.

67 Ibid., 229, 232, 234.

idea to cover the whole literature and reads into every character a sacramental kind of symbolism. Furthermore, she talks about a mystical union, i.e., by making the characters sacramental, she expects a real presence of the referent in the symbol. Such a conception of symbolism goes beyond a literary or historical sense. It is a mystical sacramental theology, which cannot find direct support from the text.

Yet Schneiders's theory has gained approval from certain scholars.[68] We can find similar ideas in the view of Painter, who disagrees that the Evangelist was a sacramentalist. In his work on John 9, he argues that there is a "universal significance" in the Evangelist's interpretation of the miracle. The healing of the blind man was not related just as an example of Jesus' miraculous power, as was in the sign source, but as an indication of the universal blindness of humankind in "spiritual perception." Thus the story becomes a narrative symbol and it becomes part of the theme of spiritual blindness.

> The man is *everyman*. . . . *blindness* is equated with the *darkness* of human existence in the world, . . . all men are blind from birth and *everyman* is in the darkness until Jesus gives him light. The dualism of light and darkness, which is equated with sight and blindness, symbolizes the dual *possibilities* of human existence.[69]

In Painter's opinion, it is symbolism that dominates the Evangelist's mind, not sacramentalism, for the evidence does not point to a sacramental interpretation, but, rather, the Evangelist has re-interpreted the sacraments in terms of his understanding of symbols.[70] The "I am" statements in the gospel, Painter argues, shows that John's use of symbols is more inclusive than just the sacraments.[71] In Painter's own definition, sacraments are part of symbols, "visibly representing something." From this onwards, he pushes the universal application of John's symbols just as Schneiders does, saying,

---

68 Culpepper endorses her definition of a symbol; see *Anatomy*, 189 and 187. Lee commends her definition as "the most helpful definition of symbol in relation to John's Gospel" (*Symbolic Narratives*, 16).

69 J. Painter, "Johannine Symbols: A Case Study in Epistemology," *Journal of Theology for Southern Africa* 27 (1979): 26–41; the article was later revised and published with the same quoted lines, "John 9 and the Interpretation of the Fourth Gospel," *JSNT* 28 (1986): 42.

70 Painter, "John 9," 44.

71 Ibid., 46–47.

"Everything is *potentially* sacramental."[72]

Amazingly, sacramentalism in this universal sense, which sounds like symbolism in a very general sense, is quite commonly accepted. Culpepper agrees with Schneiders that Jesus is the "principal symbol" and that Jesus and the characters of the gospel have "representative functions."[73] Kysar, who disagrees with the sacramentalist reading of John, is willing to endorse this new definition: "Johannine theology is the most sacramental of all the New Testament theologies in the sense that it stresses that the love of God is communicated to humans through concrete historical persons and acts."[74] In the words of Dodd, the Evangelist "writes in terms of a world in which phenomena . . . are a living and moving image of the eternal."[75] Bultmann, in his own existentialist undertaking, says, "In the Gospel of John the Jews represent the unbelieving world generally, and in the relations of the Jews to Jesus the relations of all unbelievers to the Christian Church and its message are mirrored."[76] In MacRae's terms, "οἱ Ἰουδαῖοι are symbols of 'the world' which is opposed to Jesus and to his revelation," and, by the same token, "Pilate symbolizes the state."[77] This understanding of symbolism as "universal representation" is fully taken over by Koester, who says, "The shadowy figure of Nicodemus is a useful paradigm . . . . The conversation about worship begins to reveal the universal dimension of the woman's character. . . . The beggar represents humankind. . . . Martha emerges as a paradigm of faith," and so on.[78]

The more broadly symbolism is defined, the more inclusive it is of various conceptions.

Thematic Symbolism

W. Freedman, a literary critic, observes that the literary motif may be used with a symbolic function. "The motif is not a symbol," he says, "but it

---

72 Ibid., 47. Cf. S. S. Smalley, *John: Evangelist and Interpreter* (Nashville: Thomas Nelson, 1983), 210.

73 Culpepper, *Anatomy*, 189.

74 Kysar, *The Fourth Evangelist*, 259.

75 Dodd, *Interpretation*, 143; quoted as Platonic interpretation in Painter, "John 9," 47.

76 Bultmann, *John*, 4.

77 MacRae, "Theology and Irony," 89, n. 18, citing Bultmann, *John*, 652ff.

78 Koester, "Symbolic and Representative Figures," chap. in *Symbolism in the Fourth Gospel*, 32–73.

may be symbolic."[79] The motif, unlike the symbol, may not be an event or a thing, but its cumulative effect is that it "slips into the author's vocabulary, into the dialogue, and into his imagery."[80] Culpepper endorses this view, defining a motif as follows:

> a recurrent theme, character, or verbal pattern, but it may also be a family or cluster of literal or figurative references to a given class of concepts or objects. . . . It is generally symbolic—that is, it can be seen to carry a meaning beyond the literal one immediately apparent; it represents on the verbal level something characteristic of the structure of the work, the events, the characters, the emotional effects or the moral cognitive content.[81]

As to what symbolic motifs there are in John, we may look into the perceptive treatments of G. Stemberger and Meeks. Stemberger argues that the dualistic pairs of images in John, such as light and darkness, life and death, love and hate, all point to Christ as the center of Johannine ethics. They denote the same ethical choice, and are symbolic of a radical ethical dualism.[82] Such a purely ethical reading of John's dualism may be questionable, but Stemberger nevertheless captures a recurrent theme or pattern in John which can indeed be understood as symbolic. In his own words, "On en retire l'impression que la pensée johannique tourne en rond. Cela vient de son caractère symbolique. Une affirmation symbolique est toujours une affirmation concernant le tout, elle veut tout inclure, même si, avec les divers symboles, elle a des perspectives différentes."[83] In the first part of his book he focuses on "symbolism of dualistic ethics." In the second part he moves on to other motifs, such as "water" and "combat and victory." Both of these attempts exemplify a thematic approach to Johannine symbolism.

Over against Stemberger, there is Meeks who also takes a thematic approach. While Stemberger interprets the dualism of "above" and "below"

---

79 W. Freedman, "The Literary Motif: A Definition and Evaluation," *Novel* 4 (1971): 125.

80 Ibid., 124–25.

81 Culpepper, *Anatomy*, 183, citing Freedman, "Literary Motif," 127–28.

82 G. Stemberger, *La symbolique du bien et du mal selon saint Jean*, Parole de Dieu (Paris: Éditions du Seuil, 1970), 21, 25–145, 240.

83 Ibid., 240.

as symbolic of the ethical choice of humankind, Meeks sharply opposes this view.[84] He stresses from a form critical approach that there is not any myth in the gospel that explains how some people could be from below and others from above. "Being from above," he says, is the exclusive property of "the Son of Man" (3:13). Therefore, no humankind could have the kind of faith to make the self-proclamation to be from above.[85] In his article, "The Man from Heaven in Johannine Sectarianism," Meeks exegetes the many passages related to this "descent/ascent motif," and concludes that the descent/ascent motif in John is not a symbol of unity as commonly believed, but in every instance points to contrast, foreignness, division and judgment.[86] This contrast or division signifies the alienation of Jesus from the Jews and the separation of Jesus' community from Judaism.[87] Thus we must "let the symbolic language of Johannine literature speak in its own way," according to Meeks. Even some of the *aporiae* in the gospel are seen by him as the Evangelist's intentional efforts to produce double entendre, self-contradiction, or "thematic complexes."[88]

The geographical framework of John is another thematic symbol.[89] Meeks examines the repeated statement of "Jesus' leaving Judea for Galilee" (4:43, 45, 46, 47, 54), the reference of πατρίς (4:44) to "Judea" in the Johannine context, and the recurring idea of μενείν (1:39; 2:12; 3:22; 7:1; 10:40–42; 11:54) which indicates Jesus' favor towards Galilee and Samaria instead of Judea. All these, according to Meeks, "belong within the larger theological symbolism of the gospel."[90] Thus, he says,

> The journeys to Jerusalem symbolize the coming of the redeemer to "his own" and his rejection by them, while the emphasized movement from Judea to Galilee symbolizes the redeemer's acceptance by others, who thereby become truly "children of God," the real Israel. Thus, while "the Jews" symbolize the natural people of God, who, however, reject God's messenger, "the Galileans"

---

84 "Jean rattache aussi la filiation à la symbolilque de l'origine: l'important, c'est d'où vient l'homme, ce qui détermine où il va" (ibid., 89). Note, however, Meeks's criticism in "Man from Heaven," 47, n. 11.

85 Meeks, "Man from Heaven," 68.

86 Ibid., 67.

87 Ibid., 69.

88 Ibid., 47–48.

89 W. A. Meeks, "Galilee and Judea in the Fourth Gospel," *JBL* 85 (1966): 159–69, quoted in Culpepper, *Anatomy*, 186.

90 Ibid., 165–67.

> symbolize those who are estranged from the natural people of God, but become truly God's people because they receive God's messenger.[91]

This sounds almost like what I have broadly described in the last section as "universal symbolism," but Meeks's work distinguishes itself by being grounded upon a vigorous inquiry of the literary motif, and sober references to the historical sociological context, namely, the polemic faced by the Johannine circle. So, as Meeks himself admits, it is not a "purely symbolic" concept as if it owes "little or nothing to the geographical situation of the community that shaped its traditions."[92]

Scriptural Symbolism

Whereas the Synoptics make citations of the Old Testament in establishing Messianic fulfillment in Jesus, the Gospel of John makes symbols of OT imagery. Thus OT imagery becomes a main component of John's symbolism. We have seen this in many of the symbols we have surveyed, for example, metaphorical symbols such as the shepherd (10:1–16) and the vine (15:1–8). In addition there are symbols that originate from OT historical accounts, such as "the snake in the desert" (3:14), or, more subtly, "Jacob's ladder" (1:31). Then the feasts compose a complex of symbols that points to the identity of Jesus as Christ: the Passover, the Tabernacle and the Dedication. As the Exodus forms a major theme, "manna" and even "Moses" may be seen as symbols, and they point to Christ in one way or another. Among these, the symbol of "water" not only recurs in the Gospel of John but may also have connections with various OT writings. It becomes clear that the Old Testament is a significant background to the gospel, so much so that this classification tends to be all-inclusive. Nevertheless, we may call them scriptural symbols or, as Leal classifies, "biblical symbols."[93]

The justification and importance of so calling these symbols lie in the fact that there exists a two-way relationship with Johannine symbolism: pointing to Christ and the church on the one hand, referring back to the Old Testament on the other hand. X. Léon-Dufour talks about a double symbolism intended by the author. For example, the temple made of stone

---

91 Ibid.

92 Ibid., 168.

93 Leal, "Simbolismo histórico," 338–39.

symbolizes the spiritual temple of God promised in the Old Testament, and prefigures the body of Christ, which points towards resurrection.[94] In my opinion this two-way relationship should play a significant role in the interpretation of Johannine symbolism.

Diversified Interpretations of Johannine Symbolism

Confusion and Suspicion

What I have presented above is a "mixed bag": selected references reflecting various literary or theological traits of the Gospel of John, and dissimilar interpretations by scholars of diversified interests. I assembled them under the commonly used title "symbolism," but the meaning or definition of symbolism is by no means agreed upon. Maybe the etymology of the word is the only thing agreed upon. The Greek verb συμβάλλω means "to put together," and the related noun σύμβολον means "mark," "token," or "sign," like "the half coin carried away by each of the two parties of an agreement as a pledge."[95] So we may agree that symbolism in John are expressions in the text intended to be matched with corresponding referents. But what is the nature of these referents? Is it real or ideological? How are they related to the symbols? Are they implicit meanings? Or hidden meanings? Or represented realities in the universe? How can we interpret? Where and how do we find "the other half of the coin"?

The fundamentals of the subject have not been adequately explored. Decades ago, in 1960, Leal said, "No abundan los trabajos sobre este tema, que consideramos fundamental para el estudio de San Juan."[96] Much later, in 1985, Richards said the same, that the ambiguous expressions in John have "long been noted but virtually unexplored."[97] Léon-Dufour points out that there is a drawback, "To speak of the symbolic in exegesis means running into a veritable mine field. Everywhere, you are in danger of finding 'booby traps' liable to explode the most solid systematic constructions instantly."[98] Meeks says, "It is symptomatic of the impasse in NT

94 Léon-Dufour, "Symbolic Reading," 448.
95 Friedman, *Form and Meaning*, 292.
96 Leal, "Simbolismo histórico," 329.
97 Richards, "Double Meaning," 96.
98 Léon-Dufour, "Symbolic Reading," 439.

hermeneutics that we have as yet no adequate monograph on the Johannine symbolism as such."[99]

What is it that has impeded progress? It is not that the symbolic aspect of John has not been studied. There have been many studies in history. In recent years an increasing awareness of the gospel's literary nature has inspired further works. Jones published a literary study on the symbol of water in the Gospel of John, which is a significant monograph on this subject.[100] However, as Schneiders points out, "since there do not seem to be any reliable or generally accepted criteria for the interpretation of symbols, any symbolic interpretation remains undemonstrable if not arbitrary."[101] This lack of reliable criteria has, rightly but also unfortunately, alarmed historical exegetes. Wead comments,

> Many are arising who are promoting such an [symbolic] interpretation. Yet as one inspects their work he finds a great deal of fuzziness, especially about the meaning of the term "symbolic." A vast need for clarification in the use of this term is evident.[102]

Another concern springs from what Schneiders calls a common assumption, namely, "an inverse proportion between the historical and the symbolic."[103] As early as half a century ago, Cullmann spoke of a juxtaposition between history and symbolism in scholarly thinking.

> Es ist daher falsch, wenn immer wieder in den Kommentaren "geschichtliche" und "symbolische" Erklärung der johanneischen Erzählungen als Gegensätze gegeneinander ausgespielt werden und eine Alternative aufgestellt wird, als ob im Sinne des Evangelisten eine Aussage entweder nur als historische Tatsache oder nur als Hinweis auf einen theologischen "mystischen" Sachverhalt gemeint sein könne.[104]

But how could we consider symbolism not historical if there is no clear definition of it? This distrust of symbolism has to do with the dislike of allegorical interpretation, as there is often a confusion between the two. In Wead's caution against the symbolic interpretation of John, four out of six

---

99 Meeks, "Man from Heaven," 47.

100 Jones, *Symbol of Water*.

101 Schneiders, "History and Symbolism," 371–72.

102 Wead, *Literary Devices*, 26–27.

103 Schneiders, "History and Symbolism," 376.

104 O. Cullmann, "Der johanneische Gebrauch doppeldeutiger Ausdrücke als Schlüssel zum Verständnis des vierten Evangeliums," *TZ* 4 (1948): 361.

listed reasons have to do with the denouncing of early methods such as Jewish or Christian allegorization, Platonic philosophy, or Philo's symbolic use, which had little concern about historicity.[105]

Skepticism could have been avoided if symbolism had been more discretely defined. In fact, skepticism is not typical of all historical exegetes. The following remarks of Howard, made in 1931, is still instructive today.

> We therefore distinguish between the allegorizing method . . . and the method of the Fourth Evangelist who describes what he believes to be veritable fact, but with a keen eye to the deeper revelation which the story may contain. . . . There are dramatic touches throughout the story. . . . Sometimes this approaches tragic irony. . . . By an easy transition we pass from these dramatic symbols to the mysterious sayings and constant ambiguities. . . . The writer tells the story in his own way . . . but the story is one which he has heard or read. . . . he saw the deeper meaning illustrated by the story [of miracles] which he accepted as historically true.[106]

To conclude, the historical and the symbolic are not mutually exclusive, and confusion and suspicion may be avoided. In the following sections I will try to analyze approaches that have been used, with the hope to sort out conceptions and pave the way towards making my own definition.

Form Critical Views

If historicity is in an inverse proportion to the use of symbolism, then Bultmann's view of the historicity of the Gospel of John should require that he interprets it as symbolic. And indeed, in Bultmann's view, the mythical language of John assumes no historicity but constitutes a kind of symbolic use. Nowhere in his commentary does he explicitly talk about "symbolism," but the language of John is everywhere taken as "referring to a myth." The Gnostic myth is considered a source of this language, which was modified by the author or redactor to form his own myth. Thus language is understood to be symbolic of mythical thinking. To be specific, he gathers from the unique language of John a "symbolic picture of Jesus," a "puzzle," which he attempts to solve by matching with the Gnostic picture of the "descending and ascending redeemer."[107] It is on this basis that Bultmann's

---

105 Wead, *Literary Devices*, 27–28.

106 Howard, "Symbolism and Allegory," 186–88, 192.

107 Bultmann, *John*, 7–9. See Meeks's comment on this in "Man from Heaven," 47.

commentating on John often refers to a symbolic meaning, e.g., the Jews represent the unbelieving world; Pilate symbolizes the state (I previously categorized this as "representation"). If early allegorical interpretations can be called symbolic, Bultmann's mythological explanation may well be described as symbolic. Neither of them counts on historical reality. What differs is that Bultmann begins with form critical analysis, which takes a historical posture and gives the confidence of objectivity.

Judging from the gospel's stylistic unity, Bultmann's symbolic reading of John, if so called, is far from accurate or sufficient. Bultmann's criticism is admittedly "literary oriented," because he insists that the historical source of the Johannine Jesus lies in the "form" of a myth, not in any "concept" or "philosophy" of Hellenistic thinking.[108] However, his literary analysis was interrupted by a preoccupation with the *aporiae*. His diachronic approach keeps him from seeing any symbolism in John that shows up only in a synchronic reading. This is the impasse that Meeks tries to overcome in his article "Man from Heaven in Johannine Sectarianism." Meeks follows Bultmann closely in his thorough going form criticism, maintaining that there is "a special logic for the language of myth." While other scholars suggest that the "descending/ascending" theme could be part of the history of ideas, Meeks insists on resolving it by looking into the "mythical pattern within the Johannine literature."[109] However, on the other hand, Meeks points out the flaw of Bultmann's interpretation. Bultmann argues that this mythical pattern depicted a "revealer" in the gnostic milieu posited for the Johannine group, but this argument looks for a solution only in the "extrinsic historical setting," and it ignores the literary structure of the gospel altogether.[110] It is in this context that Meeks declares, "We have not yet learned to let the symbolic language of Johannine literature speak in its own way."[111] To try to do so, Meeks applies the study of John's special language patterns to the whole literary structure, and detects the repetition

108 R. Bultmann, "Die Bedeutung der neuerschlossenen mandäischen und manichäischen Quellen für das Verständnis des Johannesevangeliums," *ZNW* 24 (1925): 100–146 (reprinted in *Exegesis* [Tübingen: Mohr, 1967], 55–104), quoted in Meeks, "Man from Heaven," 44.

109 Meeks, "Man from Heaven," 46.

110 Ibid., 47.

111 Ibid.

of the "mythical signals"throughout the gospel.[112] His attempt results in two important thematic studies, one on the geographical framework and the other on the "descending and ascending" motif of John, both of which he interprets as symbolic of characteristic viewpoints of the Johannine community. The "remarkable stylistic unity and thematic coherence" of the gospel, which Meeks uses as a basis of his work, is something that Bultmann totally ignores.

Linguistically Critical Views

The works of Bultmann and Meeks are "form critical" because they begin exclusively with the isolation of language patterns and the association of these patterns with historical antecedents. The objective of their criticism is literary, but the criterion is historical. Meeks tries to move away from the tyranny of the historical and pay more attention to the literary but he maintains his allegiance to Bultmann's historical assessment of the myth. By the same token Wead's conception of John's symbolism can be called a "linguistically critical view." It is likewise restrictive. It involves a scrutiny of the language of the literary composition in accordance with historically established rules. As pointed out above, Wead's study of double meaning is limited to words, and his assessment of the secondary meaning is governed by semantic and grammatical rules worked out from etymology and historical parallels.

In studying the σημεῖα in John, for example, Wead isolates the term σημεῖον and looks for its usage in the Old Testament, the Qumran, and other backgrounds. The result is that these signs have very little symbolic meaning.[113] In studying irony, he locates the origin of the Johannine form of irony in "Sophoclean irony" of the classical Greek plays.[114] As for metaphors, he argues from the use of the definite article that the ἐγώ εἰμι formula introduces metaphors rather than divine connotations or symbols.[115]

---

112 Ibid., 48.

113 Wead argues that signs and symbolic actions in the Old Testament were not the same, and in any case the meaning of both were "quite explicit," thus he discourages any extensive searching of symbolic meaning in John; see Wead, "The Johannine Sign," chap. in *Literary Devices*, 12–29.

114 Wead, "Irony," chap. in *Literary Devices*, 47–68.

115 Wead, "The Johannine Metaphor," chap. in *Literary Devices*, 71–94.

As for the historical root of symbols, he identifies it solely with the symbolic action of the Old Testament prophets.[116] Such is Wead's "restrictively historical" literary approach.

Wead's approach reminds us of E. Schweizer's work *Ego Eimi.*[117] The two writers interpret ἐγώ εἰμι differently. Schweizer takes it literally as "self identification of the deity."[118] Wead takes it as metaphorical. But they share the same understanding of "symbol" as an indirect language, a kind of figure of speech, "linguistically developed." Schweizer suggests that a symbol may be founded "through an incident in the history of myth, e.g., the rainbow symbolizes the grace of God."[119] Wead, likewise, considers the symbol an end result of the metaphorical process:

> [Symbols] are things which have come to represent conceptions. . . . symbols . . . are only used when an object is, possibly as a result of a common metaphor, so thoroughly associated with a conception that the object can represent the conception without the metaphorical usage. The symbol is only possible when we arrive at the final step of the metaphorical process and such a process has solidified to the place where the word can become a token for the second idea.[120]

Thus, as I quoted early in this chapter, "symbols and metaphors are related on a continuum."[121] In other words a symbol may be a non-verbal, sensual image formed at the end of a metaphorical process, when the linguistic elements have dropped out of the picture.

This "linguistically critical" approach can help us understand the play on words and the nature of metaphors, so they work well with Johannine double meaning and metaphorical symbols. However, this is also too "mechanical" or "static" an approach.[122] The isolated treatment of linguistic techniques distracts us from viewing the literary structure as a whole, even though Wead and Schweizer agrees that there is grammatical or stylistic

---

116 Wead, *Literary Devices*, 28.

117 E. Schweizer, *Ego Eimi: Die religionsgeschichtliche Herkunft und theologische Bedeutung der johanneischen Bildreden, zugleich ein Beitrag zur Quellenfrage des vierten Evangeliums* (Göttingen: Vandenhoeck & Ruprecht, 1939).

118 Schweizer, "Die mandäische Frage," chap. in *Ego Eimi*, 46–82.

119 Schweizer, *Ego Eimi*, 116.

120 Wead, *Literary Devices*, 73–74.

121 Koester, *Symbolism in the Fourth Gospel*, 6–7.

122 Such is R. W. Paschal's critique on Schweizer's concept of symbolism; see Paschal, "Sacramental Symbolism," 151–53.

unity in John.[123] Furthermore, the historical and linguistic criteria that preside over the investigation can force themselves upon the Johannine usage and hinder us from seeing its unique characteristics. These are some of the problems we also find in the form critical approach of Bultmann. In addition, linguistically critical views are not capable of dealing with abstract connections. For example, in the meticulous study of Wead, there are only limited comments on the more abstract metaphors, such as "I am the resurrection and the life" (11:25) and "I am the way, the truth and the life" (14:6).[124] The restrictive nature of this method has also excluded the possibility of sacramental references, which seem to be flimsy in critical exegesis. Schweizer's interpretation of John 6:51–58, for instance, is close to Bultmann's "sehr wahrscheinlich von zweiter hand."[125]

Linguistic/Philosophical Views

As long as the symbol is considered a literary device, it is basically a metaphor. It is agreed among literary scholars that "simile," "metaphor" and "symbol" are all on a continuum. R. W. Funk summarizes their definitions as follows:

> To say A is like B is a simile. . . . To say A is B is a metaphor, . . . in symbolic speech one speaks of B without referring to A, although it is supposed that A or an A is intended. . . . symbolism is metaphor with the primary term suppressed.[126]

While "linguistically critical views" find very little symbolism in the Gospel of John, as Wead's and Schweizer's interpretations exemplify, Funk's represents an alternative view that looks at language not as an object of investigation but as an innovative vehicle in the creation of meanings. This concept of language was first popularized among literary critics, such as P. E. Wheelwright, who pointed out that there is a "tensive" nature in language. On the one hand there are "steno-meanings" which can be communicated with exactitude, but on the other hand there is an "openness"

---

123 Wead, *Literary Devices*, 9; Schweizer, *Ego Eimi*, 82–112.

124 Wead, *Literary Devices*, 78.

125 Schweizer, *Ego Eimi*, 155–57.

126 R. W. Funk, *Language, Hermeneutic, and Word of God: The Problem of Language in the New Testament and Contemporary Theology* (New York: Harper & Row, 1966), 136–37.

in language which reflects the essential vagueness of the existing world.[127] Based on this, the use of metaphor is conceived as having a "soft" focus rather than a "sharp" focus.[128] Funk proposes:

> The logic of predication, . . . is narrowing, restricting. . . . The metaphor, by contrast, inheres in a vibrant nexus which resists reduction by prediction. It resists specificity. It intends more, much more, than it says. What it says is minimal; what it intends is maximal. Discursive speech reduces the intentionality of language as near to explicit reference as possible; metaphorical language conserves the implicit tentacles of its vision, inasmuch as it concentrates a "world" in its figure or narrative.[129]

Once the necessity of predication is done away with, a number of possibilities open up for the interpretation of symbolism in John. First, the reader can take a more active role than merely submitting to objective criticism. Second, the symbol or metaphor can now be polyvalent in meaning. Paschal's concept of Johannine symbolism, which is founded upon "the creative ability of language," reflects precisely these possibilities.

> The point is that when one juxtaposes familiar symbols in new ways, or in new contexts, new meanings and ideas are suggested. Since these new meanings depend on the inter-action of the hearer or reader, this type of symbolism tends to offer more than one level of interpretation; . . . Figurative or symbolic language can, therefore, do more than explain; it can challenge the reader to think, to probe, and to interpret.[130]

And, thirdly, a lot more symbolism can be seen in the Gospel of John with such a view than with "linguistically critical" views. Paschal, for instance, finds more symbolism in John than Schweizer.[131] With this new understanding of language the identification of symbols is no longer so restricted by rules. On the contrary, the term "symbol" has the advantage of assuming a broader meaning than even "metaphor." A word can be understood as a symbol, just as a metaphor is a symbol. Or a narrative can be symbolic, as much as a parable is symbolic. One can even say, "All

---

127 P. E. Wheelwright, *Metaphor and Reality* (Bloomington, IN: Indiana University Press, 1962), 33–44.

128 Funk, *Language, Hermeneutic, and Word of God*, 138, citing P. E. Wheelwright, *The Burning Fountain* (Bloomington, IN: Indiana University Press, 1954), 62–64.

129 Ibid., 142.

130 Paschal, "Sacramental Symbolism," 153.

131 Ibid., 151–54.

language is essentially symbolic."[132] In F. W. Dillistone's formulation, metaphor is but "the process of the continuous enlargement of man's symbolic world."[133] Or, in E. Fuchs's or A. N. Wilder's theory, the rise of the Christian gospel itself is a "speech-event" (*Sprachereignis*), meaning, "the opening up of a new dimension of man's awareness, a new breakthrough in language and symbolization."[134] Even Bultmann could have expounded more clearly his concept of salvation as "language event," if he had not been caught in a backward process of mythological interpretation. Once the use of symbols is understood in this linguistic philosophical sense, scholars find the Gospel of John most innovative in language and therefore rich in symbolism.

Dodd's Literary View

At the threshold of the rise of this new understanding of language, we encounter scholars who were historically critical and at the same time sensitive to the innovative nature of language. Fuchs's conception of the New Testament myths represents an extension of the form critical idea towards this direction. He no longer believes in the straight identification of forms with historical antecedents, but, instead, proposes that "the Gospel represented a renewal of myth" in establishing "the new style-form 'gospel.'" Similarly, "direct assimilation of pagan rhetoric" in the New Testament are "only on the margin."[135] What interests us even more, however, as related to Johannine symbolism, is the attempt of Dodd to somewhat diverge from traditional historical criticism.

> I shall assume as a provisional working hypothesis that the present order is not fortuitous, but deliberately devised by somebody—even if he were only a scribe doing his best—and that the person in question (whether the author or another) had some design in mind, and was not necessarily irresponsible or unintelligent.[136]

---

132 Lee, *Symbolic Narratives*, 29, citing E. Cassirer, *An Essay on Man* (New Haven: Yale University Press, 1947), 26.

133 F. W. Dillistone, *Christianity and Symbolism* (London: Collins, 1955), 161.

134 A. N. Wilder, *The Language of the Gospel: Early Christian Rhetoric* (New York: Harper & Row, 1964), 19, citing E. Fuchs, "Die Sprache im Neuen Testament," in *Zur Frage nach dem historischen Jesus* (Tübingen: Mohr, 1960), 261.

135 Ibid.

136 Dodd, *Interpretation*, 290.

Dodd's hypothesis is severely criticized by Ashton, who claims that "it was in response to Bultmann rather than to Dodd that scholars began once again to try *to account for* the literary puzzles of the Gospel" (italics mine).[137] But "to account for" is always a historical critical goal. To appreciate or "to discover any intelligible thread of argument" through the whole gospel is a literary goal that Dodd became a pioneer of, not Bultmann. If, as Ashton points out, Johannine scholarship has been propelled by Bultmann rather than by Dodd, then that is exactly why the study of Johannine symbolism has suffered impoverishment. It was in response to Bultmann that Meeks regretted, "We have not yet learned to let the symbolic language of Johannine literature speak in its own way," and it was after Dodd's fashion that he had begun to appreciate the gospel's "remarkable stylistic unity and thematic coherence."[138]

It is not insignificant that in Dodd's work on John the first "leading idea" he deals with in Part II is "Symbolism."[139] Dodd looks at Johannine symbols from two perspectives. He studies individual symbols historically, using the criteria he describes in Part I, "The Background." He also points out the literary structure of symbols which binds together the narrative and discourse of the Gospel of John as a whole, and this latter treatment paves his way to Part III, "Argument and Structure."[140] Because of these two perspectives Dodd is in company with two different groups of scholars. His observation of the narrative and discourse pattern of symbols in John was picked up later on by literary scholars such as Lee, who wrote "The Symbolic Narratives of the Fourth Gospel," aforementioned. At the same time, his historical interpretation of symbols attracted exegetes who picked the path of the history of ideas. Even Wead who adheres to linguistic rules appeals here and there to the history of ideas. It is notable that the final criterion of Dodd's historical study is the history of ideas (as opposed by Meeks), rather than the history of form (cf. Bultmann) or that of language (cf. Wead).

Where then do we see Dodd's notion of language as innovative? We see it in his divergence from A. Jülicher's restrictive view on the parables. Though he agrees that the metaphor or parable presents only one main point,

137 Ashton, *Understanding the Fourth Gospel*, 81.
138 Meeks, "Man from Heaven," 47.
139 Dodd, *Interpretation*, 133–43.
140 Ibid., 133–34, 143.

he agrees so only in reference to the historical context. Regarding future applications, he says that the interpretation of a parable is never really closed. The following quotation from *The Parables of the Kingdom* shows that he was aware of the innovative quality of literary language and the hearer's essential participation in making sense of it.

> By all means draw from them any "lesson" they may seem to suggest, . . .
>
> . . . the parable is a metaphor . . . arresting the hearer by its vividness or strangeness, and leaving the mind in sufficient doubt about its precise application to tease it into active thought. . . .
>
> . . . The parables, however, have an imaginative and poetical quality. They are works of art, and any serious work of art has significance beyond its original occasion. . . . a just understanding of their original import in relation to a particular situation in the past will put us on right lines in applying them to our own new situations.[141]

"Allegory" is Dodd's term for the Johannine metaphor. He considers allegory a metaphorical device just as the parable is.[142] He distinguishes between the two, as it is habitual for biblical exegetes to make formal distinctions. Yet, he does so with reserve, saying, "In making this distinction between the parable and the allegory, we must not be too rigorous."[143] So Dodd's distinction involves only a variance, not a difference. His note on "vine-symbolism" indicates this.

> we are dealing with a kind of symbolism in which the images or figures employed, although they are taken from workaday experience, derived relatively little of their significance from the part they signified. The meaning of the 'allegory' is only to a slight extent to be understood from a knowledge of what vines are as they grow in any vineyard; it is chiefly to be understood out of a rich background of associations which the vine-symbol had already acquired.[144]

So the meaning of the Johannine symbol is more removed from what the primary term stands for, and more determined by its close associations with the background. This is typically a literary definition of the symbol in relation to the metaphor. It is, for instance, similar to Wead's idea about a symbol, namely, the object is so thoroughly associated with the conception

---

141 C. H. Dodd, *The Parables of the Kingdom*, 3d ed. (London: Nisbet & Co., 1936; repr. 1952), ix, 5, 157; see also Funk's elaboration of Dodd's conception (*Language, Hermeneutic, and Word of God*, 133–52).

142 Dodd, *Interpretation*, 134–35; *Parables*, 7–8.

143 Dodd, *Parables*, 9.

144 Dodd, *Interpretation*, 137.

that the metaphorical process hides behind.[145]

Thus Dodd's definition of symbolism comes close to that of literary scholars who place symbolism on a continuum with metaphor. However, what I am trying to show is, the same definition may not lead to the same interpretation. On this continuum there are different criteria of judgment. Wead's restrictive approach prevents him from seeing symbolism in the Johannine metaphors.[146] Dodd, with an appreciation of the gospel as a whole, and a sensitivity to the nature of its literary language, dares call the Johannine metaphors either symbols or allegories. Thus he advanced more than others of his days in the study of Johannine symbolism.

Dodd' s Historical/Philosophical View

We must not forget that Dodd holds a double perspective, as pointed out above. While he gave way to a literary approach, he remained an analyst of the history of ideas. When he investigated the historical meaning of "symbol," he investigated it in the light of Aristotle, Plato, Philo, and the Old Testament. Among these criteria that he used he gave precedence to the Greek thinkers.

> 'Αληθινός properly means 'real,' as opposed to that which is either fictitious or a mere copy, as when Aristotle speaks of τὰ ἀληθινά as opposed to τὰ γεγραμμένα . . . Similarly Philo . . .
>
> . . . when the evangelist speaks of ἄρτος ἀληθινός he means that spiritual or eternal reality which is symbolized by bread, . . . Similarly he uses the term φῶς ἀληθινόν. We may then recall that Plato . . . offered the sun as a symbol or image of the ultimate reality, the Idea of Good. . . . It was probably largely through the influence of Plato that the conception of God Himself as the archetypal Light won currency in the religious world of Hellenism.[147]

So Dodd suggested that the "Platonic doctrine of Ideas" had been introduced into the Johannine texture of thought, through "religious circles with which Johannine thought has demonstrable affinities."[148]

Later on, Dodd drew upon the Old Testament idea of σημεῖον, אות, to show that the accounts of Jesus' acts, related as historical in John, were intended for symbolic meaning. The idea is that prophetic acts are meant to

145 Wead, *Literary Devices*, 73–74.

146 Ibid., 82–86.

147 Dodd, *Interpretation*, 139.

148 Ibid.

correspond with divinely ordained happenings in the real world. Dodd sees in this a correlation with the symbolic treatment of the acts of Jesus in the Fourth Gospel. Thus it was from a "rich background of associations" that Dodd derived his interpretation of Johannine symbolism. The resultant picture is that on the one hand, the symbol is absorbed into the reality it signifies, and, on the other hand, as he says, "in the symbol was given also the thing symbolized."[149] So the Johannine bread, vine, water, and light, are not merely illustrations or analogies, but they "bodies forth" the eternal idea of the respective elements. The "vine-ness" of a vine, as Dodd interprets, is defined by the eternal "Idea of Vine." Likewise, in describing the eternal Vine, one describes every vine "in every respect which constitutes its vine-ness." So throughout the gospel there is an "intrinsic unity of symbol and thing symbolized."[150]

Dodd's ideological interpretation of Johannine symbolism is quite commonly agreed upon, namely, the symbol is not merely a literary device but a sensible representation of some universal reality with which it is connected. Some describe this as "analogical." According to Painter, for example, the symbol is functionally as well as existentially related to the symbolized. Functionally, the symbol operates by analogy. Existentially, the symbol communicates something transcendent.[151] Many scholars endorse such a definition. Some generalize it as a kind of "representation," as I pointed out earlier. However, few authenticate it by Platonic thinking as Dodd does. Painter, for example, agrees that John's symbolism presupposes an epistemology, but he is not convinced by Dodd's Platonic interpretation. He proposes an epistemological definition of his own.[152]

Theological/Epistemological Definitions

According to Painter, the origin of John's symbols is to be found in "creation" itself. The gospel teaches that the *Logos* is the revealer of God and, therefore, the symbol for God in relation to the world, through whom God is known. The gospel also teaches that creation is "by the *Logos*," for

149 Ibid., 141.
150 Ibid., 140.
151 Painter, "John 9," 50–54.
152 Ibid., 47.

all things came into being through the *Logos*, instead of through acts of sheer power. Painter claims that creation by the *Logos*, who is also the agent of revelation, implies "revelation in creation." That is, whatever created can become a symbolic bearer of the revelation. Thus the world becomes "a store-house" of potential symbols which can "become" vehicles of the revelation—the variety of symbols used in the gospel, Painter argues, suggests this very point.[153]

As for when and how the potential symbols become symbolic, Painter claims that John's symbols depict an "epistemological problem," meaning, they express humankind's "quest for life."[154] Although anything created may become a symbol, those that become symbolic in the gospel are related to life and existence in the world: bread, water, light, etc. As these objects cannot ultimately sustain life and cannot satisfy humankind's perennial longing for life, they are used to "point beyond themselves to the ultimate transcendent ground (source) of all being, to God."[155]

Painter's statement on the origin and function of the Johannine symbols refers only to the theology of the text for authentication, so it may not impress historical critics too much. Nor do they impress literary critics. Lee, acknowledging that there are "insights," turns it down as being helpful only for theological understanding but not for literary analysis.[156] Culpepper, however, rates it as "perhaps the most significant article to date on John's symbolism." In Painter's conception, Culpepper observes, "the exclusive position of the sacraments is forfeited while their symbolic function in presenting the mystery of the revelation is enhanced."[157] So a theological definition is involved here and the revelatory function of symbolism is emphasized. We should note that Painter's statement takes two basic theological issues into account, namely, the quest of the human for the transcendent, and the concept of divine creation and revelation. No doubt,

153 Ibid., 47–48; I am quoting from the latter article "John 9," which was formerly published as "Johannine Symbols: A Case Study in Epistemology," with only slight difference.

154 Ibid., 50.

155 Painter further points out how Johannine symbolism took its particular form in history, i.e., it "was shaped in the struggle with the synagogue." Ibid., 48–49.

156 Lee-Pollard, "Symbolic Narratives," 25; Lee, *Symbolic Narratives*, 19.

157 Culpepper, *Anatomy*, 188.

the theology of the Gospel of John has to do with both. While biblical scholars deal with creation and revelation in John, the human quest for the transcendent is often discussed among scholars in the field of cultural, religious, and philosophical studies. Symbolism is recognized by them to be a common, religious, epistemological phenomenon. It suffices to quote from a couple of these scholars here. Dillistone writes in his book *Christianity and Symbolism*:

> The symbol is the part which stands for the whole, which signifies the whole, which represents the whole. This theory can be traced back to Plato and his followers who asserted that the part actually participates in the idea of the whole. It reveals the whole; in a certain sense it is identical with the whole.[158]

The rationale here is not to authenticate anything with Plato's theory. It rather purports that epistemological theories have always been there as a quest for the transcendent, and the symbol has been a means of this quest. We may further note the following remarks of T. Fawcett, quoted from his book, *The Symbolic Language of Religion*.

> Symbols are not created, but born out of life. They do not come into being like signs as a result of the creative faculty of man's imagination. The symbols of darkness, light and water, for example, were given to man with his existence in the world. . . . these elements in man's experience forced themselves upon him in a way he could not ignore. They were the powerful forces impinging on his being. In seeking to understand and come to terms with them, man attempted to reach through them to the reality which they mediated; he used them as symbols.[159]

Thus symbolism is not only an arbitrarily chosen means, but is born out of humankind's experiences of the world. Religious symbols exist as realities that connect humankind with the transcendent world. It follows naturally that symbols often acquire an epistemological role. In biblical literature as well as religious culture, images from the world of sense experience are taken to form symbols that speak of realities that transcend them. They do not usually represent things that are already understood, but they stand for things not yet fully known: the reality of things, the real nature of life, the frontiers of knowledge. As Fawcett points out, symbols "push beyond the

158 Dillistone, *Christianity and Symbolism*, 27.

159 T. Fawcett, *The Symbolic Language of Religion: An Introductory Story* (London: SCM, 1970), 27.

frontiers of empirical objectivity and seek a subjective appropriation of the transcendent."[160]

The scholars quoted above presume an epistemological role of symbolism. In this context Plato's theory and John's use of symbols, among others, are all epistemologies. Such a definition is inductively worked out. It does not involve any restrictive kind of criticism.

Literary/Theological Definitions

Painter does more than just define symbolism as etymology. He actually presents a theological reading of John, in which the *basis* of Johannine symbolism is located in the creation and revelation of God, which culminate in the incarnation of the Logos, and, the *function* of Johannine symbolism is to address the epistemological problem of humankind. In his conception there is clear connection between the Johannine theology of the Logos and the Johannine usage of symbols.

Prior to Painter's article (1979), other theological readings of John have been proposed. Leal uses the theological concept of the "chronos" and the "kairos" to explain the historical and the spiritual aspects of Johannine symbolism (1960). His explanations are also instructive.

> The Fourth Gospel can be historical and symbolical at the same time because its temporal horizon can embrace all the Kairos of Christ, all the history of Messianic salvation. When Jesus said that he is "the light of the world," John can think about the historical cure of the man who is blind from birth and of the spiritual and suprahistorical illumination of all the times. . . . The symbolism, then, of the fourth gospel consists in the relation that its author establishes between the acts and the historical words of Jesus with his perpetual and transcendent action in the history of the church and of the souls. That which is not seen with the open eye of history is precisely that which is symbolized, the spiritual and theological. The relation that exists between the perceptible and the imperceptible, the historical and the transcendent, is the symbolism.[161]

Schneiders also proposed a similar point (1977), namely, "a symbol is the sensible expression of the transcendent." However, she, more than anybody else, constructs her theory of symbolism around the theology of incarnation. Whereas Painter considers epistemology the key issue, and

160 Ibid., 30.

161 Leal, "Simbolismo histórico," 331–32.

creation and revelation the framework of symbolism, Schneiders stresses nothing but incarnation. In Painter's opinion, it is symbolism that dominates the Evangelist's mind, not sacramentalism. In Schneiders's opinion, the two are the same and they are everywhere intended in the gospel.

> In the Fourth Gospel . . . the notion of symbolic revelation becomes fully explicit. The Johannine concentration of all revelation and all response to revelation in the person of Jesus of Nazareth whom he designates as the Word become flesh (I, 14), that is, as the symbolization of God, is the clearest indication of this fact and the principle of all its consequences.[162]

This theology of incarnation becomes a springboard when Schneiders further develops her "sacramental principle," referred to earlier in this chapter. She freely associates the Johannine narrative with the symbolic: the disciples were symbols of Jesus, the Beloved Disciple was a symbol of the Church, the Gospel of John was a symbol of the Church's witness, and so on. This idea of symbolism involves very little critical thinking. It only opens up possibilities of theological application. However, it has been acclaimed by some as important or helpful for two good reasons.[163] First, Schneiders's theological enthusiasm is accompanied with sensible literary arguments, e.g., "if a text is essentially symbolic, then there is no literal meaning of that text apart from the symbolic meaning."[164] Beyond this, her notion of the symbol is mainly theological, e.g., the sensible expression of the whole in terms of the part, the participation of the earthly in the transcendent, the symbolic dimension of history within the revelatory tradition, and so on. This is a grand-looking definition. Theological minded readers of the gospel appreciate it. Furthermore, is it not legitimate, after all, to appeal to theology for interpretation? The symbol, taken as a literary device, is most versatile in referring to things other than or beyond itself. Johannine symbols, in particular, and especially the metaphorical and narrative symbols, are obviously presented with a revelatory claim, that they point to Christ. If historical criticism restricts this study of symbolism, and if literary analysis opens it only up to the level of the text, then solution and authentication have to be looked for elsewhere. The trend is, I think, to look into either

---

162 Schneiders, "History and Symbolism," 373.

163 Lee, *Symbolic Narratives*, 16; Culpepper does express some reserve, "One may wish to take slight exception to her definition, . . ." *Anatomy*, 187.

164 Schneiders, "History and Symbolism," 372, 374.

theology or philosophy. This is where biblical scholars begin to dialogue with Paul Ricoeur.

Philosophical/Literary Definitions

We could have mentioned Ricoeur earlier in this chapter when we looked at "Symbolism as Innovative Language," but there we began with the literary. Ricoeur, who was also influenced by a literary critic, P. E. Wheelwright, began with philosophy. While literary scholars draw upon the philosophy of language for support to go in a new direction, and the philosopher takes interest in the literature of the Bible to go after hermeneutics, the two cross paths. Ricoeur's thorough discussions on metaphor and symbolism have become a popular source for both literary scholars and philosophers who work on the subject.

Ricoeur's approach to the subject is both analytical and innovative. He suggests there are two aspects of discourse: that which explains, and that which expresses understanding and transmits new experiences to language.[165] This is in line with the modern view of language, that language is innovative of meaning. With regard to symbolism, Ricoeur works laboriously on the theory of metaphor, going back to classical traditions in his marking out of a new course for the subject. In attempting so, he affirms on linguistic grounds that "real metaphors are not translatable. . . . it offers new information."[166]

Then Ricoeur addresses directly the nature of symbol, and here he moves beyond linguistics into other disciplines, such as metaphysics, saying that the symbol differs from the metaphor by always having a non-linguistic dimension, an "external complexity." He subsequently distinguishes "the non-semantic moment" of a symbol from its semantic moment. At its semantic moment, a symbol is like a metaphor, susceptible to linguistic and logical analysis, but at the non-semantic moment it defies any "linguistic, semantic, or logical transcription."[167] It is to clarify this that Ricoeur makes the following comment on "religious symbols."

165 P. Ricoeur, "Explanation and Understanding," chap. in *Interpretation Theory: Discourse and the Surplus of Meaning* (Fort Worth: Texas Christian University Press, 1976), 71–88.

166 Ricoeur, *Interpretation*, 52.

167 Ibid., 57.

> In the sacred universe the capacity to speak is founded upon the capacity of the cosmos to signify. The logic of meaning, therefore, follows from the very structure of the sacred universe. Its law is the law of correspondences, correspondences between creation *in illo tempore* and the present order of natural appearances and human activities. . . .
>
> Such is the logic of correspondences, which binds discourse in the universe of the Sacred. We might even say that it is always by means of discourse that this logic manifests itself for if no myth narrated how things came to be or if there were no rituals which re-enacted this process, the Sacred would remain unmanifested. . . .
>
> If we now bring together the preceding analyses, I am inclined to say that what asks to be brought to language in symbols, but which never passes over completely into language, is always something powerful, efficacious, forceful. . . .[168]

I think there is a striking correspondence between Ricoeur's formulation of the symbol and Painter's theological definition of the symbol derived from the Gospel of John. Ricoeur mentions neither creation nor revelation, but there is the sacred universe in which the cosmos signifies before man can speak. Then Ricoeur talks about the law of correspondences, which correlates with Painter's conception of the Johannine use of symbols. Painter talks about the ultimate transcendent, God. Ricoeur refers to it as the sacred universe. Painter describes the function of Johannine symbolism as epistemological, while Ricoeur perceives symbolism as the reaching out of the human to the supra-human.

Philosophy expresses an upward quest for the ultimate, for God, while theology deals with revelation, which claims to have come from the other direction, from God. In the next section we will look at some theological definitions of symbolism.

Historical/Theological Interpretations

Cullmann's definition, given in "Der johanneische Gebrauch doppeldeutiger Ausdrücke als Schlüssel zum Verständnis des vierten Evangeliums," and that of Léon-Dufour, in "Towards a Symbolic Reading of the Fourth Gospel," come close to each other in several respects.[169] They

---

168 Ibid., 62–63.

169 Cullmann, "Johanneische Gebrauch," part of which is reproduced in *Early Christian Worship*, 37ff.; Léon-Dufour, "Symbolic Reading."

both reckon from the start that the Fourth Evangelist intended a theological reading, and to prove this point they both cite 20:31, "These signs have been written down in order that you might believe that . . ." Cullmann asserts that we are not dependent upon a hypothesis, "The evangelist tells us himself that his choice has been governed not by a historical principle but by an ecclesiastical or theological principle."[170] Léon-Dufour also says, "John's way of expressing himself is a result of his experience of the paschal faith."[171] There is a slight variation in their emphasis of 20:31. Cullmann identifies in 20:31 the key issue of the gospel as "believing," and, in conjunction with 30:29, stresses the relation of "seeing and believing." Léon-Dufour sees in 20:31 the "conversational character" of the gospel. That means John meant to communicate his paschal faith through a common language between himself and his readers, and that language is a double-reference language, namely, Johannine symbolism.[172]

Both scholars come up with some kind of a historical scheme in which the Johannine symbols have both a pre- and post-resurrection meaning. Cullmann draws the dividing line at the incarnation of the Logos:

> Um den Zweck seines Buches zu verwirklichen [20:31]. . . will er die Leser dazu anleiten, in den Tatsachen dieses Lebens und in den . . . gesprochenen Worten . . .ihre heilsgeschichtliche Verbindung rückwärts mit der Vergangenheit und besonders vorwärts mit der Gegenwart zu sehen, also die Linie zu ziehen, die vom Inkarnierten einerseits zur Schrift des Alten Testaments, anderseits zur Gemeinde des Erhöhten führt.[173]

It is obvious that Cullmann has a "salvation history" in view as he defines the symbolic function of John's gospel. He finds a "connexion between the historical life of Jesus and the entire history of salvation." His notion of Johannine symbolism is that the gospel "indicates in so many places the necessity of a double meaning, that enquiry into the deeper unexpressed sense [of salvation history] is to be raised to the status of a principle of interpretation."[174] This is admittedly a theological reading of the Gospel of John. However, when compared with Schneiders's view, Cullmann's view

---

170 Cullmann, *Early Christian Worship*, 38.

171 Léon-Dufour, "Symbolic Reading," 442.

172 Cullmann, *Early Christian Worship*, 40ff.; Léon-Dufour, "Symbolic Reading," 442.

173 Cullmann, "Johanneische Gebrauch," 360.

174 Cullmann, *Early Christian Worship*, 57.

is better argued because of his examination of the literature itself and his biblical exegesis. Compared with Painter's view, it has the advantage of referring back to the Old Testament and addressing the issue of salvation. Nor is there any doubt that the bountiful allusion to the Old Testament in the gospel has to do with eschatological salvation. Léon-Dufour shares almost the same view of Johannine symbolism when he says, "History is in itself run through with symbolism according to the measure of whoever reads it."[175]

If we look more carefully, then Léon-Dufour's historical scheme appears more restrictive, for he locates it in the immediate historical context of the paschal faith. He believes that the analogical relationship of a symbol is normally established in a cultural or literary framework by human intellect. So he understand the symbolism of John mainly in the context of its historical setting, and he works mainly on the "surface of the text."[176]

> The language of St John . . . comes from two different origins. There is the origin of the Jewish cultural milieu in which Jesus Himself lived, but there is also the Christian cultural milieu which inspires John's interpretation of the past. These two sources mean that there is the possibility of a double symbolism. . . .
>
> The authentic reading of the Gospel supposes that the two level of symbolism be maintained in a dialectical relationship, that is, neither one nor the other should drive its opposite number from the field. . . .
>
> . . . The symbolic operation must be situated in the two dimensions of time that are determined by the event of Easter, the time of Jesus of Nazareth and the time of the Glorified Lord.[177]

We may note that there is both a historical reference and a dialectic of Johannine theology in Léon-Dufour's interpretation. His interpretation of 3:5 illustrates this. In a Jewish milieu Jesus told Nicodemus about the rebirth of "water" and the Spirit, symbolizing the Spirit with water (3:5), but in the Christian milieu of John the text had a sacramental significance. So, by recalling "the time past of Jesus of Nazareth," John meant to bring out the "fullness of meaning" of Christian baptism and connect it with the need of spiritual rebirth.[178] Léon-Dufour emphasizes that the post-Easter Christian

---

175 Léon-Dufour, "Symbolic Reading," 437.
176 Ibid., 440–41.
177 Ibid., 440–42.
178 Ibid., 450–51.

meaning should not overshadow the pre-Easter past, but should, on the contrary, be "developed with a deeper understanding in the light of the past."[179] So we note that Léon-Dufour presumes a Christian theology, and he expects to be able to deepen that theology by looking into the pre-Easter meaning of the Johannine symbols.

Both scholars end up with a historically oriented scheme. Léon-Dufour's scheme looks back to the Jewish setting immediately prior to Easter, while Cullmann's scheme goes all the way back to the Old Testament history of salvation. Léon-Dufour focuses mainly on the New Testament, while Cullmann has both Testaments in view. They both have theological assumptions. We may categorize theirs as the "historical theological approach."

Our Methodology

What kind of a treatment on Johannine symbolism is needed now? Culpepper has suggested,

> a treatment is needed that (1) is based on adequate definitions, (2) is sensitive to movement and development in the gospel, (3) relates the metaphors, symbols, and motifs to one another, and (4) analyzes their function within the gospel as a literary whole.[180]

In the next chapter, as we focus our study of symbolism on "water," we will begin with a literary approach. We will look into "metaphors, symbols, and motifs" that are related to water, and observe their "movement and development in the gospel." We will try to interpret the use of water "within the gospel as a literary whole." These should match with three out of Culpepper's four expectations, which presuppose a literary interest.

However, a purely literary definition cannot be an "adequate definition." The study of Johannine symbolism has to satisfy historical, philosophical and theological investigations as well. We will attempt here a balanced treatment, though such an attempt will not be void of presuppositions.

---

179 Ibid., 446.
180 Culpepper, *Anatomy*, 188–89.

An Integrative Approach

Most of the theories analyzed above take a "mixed approach." Schneiders's theory begins with literary analysis and ends up with extensive theological applications. Dodd is sensitive to the literary nature of the text but historically critical towards the ideology of the gospel. Meeks insists on a mythological reading in the Bultmannian style but keeps his eyes open to the overall structure of the gospel. Even Wead, whose method seems so restrictive, makes ideological investigations besides form analysis. I can go on and on. The fact is that an exclusively literary interpretation or an exclusively historical one seldom holds. Even Ashton, who disagrees with literary approaches to John, talks about a synchronic reading of the gospel.[181] There is nothing wrong with taking a historical approach but everything wrong with taking it exclusively. Theological "reading in" is unacceptable but a theological interpretation supported by literary and historical observations is in every way justifiable. In this book we take different approaches into consideration but rule out the most restrictive methods. Bultmann's solution of the Johannine puzzle of Jesus is not as preferable as Meeks's, for example, because Bultmann limits himself to a diachronic view but Meeks looks also at the literary development of the full text. For the same reason interpretations that begin and end with reader response are not being considered here.[182]

If a mixed approach is taken, which takes priority in interpretation? The literary, the historical, or the theological? Here we note that there are goals and presuppositions that govern the methodology. There is, for example, an endless effort in shaping up the Johannine text in Bultmann's work, because the goal of it is to recover the history behind the text. Form criticism is the rule and process, and the presupposition is a mythical pattern for John in the history of religion. Meeks shares the same presupposition but somewhat diverges in the goal and therefore the method. In these cases historical criticism becomes the "master" in the determination of the meaning

---

181 After condemning the views of Staley, Segovia, Culpepper, and Mlakuzhyil rigorously in a row, Ashton almost contradicts himself by saying that it is necessary to work on John as an integrated narrative; J. Ashton, "Narrative Criticism," chap. in *Studying John: Approaches to the Fourth Gospel* (Oxford: Clarendon Press, 1994), 141–65.

182 For example, L. Eslinger, "The Wooing of the Woman at the Well: Jesus, the Reader and Reader Response Criticism," *Literature and Theology* 1 (1987): 167–83.

of the symbols of John.

An Open Investigation

Traditional critical methods cannot satisfy the study of symbolism because, as "masters," they bring language too much under control. By studying only the "literary" peculiarities of John and only "historically" critically, the symbolism therein is missed out. The following quotation from Fawcett explains the problem.

> The age of radical criticism in the later nineteenth century was characterized by the intent . . . to take all biblical statements as physical fact and argue their validity on that basis. Only with the recognition that these writings were often poetic and symbolic could the misguided arguments of that era be brought to an end. . . . *Progress in understanding scripture may in fact be said to be proportionate very largely to the extent to which its symbolic character is recognized.*
>
> In the age of rationalism . . . and of materialism . . . it appeared to many that man had overcome the need for symbols and could know the world as it is. . . . Others, however, had already recognized the permanence of the symbol and not merely in the religious but also in the scientific sphere. Thus Herbert Spencer remarked that: 'Ultimate religious ideas and ultimate scientific ideas alike, turn out to be merely symbols of the actual, not cognitions of it' (italics mine).[183]

If the scientific method recognizes only codes and signs, not symbols, then, likewise, biblical criticism ignores what it cannot scrutinize. That is the situation we see in Bultmann, Wead, and others. As Fawcett points out, progress in interpretation is being restricted because of the authoritative status we have given to criticism. Whether we are ready to relinquish that depends on our recognition of what more is to be known.

In this book, symbolism is understood as epistemological, as Dodd, Painter, and Ricoeur suggest. It expresses that which science cannot exhaustively know, or, in terms of biblical symbolism, it proclaims the transcendent truth, the authority of which goes beyond that of criticism. Painter's formulation of Johannine symbolism is specially relevant in this respect, namely, there is an epistemological function in the use of symbols in John, and the foundation of it is located in the creation and revelation of the Logos.

---

183 Fawcett, *Symbolic Language*, 31–32. Spencer's remark comes from *OED*.

Symbolism, thus defined, may not always be interpreted with precision, or be expounded exhaustively. Precision and exhaustiveness belong to the domain of criticism, which, when dealing with symbolism, cannot avoid ambivalence because symbols are versatile in their power to signify. When we think of the vast unknown that calls for the use of symbolism, we expect to read in the symbol a richness of expression and a possibility of multiple meanings. In this book, we will allow for multiple meanings as well as inconclusive investigations.

An Exploration of Revelatory Contents

Our goal is to search for the revelation about Jesus presented in the Gospel of John through water symbolism. This goal matches with the purpose disclosed at the beginning and towards the end of the gospel itself. "No one has ever seen God, but God the only Son, who is at the Father's side, has made him known" (1:18); "Jesus did many other miraculous signs in the presence of his disciples, which are not recorded in this book. But these are written that you may believe that Jesus is the Christ, the Son of God, and that by believing you may have life in his name" (20:30–31). Here we follow the "historico-theological" approach of Cullmann and Léon-Dufour and consider the Johannine symbols a means of proclaiming Jesus as the revelation of God.

O'Day summarizes the issue of "revealer and revelation in the Fourth Gospel" in three terms: the *Dass*, the *Was*, and the *Wie* of revelation.[184] In this book we reckon the three functions of Johannine symbolism: the *Dass*, the *Was*, and the *Wie* of revelation. By *Dass* we refer to the identity of Jesus. It was Bultmann who first defined the *Dass*, "Jesus reveals nothing but that he is the revealer."[185] However, we must break away from Bultmann's restrictive *Dass*, because the Johannine symbols tell us more than just Jesus' identity. The metaphorical and narrative symbols, in particular, reveals further truths about Jesus, such as his power and his salvation, and also truths taught by Jesus, such as eschatology and the Holy Spirit. We summarize these as the *Was*, and *Was* stands for christological

184 O'Day, "Narrative Mode," 657.

185 R. Bultmann, *Theology of the New Testament*, trans. K. Grobel (London: SCM, 1955), 66.

dogma in E. Käsemann's original sense.[186] All these constitute a wealth of revelatory contents. Our goal is to explore it through water symbolism.

As for *Wie*, the form or fashion of revelation, one would like to make some theological claims about John's literary devices, as literary scholars do. O'Day, for instance, says that irony in John is revelatory. Along the same lines the most attractive theory is Schneiders's treatment of Johannine symbolism as incarnational. However, though there may be an analogical relation between symbolism and incarnation, the effectiveness of Johannine symbolism as a form of revelation lies not in its analogy to incarnation. It lies in its versatility and elusive nature, which defy our demand for precision. In the Johannine narrative, every time a symbol is evoked, whether it is an ἐγώ εἰμι statement or a σημεῖον or just an irony, we are led to a heightening of curiosity, a search for further knowledge about something transcendent, namely, "who" Jesus is or "what" he teaches. So the symbol brings in an enigma. Yet, at the same time, by using a symbol, the author of the gospel clarifies the enigma. As said above, the symbols in John, though elusive, are used not to conceal but to reveal. My view is that the author had not intended any puzzle. He composed with symbolism only because that was "how" revelation came. He had received and understood it, and he intended to clarify and pass it on.

The way the Johannine symbols work may be seen as similar to how the kingdom parables work. They create a dynamics or dilemma of "concealing and revealing at the same time" (cf. Mark 4:11–12), and that is the way it is with God's revelation to humankind. In the Synoptics and in John, respectively, parables and symbols are *Wie*'s of revelation.

A Canonical Search

In this work we will not stop at critical analysis but attempt an open search. Historical and literary methods will be our helpers, rather than masters, in pursuing the theological meaning of "water" in the Gospel of John. If we are not satisfied with hard and fast conclusions, we will have to expect some fuzziness in the work. Such a work may look nebulous, but it has a clear focus on "water," and a special reference to John 4.

There will be three more chapters in this book. In the next chapter a

---

186 E. Käsemann, *The Testament of Jesus, According to John 17* (Philadelphia: Fortress, 1968).

literary approach will be taken to study the overall structure of water symbolism in the gospel. In the third chapter there will be an exegetical study on John 4, where "the living water" will be interpreted in its historical context. In the fourth chapter we will make "an open search," to locate water symbolism in its "salvation historical" context, after Cullmann's fashion. This will be a biblical or canonical search.

We have chosen Painter's framework to begin with, locating the foundation of Johannine symbolism in the Logos's creation and revelation and defining its function as epistemological. If humanity's search for the unknown is our starting point, and God's creation is our open end, then biblical revelation will be our field. Between the restrictive domain governed by traditional criticism, and the transcendent unknown which Johannine symbolism claims to reveal, we want to trace water symbolism down the canonical context of the gospel. We presuppose that the Old Testament form the main source of water symbolism in John, and it provides the guidelines and boundaries for our open search. We also presuppose a history of revelation in these "scriptures." According to the gospel, this history culminates in the Logos' incarnation. It is in the context of this history that we study water symbolism in chapter four of this work. Cullmann's conception is instructive towards this understanding. "In the life and words" of Jesus the Christ, the Son of God (20:31), there is a "salvation historical relation backwards and forward." It leads from the incarnation of the Logos "to the writing of the Old Testament on the one hand and to the community of the exalted one on the other."[187]

It is in the theological context of salvation history that we call this work an eschatological interpretation. It will be worked out in the subsequent chapters with a literary emphasis, a historical emphasis, and then a biblical theological emphasis.

---

187 Cullmann, "Johanneische Gebrauch," 360.

CHAPTER TWO

THE LITERARY DEVELOPMENT OF JOHANNINE WATER SYMBOLISM

In this chapter we are concerned with two questions. First, "Where is water symbolism located in the overall structure of the Gospel of John?" Second, "How is water symbolism in John 4 related to Johannine water symbolism in general?" These questions are important because the mention of water is extensive in this gospel. It is sometimes significant and explicit, e.g., in reference to John's baptism, in Jesus' dialogue with Nicodemus about the new birth, in Jesus' discussion with the Samaritan woman about eternal life, and so on. It is sometimes implicit or inconspicuous, e.g., in the account of Jesus' walking on the sea, in the healing of the blind at the pool of Siloam, and in the intriguing passage which tells us that blood and water flew out from the pierced side of Jesus' body (19:34). It is uncertain whether the author of John intends a symbolic meaning in every mention of "water," or how many of the symbolic references are theologically significant.

Water symbolism in John is thus treated not only as "metaphorical" symbolism but also as "thematic" symbolism. My expectation is that a study of its occurrence throughout the gospel will guide us into a fuller understanding of its meaning. As Meeks says, "the reader cannot understand any part of the Fourth Gospel until he understands the whole."[1] In this chapter we are dealing with the whole of water symbolism in John.

Previous Works on Johannine Water Symbolism

There have been comparatively few attempts on this topic. B. Olsson wrote a "text-linguistic analysis" on John 4 in 1974 and remarked that a detailed analysis of water symbolism in the Gospel of John was needed, as

1 Meeks, "Man from Heaven," 59.

no such analysis existed.[2] What Olsson contributed at that point was only an excursus on "living water in John," several pages long, addressing the symbolic use of water in chapters 4 and 7. Around the same time, L. Sciberras wrote a thesis on "Water in the Gospel of St. John According to the Greek Fathers and Writers of the Church."[3] He went through the symbol of water in chapters 2 to 5, 7, 9, 13, and summarized the views of ancient writers such as Origen, Ammonius of Alexandria, and Cyril of Alexandria, but he did not exegete the passages or comment on the overall structure. Since then several dissertations or monographs on the topic have been published. These works, in their respective ways, all try to grapple with the existing pattern or structure of Johannine water symbolism.

A Three-Stage Development of the Symbol

In a doctoral dissertation written in 1982, "Le symbolism de l'eau dans le Quatrième Évangile," E. Becerra studies all the accounts in John in which he comes across the use of water symbolism.[4] The order in which Becerra arranges these accounts is worth noting. It reflects his way of interpretation of these symbols, as well as his understanding of the overall structure.

The Water of Baptism and Purification	
A. The baptism of John the Baptist	(John 1)
B. The changing of water into wine at Cana	(John 2)
The Water and Sprit of the New Birth	
I. The dialogue of Jesus with Nicodemus	(John 3)
II. The washing of the feet	(John 13)
The Living Water of John 4	(John 4)
The Stream of Living Water of John 7	(John 7)
The Water of the Pierced Side of Jesus	(John 19)[5]

2 B. Olsson, *Structure and Meaning in the Fourth Gospel: A Text-Linguistic Analysis of John 2:1–11 and 4:1–42*, trans. J. Gray, Coniectanea biblica, New Testament 6 (Lund: Gleerup, 1974), 212.

3 L. Sciberras, "Water in the Gospel of St. John According to the Greek Fathers and Writers of the Church" (thesis for the licentiate, Studium Biblicum Franciscanum, Jerusalem, 1974–75).

4 E. Becerra, "Le symbolisme de l'eau dans le Quatrième Évangile" (diss., Université des Sciences Humaines de Strasbourg, 1982).

5 Ibid., 295–99.

Becerra's order basically follows the sequence in the gospel. However, "the washing of feet" (John 13) is moved forward and placed next to "Jesus' dialogue with Nicodemus" (John 3) under the topic "the water and spirit of the new birth." That means, Becerra associates the washing of feet with the death of Jesus, which he interprets as instrumental to regeneration. Becerra calls this association a "symbolic interpretation." As Jesus humbled himself and washed the disciples' feet, he "symbolically" declared their purification at the same time.[6]

Becerra intends to strike a balance between literalism and allegorical interpretation. He exegetes the passages historico-grammatically, but simultaneously looks out for "the allusive sense,"—which, he declares, "the concrete representation or real language do not prevent us to perceive."[7] His conception regarding symbolism is that language can be susceptible to a wealth of meaning "beyond the dimension of the real primary sense."[8]

As for the overall structure, Becerra's thematic outline does not seem to reflect the narrative movement of the gospel as a whole. His interpretation of individual passages distorts his perception of the structure. Thus he moves John 13 up to be placed with John 3 under "new birth." In fact he groups it with the first three chapters in John together, and interprets the "water" there, whether of "baptism," or of "new birth," as having to do with "purification." So "the washing of feet" also symbolizes purification. As for the living water in John 4, he interprets it as "revelation," "wisdom," or "the law of the new order."[9] As for the stream of living water in John 7, he interprets it as "the eschatological work of the Holy Spirit."[10]

Thus, Becerra observes, "in the mind of the evangelist, water symbolism seems to develop in three periods or stages."

> a. La première étape montre l'eau comme symbole de purification dans un contexte très proche de l'Ancien Testament . . .

---

6 Ibid., 177.

7 Ibid., 9.

8 Note that he endorses Ricoeur's definition, "J'appelle symbole toute structure de signification," and so, "Le symbolisme où sens indirect oblique alors une interprétation qui consiste à déchiffrer le sens caché dans le sens apparent, à déployer les niveaux de signification impliqués dans la signification litérale" (ibid., 4–5), citing P. Ricoeur, *Le conflit des interprétations. Essais d'herméneutique* (Paris: Édition du Seuil, 1969), 16.

9 Ibid., 211.

10 Ibid., 240.

> b. La deuxième étape se voit le plus clairement dans le dialogue de Jésus avec la Samaritaine. . . . Jésus, le nouveau Jacob, qui apporte l'eau vive (la révélation, la sagesse ou la loi du nouvel ordre) à tous ceux qui la demandent . . .
>
> c. . . . Jn 7 souligne d'une façon particulière qu'après la glorification de Jésus l'Esprit Saint serait donné. Nous voyons donc comme une troisième étape, dans l'emploi du symbolisme de l'eau, l'annonce directe de Jn 7,37–39: l'oeuvre eschatologique du Saint Esprit . . .[11]

The weakness of this proposal is twofold. First, it fails to see any unifying factor in the use of water in John. Although Becerra derives his topics from careful exegesis, his topical outline ends up rather forced. The symbolic meaning of water also ends up stifled, as the passages get confined to the three stages. Second, Becerra does not cope with the decreasing use of water symbolism towards the end of the gospel. The latter two of his three stages are too scantily represented to be called a stage (respectively, just John 4 and John 7). "The water from the pierced side of Jesus" (John 19) is not assigned to any of the stages at all.

On the other hand, the strength of Becerra's interpretation lies in his interpretation of "the washing of feet" as one of the symbolic references to the death of Christ. This brings to our attention an important linkage between water symbolism and the death motif in John. Running through the gospel, we see a series of symbolic sayings that point to Christ's death, namely, the lifting up of the serpent (3:14), the giving of Christ's flesh (6:51), the laying down of the shepherd's life (10:15), the dying of a kernel of wheat (12:24), etc. Here in the "washing of feet" we see an overlap between the symbol of water and the motif of Christ's death, which is a key to unlock the intricate "thematic structure" of John's gospel. We will look into this again later on in this chapter.

"Water Units" Embedded in Narrative Sections

J. A. Kowalski, in her dissertation written in 1987, "Of Water and Spirit: Narrative Structure and Theological Development in the Gospel of John," demonstrates a better sense of the varying intensity of water throughout the gospel.[12] Unlike Becerra and others who exegete the water

---

11 Ibid., 259–61.

12 J. A. Kowalski, "'Of Water and Spirit': Narrative Structure and Theological Development in the Gospel of John" (diss., Marquette University, 1987).

passages one by one and offer a flat structure of water in John, Kowalski bases her study of water symbolism on the narrative structure of the full text:

> Some sections carry more than one reference to water, and others treat water in passing, by inference, or in retrospect, referring to a previous occasion. . . .
>
> Some have treated the episodes individually, and have based their interpretation on information carried within discrete episodes . . . exegetes who focus on only one unit may overlook the possibilities of exposing their interpretation to the corrective or affirmative critique of other Johannine "water" units.[13]

Kowalski's work includes two stages. First, applying some of M. Sternberg's criteria of literary analysis, namely, the narrator's representation of time, the distribution of gaps, and the ordering of materials, she deduces the intended structure of the gospel. There are twelve sections in the structure she proposes, each with two to several units. Second, going through all units and sections, Kowalski looks into two "dynamics" of the gospel, namely, the emphasis on time and timing which the narrator employs, and the appearance of water as a recurring motif. Kowalski claims that both aspects are pervasive in the gospel, and that "they occur in all sections, and seem to affect many critical issues in the 'story.'"[14] The prevalence of water in the gospel, as Kowalski sees it, can be seen from the wide distribution of sections or units in which water appears. In the outline that follows, the "water units" located by Kowalski are marked by asterisks.

I. 1:1–2:11 Introduction to Characters and Story		
*	A. 1:1–1:28	John: baptism of *water*
	B. 1:29–1:51	Jesus: baptism of Holy Spirit
*	C. 2:1–2:11	Jesus: *water* changed to wine
II. 2:12–3:21 Jerusalem (First Passover)		
	A. 2:12–2:22	Jesus and disciples: Temple cleansing
*	B. 2:23–3:21	Jesus and Nicodemus: *water* and Spirit
III. 3:22–4:42 Judea and Samaria		
*	A. 3:22–4:3	John and Jesus' disciples: *water* baptism
*	B. 4:4–4:42	Jesus and Samaritan woman: living *water*
IV. 4:43–4:54 Galilee		
*	A. 4:43–4:46a	Galileans and Jesus: . . . *water* to wine
	B. 4:46b–4:54	Gentile official: response to Jesus' word

---

13 Ibid., 52, 58.

14 Ibid., 2.

V. 5:1–5:47 Jerusalem (A Feast of the Jews)
* A. 5:1–5:9a Jesus: healing at the *Pool* of Bethzatha
B. 5:9b–5:47 Jews: response to healing
VI. 6:1–6:71 Sea of Galilee and Capernaum (Second Passover)
* A. 6:1–6:15 5000: being fed by the *Sea* of Galilee
* B. 6:16–6:21 Jesus: walking on the *Sea* of Galilee
C. 6:22–6:71 Jews: response to both events
VII. 7:1–10:39 Jerusalem (Feast of Tabernacles and Dedication)
* A. 7:1–8:59 Jesus: speaking on "River of Living *Water*"
* B. 9:1–9:39 Jesus: healing at the *Pool* of Siloam
C. 9:40–10:21 Jesus and Pharisees at Tabernacles: conflict
D. 10:22–10:39 Jesus and Jews at Dedication: conflict
VIII. 10:40–11:53 Bethany (Across Jordan, . . . Judea)
* A. 10:40–11:6 Jesus across Jordan: where John *baptized*
B. 11:7–11:46 Lazarus: being raised from death
C. 11:47–11:53 Pharisees: plotting Jesus' death
IX. 11:54–19:27 Ephraim . . . Jerusalem (Third Passover)
A. 11:54–11:57 Jews at Ephraim: speculating on Jesus
B. 12:1–12:11 Mary at Bethany: anointing Jesus' feet
C. 12:12–12:50 Jews and Greeks at Jerusalem: reaction
* D. 13:1–13:30 Jesus at Jerusalem: *washing* disciples' feet
E. 13:31–17:26 Jesus at Jerusalem: "Farewell Discourses"
F. 18:1–19:27 Jesus at Jerusalem: arrest and trial
X.* 19:28–19:37 Jesus' Death (Blood and *Water* from Jesus' Side)
XI. 19:38–20:31 Disciples' Response to Jesus' Death
A. 19:38–20:10 Diciples: immediate reactions to the death
B. 20:11–20:18 Resurrection appearance to Mary
C. 20:19–20:31 Resurrection appearance to other disciples
XII.* 21:1–21:25 The *Sea* of Tiberias: Resurrection Appearances[15]

Thus Kowalski made an attempt to grasp the narrative movement of the gospel. She reminds us that John's use of water should be studied in the overall narrative framework. However, she never distinguishes between the incidental mention of water and the symbolic use of it, so the prevalence of water units in her outline describes only the general appearance, not the symbolic use. As she treats the author solely as a "narrator" and never a writer of discourse or redactor, she fails to see the possibility of a topical arrangement of materials. In her view there is no isolation of the prologue, nor is there any transition between chapters 12 and 13. Some of the sections

15 Kowalski's outline (ibid., 17–18) is rewritten here, with emphasis on "water."

seem disproportionately long, e.g., VII and IX. Some are very short, e.g. X.

Kowalski's consistently "narrative" approach is applied also to the second part of the work. In studying the "water units," her assumption is that many of the "gaps" where the meaning of water is withheld are "filled" (offered an explanation) later on in the story. For example, the function of John's water baptism mentioned in 1:26 (unit IA) is explained at 1:31 and 1:34 (unit IB) as "to reveal Jesus by John's 'witness'"—a partial filling of the gap. The gap is completely filled when, still later, in 5:33–38 (unit VB), the temporary witness of John's baptism is said to be replaced by the witness of "the Father's Word (τὸν λόγον)."[16] Thus Kowalski makes a lot of "links" throughout the text between "water" and "God's Word." In her interpretation the mention of water can almost invariably be ascribed to the Word of God.[17]

As Kowalski takes a synchronic approach, she makes no reference at all to the historical background. Yet she also neglects the fact that some mention of water arises out of a discourse rather than a narrative (cf. 1:31, 7:35). In doing so she cannot possibly remain objective in interpreting. It is quite forced to say that all the uses of "water" can be connected to the mention of "God's Word." Such a preconceived connection detaches the symbol from its immediate context and distorts its symbolic sense.

Kowalski is to be commended, however, for studying the use of water in John as a connected whole, just as the gospel text itself stands as a narrative whole. If the author of John has intended any "pattern" at all for the use of water, that pattern may well be seen more clearly in the context of a narrative development of the gospel, rather than in truncated passages alone.

"Like a Stream on a Hillside"

In the last chapter I have quoted Koester's view on the distinction between "metaphor" and "symbol." I now refer to his view on the literary context. His book, *Symbolism in the Fourth Gospel*, published in 1995, is a bold attempt to study all the uses of symbolism in John's gospel.[18] Koester's conception of symbolism is close to what I formerly described as

16 Ibid., 72.
17 Ibid., 57.
18 Minneapolis: Fortress, 1995.

commendable. He locates the foundation of symbolism in the creation and revelation of God.[19] He presumes the versatility of symbolic language and its reference to "transcendent reality." Instead of taking a restrictively historical approach, or, in his own words, working only on "the cultural context," he looks extensively into the "literary context" of Johannine symbolism. In this respect Culpepper seems to have influenced him greatly. This can be seen in his definition of Johannine symbolism in terms of "core" and "supporting" symbols, which Culpepper calls "core" and "peripheral" symbols.[20] "A recurring cluster of core and supporting images creates a motif," Koester proposes. So some chapters of his book are devoted to the major motifs, e.g., "light and darkness," "water" and "the crucifixion."

Koester claims to be sensitive to the literary nature of the subject. He also reckons the ambiguity of symbolic language:

> A challenge for interpreters is to discern which images in John's Gospel should be understood symbolically. . . . We can chuckle when Nicodemus is tripped up by the prospect of being "born" again . . . But as we make our way through the narrative, we may find that our own footing is not so sure. We may be confident that a statement like "people loved darkness rather than light" (3:19) is symbolic, but does this mean that all references to darkness and night are symbolic?[21]

Such a note cautions us against calling every mention of water "symbolism." In fact, Koester does not treat every incidence of water under the chapter "water." "The washing of feet," for instance, is discussed under "symbolic action." So is the breaking of "bread," which Culpepper enlists as one of the three core symbols. Behind all these is Koester's evaluation of the varying intensity of symbols throughout the narrative. "The primary symbol in the [Cana] episode," he evaluates, "is the transformation of water into wine, and the supporting symbols are the stone jars that held the water."[22] So Koester discusses it twice: as a core under "symbolic actions" and as a supporting symbol under "water." In works prior to Koester's, the use of water symbolism is "flatly" perceived. To interpret water symbolism in a

19 He seems to locate it also in the incarnation (ibid., 2–3), but he does not state or support his theory as clearly as Painter does.

20 Ibid., 5; Culpepper, *Anatomy*, 189.

21 Koester, *Symbolism in the Fourth Gospel*, 7.

22 Ibid., 11.

passage, one only sees if there is, or not, but never its relative significance. Koester, however, points out the variation between the core and the supporting. Thus he addresses the characteristic development of water symbolism as being "flexible," or "conforming to the contours of the narrative." Note the following observation of Koester's.

> The water motif in the Fourth Gospel is less consistent than that of light and darkness. Like a stream on a hillside, it maintains a general direction of movement while readily conforming to the contours of the narrative through which it flows. The significance of water is almost always connected with washing or drinking. There is an easy movement from one type of action to the other, and both may have the same meaning. The jar . . . baptism . . . living water . . . the pool of Siloam . . . sea . . .[23]

This perception can free us from expecting consistency in the representation of water in John. We still need, however, examine how it integrates with other symbols or motifs to constitute the narrative whole, something Koester does not proceed to do. A disappointment with Koester's work may be that he aims at including too much. He topically covers all kinds of symbolism and he works through all of the chapters in John. He copes with all the instances in which he finds water symbolism and treats some of them even twice. With such a full agenda, his treatment becomes like a running commentary through the passages with minimal scholarly interaction. Little is said about how the pattern of water symbolism in John resembles "a stream on a hillside."

Koester does offer a brief statement on the overall structure: "The fundamental structure of Johannine symbolism is twofold. The primary level of meaning concerns Christ; the secondary level concerns discipleship."[24] In my opinion this is a summary of the theological use of Johannine symbols, rather than a literary structure.

Narrative Sections Consecutively Arranged

A full monograph on the subject eventually got published in 1997. L. P. Jones, in *The Symbol of Water in the Gospel of John*, offers the most

---

23 Ibid., 156.
24 Ibid., 12–15.

extensive treatment to date.[25] He considers water "a literary device within the narrative," and analyzes all the twelve narrative sections in John that feature water as a symbol.[26] His approach is purely literary and synchronic. The study of each narrative section includes three steps: a description of its narrative context, an examination of the literary structure and development, and an investigation of the meaning and function of water within it. The arrangement is all the time neat, and it follows the order in which the narrative sections appear. Here is an outline given at the end of chapter 1 of Jones's book:

> The following chapter [2] will examine the narrative sections involving water at beginning of Jesus' ministry (1.19–34; 2.1–11; 3.1–21; 3.22–30). Chapter 3 will examine the narrative sections in which water appears in the initial journeys from Galilee and Jerusalem. . . . Chapter 4 will examine the two narrative sections in which water appears in the final journey to Jerusalem (7.37–44; 9.1–44). The final exegetical chapter will examine the narrative sections in which water appears during the narrative of the 'hour' . . . (13.1–20; 19.28–37) [27]

Jones claims to have attempted after Koester's fashion to remain sensitive to the movement of the narrative. However, he is sensitive only to the surface flow of the gospel narrative. Quite like Becerra and others, he exegetes the water passages one by one but ignores the varying intensity of the symbolic use of water. The flat structure he composes must have appeared to him sufficient, for what he concentrates on is only the literary aspect of the appearance of water in John.

The Use of Water Symbolism throughout the Gospel

Here I will go through the appearance of water in John to establish a preliminary "map." My exploration is based on the perception that the gospel is an "episodic" narrative.[28] The episodes in the initial chapters, up to chapter 4, are mainly narratives, though there are short intervening discourses. The episodes in the central portion of the gospel, between chapters 5 and 12, are

---

25 Sheffield: Sheffield Academic Press, 1997.

26 Ibid., 34.

27 Ibid., 35.

28 Both Culpepper and Ashton recognize that the gospel's plot is episodic (Culpepper, *Anatomy*, 89; Ashton, "Narrative Criticism," 158); cf. Dodd's view of the gospel structure, *Interpretation*, x.

narrative-discourse complexes with long intervening discourses. The last few chapters are made up of the farewell discourse (chapters 13 to 17), which is one long episode, and then the passion and resurrection accounts, composed mainly of narratives. This is a rough but truthful picture of the gospel's literary structure, which will be useful in our exploration.

Incidental References to Water

There are three passing remarks that should not be interpreted symbolically although they either carry the word "water" or refer to some situations that involve water.

3:22–24. The first of these passing remarks is found at 3:22–24, Μετὰ ταῦτα . . . ἦν δὲ καὶ ὁ Ἰωάννης βαπτίζων ἐν Αἰνὼν ἐγγὺς τοῦ Σαλείμ, ὅτι ὕδατα πολλὰ ἦν ἐκεῖ, καὶ παρεγίνοντο καὶ ἐβαπτίζοντο. Since Σαλείμ means "salvation" and Αἰνών is the transliteration of the Semitic word meaning "springs," a symbolic reading has been suggested: "the baptism of John was 'near' Jesus' salvation," but commentators have generally dismissed this interpretation.[29] A reader who has been struck by the frequent mention of water in the initial chapters might interpret the words ὅτι ὕδατα πολλὰ ἦν ἐκεῖ as a hint at the former dependence on the rite of purification, in contrast to the wonders of Jesus' present salvation. But one should note that this sentence is just one of the explanatory insertions characteristic of John. In fact Jesus was baptizing just as John did at that time, and the author could have associated Σαλείμ with Jesus if he desired a symbolic connection, but he has not. My interpretation is that 3:22–24 is just a subsidiary remark written or edited by the author to clarify the setting of the ensuing episode: the topography (Ἰουδας, Σαλείμ, Αἰνών), the chronology (Μετὰ ταῦτα . . . οὔπω γὰρ ἦν βεβλημένος εἰς τὴν φυλακὴν ὁ Ἰωάννης), and the accompanying scene (καὶ παρεγίνοντο καὶ ἐβαπτίζοντο).

I am more inclined towards seeing a connection between the ensuing episode of this statement, the Baptist's response to the debate on ceremonial washing (3:25–30), and previous episodes, namely, the Baptist's testimony that he is not the Christ (1:19–28) and Jesus' changing water into wine at Cana (2:1–11). Using Sternberg or Kowalski's terms, the "gaps" which

29 Bultmann, however, believes that the evangelist has this association in mind (*John*, 170, n. 9).

were left opened in the earlier episodes are now filled. The Baptist, who said he was not the Christ, now further explains he is like the friend who attends the bridegroom. The miracle at Cana in which the choice wine was left till the end is now furthered with a reference to the eschatological wedding, in which the Christ is the real bride.[30] While the statement ὅτι ὕδατα πολλὰ ἦν ἐκει does not carry any symbolic sense by itself, the ensuing episode teaches the eschatological meaning of ceremonial washing. When John the baptist says, ἐκεῖνον δεῖ αὐξάνειν, ἐμὲ δὲ ἐλαττοῦσθαι (3:30), he implies that ceremonial washing is preparatory to eschatological salvation, and that eschatological salvation is symbolized by the joyful event of the bridegroom's wedding.

4:46. Another incidental reference to water occurs at 4:46, Ἦλθεν οὖν πάλιν εἰς τὴν Κανὰ τῆς Γαλιλαίας, ὅπου ἐποίησεν τὸ ὕδωρ οἶνον. The literary use of it, however, is not so incidental. The sentence is again a typical explanatory note on the topographical setting of an ensuing episode. It forms part of the inclusion, which delimits the account of healing of the official's son (4:46–54). It stands in close affinity to another inclusion, 2:1 and 2:11, which delimits the account of a previous episode, the change of water into wine (2:1–11). Both inclusions (4:46, 54; 2:1, 11) stress repeatedly that the place of Jesus' miracle was Cana, and give an explicit numbering of the miracle at the end. The resemblance between the miracles is well known.[31] These have caused interpreters to either attribute the two periscopes to the same source, or structure the gospel with a clear division at 2:1–4:54, "from Cana to Cana." The mention of water at 4:46, ὅπου ἐποίησεν τὸ ὕδωρ οἶνον, plays a strong literary role in this connection, but it is unlikely that symbolic meaning is intended here.

10:40. In this verse, we find another passing remark, καὶ ἀπῆλθεν πάλιν πέραν τοῦ Ἰορδάνου εἰς τὸν τόπον ὅπου ἦν Ἰωάννης τὸ πρῶτον βαπτίζων καὶ ἔμεινεν ἐκεῖ. Though John's baptism involves water, there is no explicit use of the water symbol here. The function of this remark is, seemingly, to "recall the first encounter John had with Jesus."[32] The topography of Jesus' movement is also stressed. It forms part of the total

---

30 Cf. Kowalski, "Of Water and Spirit," 80–82, 90–91.

31 Their general pattern and literary context are the same (See Brown, *John*, 1:194).

32 Kowalski, "Of Water and Spirit," 110.

statement (10:40–42) which summarizes Jesus' public ministry.[33] The reference to John's testimony to Jesus and the initial place of John's baptism echoes a very early statement, 1:28, ταῦτα ἐν Βηθανίᾳ ἐγένετο πέραν τοῦ Ἰορδάνου, ὅπου ἦν ὁ Ἰωάννης βαπτίζων. An inclusion may be suggested here. Carson argues for the symbolic meaning of this reference: the identification of Jesus as the Lamb of God (1:28–29) and the anticipation of his death as a sacrifice for the people (11:45–53).[34] This symbolism, however, has no direct bearing to our study here.

Symbolic References That Are Uncertain

Here I will discuss three incidents in which water is mentioned or involved but its symbolic meaning is unclear or implicit. Interpretations on these passages have been controversial.

5:1–15. The episode of the healing at Bethesda (5:1–15) was interpreted by most early church fathers with a symbolic reference to Christian baptism: the pond of Bethesda heralded the future sacrament of baptism with the forgiveness of sin and the giving of grace.[35] Tertullian finds baptismal significance in the healing power of the waters stirred by the angel.[36] However, the omission of 5:4 in early textual witnesses makes it appear as if this stirring action bears little significance in this episode. If that note had been original in the text, there might have been some agreement about the symbolic meaning of water here. But not so nowadays. Becerra does not include this passage at all in his work. Even Brown admits, "The theme of water is incidental to the story; it has nothing to do with the healing; the primary emphasis is more on the Sabbath setting than on the healing as such."[37] But "certainly," Brown wavers, "some of this symbolism is possible." Dodd suggests that the water here symbolizes "law given through Moses," which is "powerless to create the will to live," and that over against it is set "the life-giving word of Christ."[38] But Dodd does not give any

33 Brown, *John*, 1:414.

34 D. A. Carson, *The Gospel According to John* (Grand Rapids: Eerdmans, 1991), 147, 400.

35 Sciberras, "Water According to Greek Fathers," 69–73.

36 Tertullian, *De Bap.* v 5–6, SC 35:74, quoted by Brown, *John*, 1:211.

37 Brown, *John*, 1:211.

38 Dodd, *Interpretation*, 319–20.

historical or literary support to this seemingly allegorical interpretation.

Yet the theme of water is not altogether incidental if the invalid's longing to be put into the water is taken into consideration. The words ἄνθρωπον οὐκ ἔχω ἵνα ὅταν ταραχθῇ τὸ ὕδωρ βάλῃ με εἰς τὴν κολυμβήθραν . . . disclose an expectation of some power in the water. Furthermore, the symbolic use here becomes clearer if we view it in the context of the preceding episodes in chapters 1 to 4. There is consistently a juxtaposition of water with what Jesus brings about. In John's testimony water is juxtaposed with the Holy Spirit with which Jesus will baptize (1:19–34). In the miracle at Cana water fills the jars but wine is drawn out (2:1–11). In Jesus' discourse with Nicodemus about rebirth water is mentioned side by side with spirit (3:1–21). In Jesus' dialogue with the Samaritan woman, Jacob's water is superseded by the living water of Jesus (4:1–26). So, now, in 5:1–15, the long awaited healing by Bethesda water is replaced by the instant healing brought about by Jesus. This episode is, admittedly, not placed inside the Cana inclusion (2:1–4:54) in which we find previous "water episodes."[39] With its sabbath motif, it actually commences the next section that follows, chapters 5 to 12, in which conflict escalates. But the Gospel of John denies any rigid structure that disrupts its thematic flow. If it is arguable that the episodes 2:1–11, 4:46–54 and 5:1–15 have come out of the same "signs source," then these pericopes bear enough resemblance to be read as adjacent accounts artfully placed together.[40] The use of water as a symbol might well be a connective intended by the author. A symbolic interpretation of water in 5:1–15 is, therefore, suitable.

6:35, 55. There are two consecutive miracles in John 6, Jesus' multiplication of the loaves and walking on the sea (6:1–15, 16–21), with an ensuing discourse on "the bread of Life" (6:22–71). Kowalski enlists both miracles as "water units" on account of the phrases τῆς θαλάσσης τῆς Γαλιλαίας τῆς Τιβεριάδος (6:1) and ἐπὶ τὴν θάλασσαν (6:16), but it is really forced to see "water" in "sea." However, if we read carefully through,

39 D. W. B. Robinson, in suggesting a ritualistic interpretation of "water" in John 3:5, points out the theological coherence of some of the episodes in John 1 to 3, but he does not include 5:1–15 among them; see Robinson, "Born of Water and Spirit: Does John 3:5 Refer to Baptism?" *RTR* 25 (1966): 20.

40 R. T. Fortna, *The Gospel of Signs: A Reconstruction of the Narrative Source Underlying the Fourth Gospel*, SNTSMS 11 (Cambridge: Cambridge University Press, 1970), 15–22, 108, 235–45.

we should note when Jesus says, Ἐγώ εἰμι ὁ ἄρτος τῆς ζωῆς· ὁ ἐρχόμενος πρός ἐμὲ οὐ μὴ πεινάσῃ, καὶ ὁ πιστεύων εἰς ἐμὲ οὐ μὴ διψήσει πώποτε (6:35), he is speaking of the impotence of bread and water on this earth. The word ὕδωρ is not mentioned, but the theme of "dissatisfaction with water" continues here (cf. 4:13), as Jesus continues to offer himself as "the water that satisfies." So there is implicit water symbolism here.

It is actually significant that the water motif and the bread motif merge here. The symbol of water and the symbol of bread are behind the words οὐ μὴ πεινάσῃ, καὶ . . . οὐ μὴ διψήσει πώποτε, appositionally related. Thus we witness the interlocking of two major symbols, thematic and metaphorical. These "core symbols," as Culpepper and Koester call them, have their "domains" in the text, and their domains overlap one another. Illustrative of this point is a "penta-partite" outline proposed by E. C. Webster for the structure of the gospel:

Christological statement i: The pre-existent Son 1:1–18
I. Jesus: the source and giver of life (1:19–5:18)
Christological statement ii: The son of man, judge of all 5:19–47
II. Jesus: sustainer of life amidst the hostility of the world (6:1–8:30)
Christological statement iii: The Son who frees from sin & death 8:31–59
III. Jesus: light & life, the penultimate signs (9:1–12:22)
Christological statement iv: The Son of man, lifted up 12:23–50
IV. Example & promise: abiding love & the Counselor (13:1–16:33)
Christological statement v: The Son glorified ch. 17
V. Death & resurrection (18:1–21:25)[41]

Webster's outline was obviously constructed with christology in mind, and since Johannine symbols are often christological in nature, most of the units feature some significant symbols, and the outline reflects the flow of one core symbol into another:

1:19–5:18	(Water) Jesus, the source . . . of life
6:1–8:30	(Blood) Jesus, sustainer of life . . .
9:1–12:22	Light & life . . .
Chapters 13–16	(Spirit) Abiding love
Chapters 18–21	Death and resurrection . . .[42]

---

41 E. C. Webster, "Pattern in the Fourth Gospel," in *Art and Meaning: Rhetoric in Biblical Literature*, ed. D. J. Clines, D. M. Gunn and A. J. Hauser (Sheffield: JSOT, 1982), 230–57.

42 Webster's "theological" headings for the units are listed here (ibid., 252–53).

Just as shown above, in chapters 1 to 5 there is a prominent use of the water symbol. In chapter 6 it is taken over by the symbol of bread, though Webster gives it the heading of "blood" on account of the words ἡ γὰρ σάρξ μου ἀληθής ἐστιν βρῶσις, καὶ τὸ αἷμά μου ἀληθής ἐστιν πόσις (6:55).[43] Thus, we can be quite sure that the symbol of water does not totally disappear because of the rise of the symbol of bread but, rather, lingers on. In fact, at 7:38, it is loud and clear in Jesus' saying, ὁ πιστεύων εἰς ἐμε . . . ποταμοὶ ἐκ τῆς κοιλίας αὐτοῦ ῥεύσουσιν ὕδατος ζῶντος. Likewise, although the symbol of light, as Webster suggests, appears to begin in chapter 9 with the episode of the healing of the blind as a narrative symbol, it is actually presented earlier with Jesus'saying, Ἐγώ εἰμι τὸ φῶς τοῦ κόσμου, as a metaphorical symbol (8:12). Thus the domains of the core symbols of the gospel overlap one another.

While the symbol of water coheres more with the initial chapters, the other core symbols cohere with the narrative-discourse complex in the more central portion of the gospel such as the bread of life discourse. In the former case the symbol is often a "narrative symbol," e.g., the changing of water into wine, the healing of the invalid beside the pool. In the latter case the symbols often take the form of an ἐγώ εἰμι statement. It is significant, therefore, that ἐγώ εἰμι ὁ ἄρτος τῆς ζωῆς (6:35) is the first of such statements in the gospel. "Water," though the prevalent symbol of the initial chapters, is never presented as a symbol of the divine, and is never introduced by the words ἐγώ εἰμι. With the emergence of the symbol of bread, however, these words begin to appear. This may even be one of the reasons why the account of Jesus walking on the sea is cruder in John than in Matthew and Mark. In this shorter and yet more striking report of the episode, Jesus' identification of himself to the terrified disciples stands out as an emphasis, ἐγώ εἰμι(6:20)! The author's tradition or his handling of the tradition is such that the divinity of Jesus is especially highlighted.[44] Thus this episode anticipates further christological revelation, and to that end the seven "ἐγώ εἰμι" sayings of Jesus emerge.

9:1–12, and the change in the use of the symbol. Water is not literally mentioned in the account of the healing of the blind man, but it plays a part in the event, as Jesus said to the man, ὕπαγε νίψαι εἰς τὴν κολυμβήθραν τοῦ

---

43 Ibid., 253.

44 Cf. Brown, *John*, 1:254–55; Carson, *John*, 275–76.

Σιλωάμ (ὃ ἑρμηνεύεται 'Απεσταλμένος), and the man went and washed and returned being able to see (9:7). Early church fathers unanimously interpret the washing in Siloam as Christian baptism.[45] Along with the account of the healing of the invalid in chapter 5 and that of Nicodemus in chapter 2, this was one of the three great Johannine readings used in preparing catechumens for Baptism in the early Church.[46] Although modern interpreters tend to discard this as allegorical, there are good reasons to locate a symbolic use of water in the narrative. First of all, the author spells out the meaning of the Hebrew name שלח, the sent one, interpreted by the Jews as the Messiah.[47] And "the sent one" is exactly what Jesus claims to be, a christological claim throughout the gospel: 3:16–17, 34; 4:34; 5:23–24, 30, 36–38; 6:29, 38–39, 44, 57; 7:16, 28–29, 33; 8:18, 26, 29, 42; 9:4; 10:36; 12:44, 45, 49; 13:20; 14:24; 15:21; 16:5; 17:3, 18, 20–26; 20:21. So the symbolic meaning of the name of the pool is evident. Then, in the original setting, the pool of Σιλωάμ was also the source from which water was drawn for the water pouring ceremony conducted at the feast of Tabernacles (7:2). Readers familiar with this ritual would not have missed the significance. The question is whether the washing itself symbolizes anything, and if it does, whether it is part of water symbolism in John at large.

Two symbolic interpretations have been proposed for the washing. First, "sacramental symbolism" may be intended here. Alternatively, we may broaden the symbolic meaning of washing to "salvific bath," which means that sinners must be "washed in the fountain of cleansing water at Calvary."[48] This latter interpretation complies with Painter's view of "symbolism as universal representation," and is probably accepted by a wider circle of scholars. At any rate Σιλωάμ symbolizes Christ in both cases. And both interpretations affirm the use of water symbolism in 9:1–12.

Important to our understanding is actually the contrast of water symbolism here with elsewhere. In previous episodes, water symbolizes the old rites or salvific means, or earthly resources, which Jesus has come to supersede. On this basis one may not agree that the water of Σιλωάμ

45 Sciberras, "Water According to Greek Fathers," 80–88.

46 Brown, *John*, 1:211.

47 The name probably alludes to Isaiah's words in 8:6, "this people has rejected the gently flowing waters of שלח."

48 B. H. Grigsby, "Washing in the Pool of Siloam—A Thematic Anticipation of the Johannine Cross," *NovT* 27 (1985): 227–35.

symbolizes Christ, though the name Σιλωάμ symbolizes Christ. Such is Carson's sentiment: "the suitability of drawing attention to Siloam may have depended simply on its name."[49] But my opinion is that we must not expect the use of a certain symbol in John to be so rigid and restrictive. If the water motif in John is "like a stream . . . readily conforming to the contours of the narrative through which it flows," then there is reason to expect change in the direction it goes.[50] In the initial episodes of the narrative, up to 5:1–15, water is repeatedly juxtaposed with Jesus' blessing. In the central portion of the gospel where longer discourses are interspersed, the contour has changed, and water is no longer juxtaposed as before. It looks as if water symbolism has ceased after these discourses appear. Actually, as I have shown above, it is still there implicitly, complementary to the bread symbol (6:35, 55). In fact, in the middle of this narrative-discourse complex an important statement stands out, Ἐάν τις διψᾷ ἐρχέσθω πρός με καὶ πινέτω . . . ποταμοὶ ἐκ τῆς κοιλίας αὐτοῦ ῥεύσουσιν ὕδατος ζῶντος (7:37–38). Like a sudden fall in the middle of a gentle stream, this statement brings forth the symbol of water in a captivating manner. From there on the water symbol remains significant, and it now represents Jesus' own blessing. To map the use of the symbol on the contour of the narrative, we may say that it has entered a new phase at the appearance of this statement. It is becoming less frequent but more important. Its significance has changed. Formerly a contrast against Jesus' blessings, it is now symbolic of Jesus' blessings. It is in this context that we must interpret the symbolic meaning of water in 9:1–12, as identification with Jesus rather than juxtaposition. Subsequent to 9:1–12, there are two more episodes, in 13:1–11 and 19:28–37, to be studied later, in which the water symbol is similarly used. These incidents belong to the same phase in the contour.

Its Clearer Use in the Initial Chapters

In the initial chapters, because there is a consistent "juxtaposition" between water on the one hand and Jesus' salvation and blessings on the other, the use of water symbolism is clear.

1:14–34, the "fountainhead." Johannine water symbolism begins with water baptism. The meaning of water baptism as a rite is well recognized.

---

49 Carson, *John, 365.*

50 Cf. Koester, *Symbolism in the Fourth Gospel*, 156.

It symbolizes purification. The rite was commonly practiced, but John the Baptist practiced it outside of mainstream Judaism, giving the impression that he was the "end-time" figure.[51] It is debatable as to whether and in what way he was associated with the Qumran community. He certainly shared the eschatological expectation of his times, looking forward to a time of repentance when God would cleanse his people from sin and grant them a new heart (Ezek 36:25; cf. Ezek 36:22–31; Jer 31:31–34).[52] Both the Gospel of John and the Synoptics declare that he was heralding the Christ, ὁ ἐρχόμενος, but the Johannine tradition asserts more strongly the following points. First, John baptized in order to testify to or identify Jesus, for he said, κἀγὼ οὐκ ᾔδειν αὐτόν, ἀλλ' ἵνα φανερωθῇ τῷ Ἰσραὴλ διὰ τοῦ το ἦλθον ἐγὼ ἐν ὕδατι βαπτίζων (1:31). Second, the coming of interrogators from Jerusalem shows that an incipient opposition to the Christ began as early as John's baptism, prior to Jesus' coming on the scene (1:19–28). Third, at stake was the question, "who is the eschatological figure" who will bring in the salvation which the water baptism of John symbolizes or anticipates? In Jewish understanding, the Christ, Elijah, and "the prophet" were principal eschatological figures.[53] By referring to these figures the Jerusalem authorities challenged the Baptist's authority, Τί οὖν βαπτίζεις (1:25)?

In our study of the narrative of the gospel, whereas the interrogation anticipates future opposition from Jerusalem, the Baptist's answer to the interrogation sets the stage for the subsequent use of water symbolism: Ἐγὼ βαπτίζω ἐν ὕδατι· μέσος ὑμῶν ἕστηκεν ὃν ὑμεῖς οὐκ οἴδατε, ὁ ὀπίσω μου ἐρχόμενος, οὗ οὐκ εἰμὶ ἄξιος ἵνα λύσω αὐτοῦ τὸν ἱμάντα τοῦ ὑποδήματος (1:26–27). The Baptist, who was challenged as if he was the eschatological figure, is juxtaposed with the real eschatological figure, the Christ, who was about to come in glory. This relation may be interpreted as symbolic in

---

51 It has been pointed out that whereas baptism was self-administered (candidates baptized themselves), John the Baptist himself administered it for the candidates. So it appeared as if he was the end-time figure administering the end-time rite with great authority. See Carson, *John*, 145.

52 Cf. J. A. T. Robinson, "The Baptism of John and the Qumran Community," *HTR* 50 (1957):175–91.

53 However, they were not necessarily expected to baptize at their appearing (G. R. Beasley-Murray, *John*, WBC, vol. 36 [Waco, TX: Word Books Publisher, 1987], 24; contra Bultmann, *John*, 88).

an eschatological sense. If water baptism symbolizes salvific cleansing brought about by the eschatological Christ, this symbolism works in an eschatological framework, in which the symbol prepares or anticipates the symbolized. Just as John the Baptist prepared the way for the eschatological Christ (2:23), his baptism anticipates salvific cleansing of the eschatological kingdom. So water anticipates the eschatological means of purification, which the gospel eventually comes to reveal as the Holy Spirit (7:37–39). Thus the stage is set for the symbolic use of "water" in the subsequent episodes. And, if we take a look at the end point of the "drama," before the curtain falls, the purpose of the gospel is stated again as follows: ἵνα πιστεύσητε ὅτι Ἰησοῦς ἐστιν ὁ Χριστὸς ὁ υἱὸς τοῦ θεοῦ, καὶ ἵνα πιστεύοντες ζωὴν ἔχητε ἐν τῷ ὀνόματι αὐτοῦ (20:31). This further confirms that the question at stake is, as stated right from the beginning, "Who is the eschatological figure who will bring in the salvation which the water baptism of John symbolizes?"

In the author's master design of the gospel, therefore, the identification of the eschatological Christ is "like a fountainhead" to the subsequent and successive use of water symbolism and John's testimony to Jesus marks the starting point.

2:1–11. In the Cana episode "water" seems to play only a secondary role. As related earlier, Koester's view is that the primary symbol here is the transformation of water into wine, which is a symbolic action. The supporting symbols are the stone jars that held the water.[54] Here I propose that the symbolism in the episode should be interpreted as an integrated whole. It is true that there can be several points of significance in relation to the episode. (1) Preeminent is the revelation of Jesus' glory in his action. The author himself underscores this (2:11). (2) Important also is the symbolic meaning of the wine. Some scholars accentuate the fact that in the Greco-Roman world wine represents the presence and benevolence of the deity.[55] In the discernibly Judaistic background of the gospel, however, wine is a feature of the eschatological feast (Isa 25:6), an eschatological gift given by the Messiah. R. Schnackenburg summarizes:

> In the O.T. (Amos 9:13; Hos 2:24; Joel 4:18; Is 29:17; Jer 31:5) and in late Judaism (Enoch, 10:19; Apoc Bar Syr, 29:5; Or Sib, II, 317f.; III, 620–4; 744f.)

---

54 Koester, *Symbolism in the Fourth Gospel*, 11.
55 Cf. ibid., 80–81.

> wine in abundance (along with oil or milk) is a sign of the age of salvation; in the ancient blessing of Jacob it is a characteristic of the Messiah from Judah (Gen 49:11f.).[56]

And, (3) possibly, the stone jars which held water for ceremonial washing (2:6) hints at Jesus' break with Judaistic rites or the substitution of the law with Jesus' truth and grace (cf. 1:17). This polemic idea of "replacing the old with the new" seems to find support also in the next episode (2:13–22) in which Jesus talked about the destroying of the temple and the raising of it in three days. Koester's singling out of the stone jars as a symbol may have been caused by this "replacement" idea.[57] If water symbolizes only what the stone jars stand for, namely, Judaistic rites about to be replaced, its role is very limited indeed. But I disagree with interpreting the gospel solely as a polemical document. As Schnackenburg says, "it is not certain that the evangelist is really so hostile to Jewish purification . . . since he also mentions ritual customs without disparagement (cf. 7:22; 11:55; 18:28; 19:40)."[58] The relation between the juxtaposed old and new, as I perceive it, is one of "anticipation and fulfillment," rather than "renouncement and replacement." Just as John the Baptist prepares for the way of the eschatological Christ, and thus provides a "fountainhead" for the use of water symbolism in John, the former ritual represented by the water in the stone jars anticipated the imminent blessing represented by the wine made by Jesus.

If juxtaposition signifies anticipation and fulfillment rather than renouncement and replacement, then the points sketched out above should not be understood as discrete, but understood as various aspects of the total significance. At the eschatological hour (cf. οὔπω ἥκει ἡ ὥρα μου, 2:4) the Christ who comes in glory (2:11) will satisfy the anticipation of his people (symbolized by water in the stone jars) with blessing (symbolized by the choice wine). I perceive in 2:1–11, therefore, an integrative symbol made up of one symbolic action (Jesus' σημεῖον) and two symbolic objects (water and wine). Water is one of these three aspects of the total significance, standing for the old rites. Its symbolic use is subtle but clear, though it looks inconspicuous.

---

56 Schnackenburg, *John*, 1:338.

57 Cf. Beasley-Murray, *John*, 36; Carson, *John*, 173.

58 Schnackenburg, *John*, 1:339.

By being part of the total symbol in 2:1–11, "water" participates in the overall intent of the gospel, to testify Jesus as the Christ who brings in eschatological blessings. Further down in the gospel we will see the symbol recur with varying intensity. It is sometimes obvious, sometimes subtle, but it always contributes to the overall eschatological message. That message runs from the "fountainhead" of water symbolism (1:26, 31, 33, the Baptist's testimony) all the way to the end of the "drama" (20:31, a recapitulation). The stone jars are comparatively limited in their symbolic function, sticking out here once and then dropping out for good. The water symbol, however, comes into play again and again.

3:1–15. Here water is mentioned again in juxtaposition to something else, the Spirit, or spirit (πνεῦμα). In this episode, however, water does not appear as an object of Jesus' action. It is mentioned as a means of rebirth in the discourse of Jesus with Nicodemus: 'Αμὴν ἀμὴν λέγω σοι, ἐὰν μή τις γεννηθῇ ἐξ ὕδατος καὶ πνεύματος, οὐ δύναται εἰσελθεῖν εἰς τὴν βασιλείαν τοῦ θεοῦ (3:5). The interpretation of "water" in this passage is notoriously controversial. One main cause for disputes is that the two words, "water and spirit," can be construed either as constrastive or as appositional. Central to my thesis, however, is that "water," as a symbol, is versatile in its meaning so that an overly discriminative interpretation may not be appropriate. If it refers to spiritual cleansing, for example, may it not hint at a baptism of repentance at the same time?[59] Controversies have nevertheless produced a number of interpretations to be scrutinized here: water in the womb, celestial waters, spiritual water or spiritual birth, spiritual renewal, John's baptism, Christian baptism, Jewish cleansing rites, water as the Torah, water as "wind," water as "the Spirit" and so on.[60]

Some of these interpretations are inconclusive. "Water in the womb" seems to fit into the literary context, because Nicodemus was referring to "the womb" in his query of Jesus' earlier remark (3:3–4), and, if "water" is

---

59 The Gospel of John does not call John's baptism a "baptism of repentance for the remission of sins," as do the Synoptics. However, this omission is congruous with the gospel's emphasis on the merely preparatory role of the Baptist to Jesus' ministry; see Dodd, *Historical Tradition*, 275; D. W. B. Robinson, "Water and Spirit," 21.

60 L. Belleville classifies them impressively into six topical groups: "ritualistic views," "symbolic usage," "physiological views," "implied dualism," "cosmological" and "figurative usage"; see Belleville, "'Born of Water and Spirit:' John 3:5," *TrinJ* 1 (1980): 125–41.

interpreted as the natural birth of the flesh, a structural balance between 3:5 and 3:6 can be maintained. However, there is no parallel use of "water" in ancient or contemporary writings to support this view.[61] Furthermore, if life of the flesh were in view here, as G. M. Burge points out, the use of ἐξ αἵματος would have been more appropriate.[62] Another inconclusive interpretation is "celestial waters" or "spiritual seed," which presumes that the phrase "water and spirit" is a hendiadys. Celestial water refers to God's semen in contrast to the semen of the flesh. To support this view, H. Odeberg has collected a long list of evidences from Jewish mysticism and Hellenistic sources.[63] However, these evidences are considered late by recent scholars, and therefore unconvincing.[64] The symbolic use of "water" in reference to the Torah is also inconclusive. Although parallel uses can be found in rabbinic literature, there we do not find any concept of "birth of water."[65] Nor is "water" the symbol most frequently used in rabbinic literature for God's word.[66] In any case it is really "Jesus' words" that is distinguished in the gospel as life-giving, rather than the Torah understood by the Jews (cf. 6:63; 15:3). Water as "wind" is yet another inconclusive interpretation, which interprets πνεῦμα also as "wind" and reads "water and spirit" as a hendiadys. According to Z. Hodges this double metaphor was used by Jesus to evoke OT imagery representing God's vivifying work.[67] The difficulty with this is that πνεῦμα cannot possibly mean "wind" in John 3:6, and so inconsistency results. Πνεῦμα, actually, is hardly ever used as "wind" in the New Testament.

A more acceptable interpretation is "spiritual birth," which is Origen's

---

61 Another "physiological" interpretation, "water as male semen," finds support in a few rabbinic writings but they are rare and late; see Belleville, "Water and Spirit," 132; and Carson, *John*, 191.

62 G. M. Burge, *The Anointed Community: The Holy Spirit in the Johannine Tradition* (Grand Rapids: Eerdmans, 1987), 161; cf. Belleville, "Water and Spirit," 131.

63 H. Odeberg, *The Fourth Gospel Interpreted in Its Relation to Contemporaneous Religious Currents in Palestine and the Hellenistic-Oriental World* (Uppsala: Almquist & Wiksell, 1929), 48–71.

64 E.g., Barrett, *John*, 209; Carson, *John*, 193.

65 Carson, *John*, 193.

66 Belleville, "Water and Spirit," 130.

67 Z. Hodges, "Water and Spirit—John 3:5," *BSac* 135 (1978): 206–20.

interpretation of water in 3:5.[68] Close to this is Calvin's view, that water is "the Spirit," or "water, namely, the Spirit."[69] This hendiadys interpretation renders the καί epexegetic. A strong support to this view is that in John 7:39 "water" is directly interpreted as "the Spirit." The question is then why water should be mentioned at all. Origen rationalizes this by saying that "water" differs from "spirit" in "conception," though not in "substance."[70] L. Belleville, in a full discussion of this verse, adopts this explanation, but to adapt it to her own view she renders it a "figurative usage" and expands the meaning of "water" to include specifically "the purifying work of God's Spirit."[71] She also finds a convenient solution in reckoning the two anarthrous nouns to be both "descriptive of the nature of birth" rather than indicative of the identity of the agent. Thus she comes up with the elaborate idea: water refers to "that which purifies and renews," and spirit refers to "all that belongs to God and the heavenly or spiritual world."[72]

This figurative usage may be commendable, but not so if it is forced out of a prejudice against the more literal interpretation of water baptism. This prejudice can be found in Belleville, as she expresses a fear of "confining salvation to an outward sign" and prefers to interpret water "without any direct connection with literal baptism."[73] Nor is it uncommon for scholars with the same fear to discriminate against "ritualistic views."[74] It is, however, precisely in the ritualistic context of prophets such as Ezekiel that water and spirit are associated as symbols of cleansing and renewal. It is illegitimate to say that there is no direct connection between the figurative

---

68 D. W. B. Robinson carefully points out that elsewhere Origen uses John 3:5 with reference to Christian baptism, but in "Fragment 36," which reflects Origen's work at the primary level of interpretation, water is expounded as spiritual birth; see Robinson, "Water and Spirit," 22, n. 5, citing A. E. Brooke, *The Commentary of Origen on St. John's Gospel: The Text Revised with a Critical Introduction and Indices*, vol. 2 (Cambridge: Cambridge University Press, 1896), 249ff.

69 Calvin, *Commentary on the Gospel According to John*, vol. 1 (Grand Rapids: Eerdmans, 1949), 109–112.

70 Brooke, *Commentary of Origen*, 2:249ff.

71 Belleville, "Water and Spirit," 134.

72 Ibid., 135–41.

73 Ibid., 130.

74 The ritualistic views, as categorized by Belleville, are also well endorsed by scholars (ibid., 125–30); cf. Carson, *John*, 191–93.

use of water and water rituals. On the contrary, a "ritualistic" sense of water as symbolic of cleansing and renewal may well be more preferable than a purely figurative sense, which precludes literal baptism.

Along this line, Burge interprets water in 3:5 as baptism, and the second noun as "the Spirit" rather than just the nature "spirit."[75] However, there is flexibility in John's symbolic language, as Burge points out:

> what we most likely have is a hendiadys in which both terms should be coordinated in order to give a single concept. This means that 3:5 reflects the typical Johannine idiom of "pairs in tension." The significance of the one spills over into the other; and as often is the case, the accent falls on the second noun.[76]

In this explanation there is mutuality with the concept, but the coordination of the nouns does not have to be strained to mean "identity in substance." As regards the simulation between the two, Burge says, water baptism can point in one of two directions: either "as close and inseparable to Spirit baptism," or "depreciated and used as a symbol of spiritual cleansing."[77] In any case, Burge himself emphasizes, "these options do not have to be mutually exclusive."[78] Just as said above, if water refers to spiritual cleansing, may it not hint at the significance of a baptism of repentance at the same time, and vice versa? May it not also allude to the agent of rebirth, the Holy Spirit, whose advent becomes pronounced later on in John 7:39? It seems best to allow more than one meaning in the use of "water" in John 3:5, if it is indeed a symbolic use.

Burge's interpretation involves the background of the Johannine church, in which he sees a problem with Christian baptism. In his own words, "the use of baptismal language in John 3 suggests that the Evangelist is addressing a situation in which sacramental abuse may have been close at hand."[79] This does not necessarily exclude the possibility that Jesus himself used the same language. In that original setting there was Judaistic water cleansing as well as baptismal activities going on. Nicodemus should

---

75 Burge, *The Anointed Community*, 157–78.

76 Ibid., 166, citing K. Barth, *Church Dogmatics*, vol. 4, tran. G. W. Bromiley, ed. G. W. Bromiley and T. F. Torrance (Edinburgh: T. & T. Clark, 1969), 121.

77 Ibid., 167.

78 Ibid.

79 Ibid., 170.

have naturally thought of the old rite on hearing the word ἐξ αἵματος.[80] In chapter one of this present work, an account was given of Cullmann's and Léon-Dufour's "historical and theological" definitions on Johannine symbolism. The idea is precisely that the gospel was written for a symbolic reading with double or multiple references, so that Jesus' historical life in the Jewish milieu was connected on the one hand with OT salvation history, and on the other hand with ecclesiastic theology in the Christian milieu. Thus Léon-Dufour, pondering on the various milieus, interprets "water" in John 3:5 with a triple meaning: the Holy Spirit, the need for spiritual rebirth and Christian baptism. The OT background of this is, no doubt, the eschatological sprinkling of water prophesied in Ezek 36:25–27, which leads to the gift of a new heart and the Spirit. Ezekiel's ritualistic language is significant here in that it validates the eschatological meaning of water rituals. So we may say that "water" in John 3:5 stands for water rituals, which take root in OT prophecies on the Spirit and lead on to Christian baptism. Thus the major sense of the symbol has to do with the baptism that points to the eschatological kingdom, in which the Holy Spirit brings about spiritual cleansing. The accent on water baptism in the initial chapters affirms this sense.[81] It is not surprising that a number of scholars have interpreted "water" in John 3:5 as water baptism.[82]

The reference of "water" to baptism fits in well with the overall narrative structure of the initial chapters. We have earlier pointed out that there is a connection between 3:22–30 (the Baptist's comment on ceremonial washing, and his reference to Jesus as the bridegroom), 1:19–28 (the Baptist's testimony that he is not the Christ), and 2:1–11 (Jesus' changing water into wine in a wedding at Cana). The picture is now more complete

---

80 Earlier commentators such as Godet and Westcott were content to say that Nicodemus should naturally think of the old rite on hearing the word ἐξ αἵματος. See F. L. Godet, *Commentary on John's Gospel* (New York: Funk and Wagnalls, 1886; repr., Grand Rapids: Kregel Publications, 1978), 397; B. F. Westcott, *The Gospel According to St. John: The Authorized Version with Introduction and Notes*, repr. ed. (Grand Rapids: Eerdmans, 1973 [1908]), 50. A couple of scholars query about the Baptist's fame in producing such a thought. E.g., Carson, *John*, 193.

81 D. W. B. Robinson points out that the theological coherence of the initial chapters of John confirms this ("Water and Spirit," 20).

82 Barrett, *John*, 208–9; Beasley-Murray, *John*, 49; Burge, *The Anointed Community*, 162.

as we add to it the present passage, 3:1–15 (Jesus' instruction about the new birth, ἐξ ὕδατος καὶ πνεύματος). In all these chapters of the gospel, there is a use of the water symbol in one way or another. That usage comes in the form of juxtaposition. That juxtaposition symbolizes an eschatological expectation and its corresponding fulfillment brought about by Jesus, and the former anticipates or prepares for the latter. Water, in these chapters, is used mainly as a symbol standing for the anticipating party. The significance of the part it plays varies slightly from episode to episode, but the message it pronounces is consistent: Jesus is the Christ who brings in eschatological salvation and blessings.

Along this line we may say that the juxtaposition of "water" and "spirit" in 3:5 is governed by an eschatological relationship. "Water" in 3:5 refers to the ritualistic cleansing with water, or water baptism, the symbolic expression of repentance, the anticipatory rite. The "spirit" refers to the eschatological fulfillment, the coming of the Spirit, the new heart as an eschatological gift. Both are instrumental to the new birth. One anticipates, and the other fulfills. In post-Easter times the fulfillment has come and the two may become one. So, as Burge says, the significance of the one spills over into the other; and, as often is the case, the accent falls on the second noun.

Its Double Role in Chapters 4 and 7

Water in the initial chapters symbolizes either the old rites or John's baptism, both of which are preparatory. In chapters 4 and 7, however, water plays a double role, because it sometimes stands for the old rites and sometimes stands for the eschatological blessings of Christ. There is, therefore, an expansion of the usage and significance of the symbol. We may say that the use of "water" earlier in John 3:5 is incipient of this double role. Even if the major sense there has to do with baptism, the symbol points to the eschatological Spirit which brings about spiritual cleansing.

4:1–42. One can immediately sense this expansion of use by noticing how extensively water is mentioned throughout John 4. The episode took place at the well of Jacob. The traditional supply of water for the Samaritans provided an immediate context. Then the encounter of Jesus and the woman revolves around the gift of water: Jesus asked her for water and at the same time offered "living water." This triggered a conversation that led to a revelation of Jesus' identity as the Messiah, the eschatological Christ, and upon learning about this the woman ἀφῆκεν οὖν τὴν ὑδρίαν αὐτῆς ἡ γυνὴ καὶ ἀπῆλθεν . . . (4:28). Thus one constantly comes across "water" in reading this passage: 4:7, 10, 11, 13, 14, 15, 38. More significantly, "water" does not only paint a background in this episode, it is directly used by Jesus as a symbol alluding to eternal life: Εἰ ᾔδεις τὴν δωρεὰν τοῦ θεοῦ καὶ τίς ἐστιν ὁ λέγων σοι, Δός μοι πεῖν, σὺ ἄν ᾔτησας αὐτὸν καὶ ἔδωκεν ἄν σοι ὕδωρ ζῶν (4:10). It is mostly in the ensuing conversation between Jesus and the woman regarding this symbolic saying that water is mentioned again and again (4:11–15). Because of the frequent mention and dominant use of water in this episode, we will exegete this passage more fully in the next chapter. It suffices here to point out how the use of water symbolism here relates to elsewhere in the gospel.

Theologically speaking, the passage joins in repeating the same eschatological message which finds its way down from the "fountainhead," namely, Jesus' identification as the Messiah, the Christ (4:25). When Jesus says, Εἰ ᾔδεις τὴν δωρεὰν τοῦ θεοῦ καὶ τίς ἐστιν ὁ λέγων σοι (4:10a), he is referring to the eschatological gift of God and himself as the bringer of the gift. When he says, σὺ ἄν ᾔτησας αὐτὸν καὶ ἔδωκεν ἄν σοι ὕδωρ ζῶν (4:10b), he is implying that "living water" symbolizes God's eschatological gift, and he himself, the giver of that gift, the Messiah, is symbolized as the source of living water. Thus the eschatological message rings loud and clear. "Water," for the first time, stands decisively for the gift of eschatological fulfillment.

As for the juxtaposition typical of the initial episodes, the interesting arrangement here is that water is now found on both sides of the juxtaposition, symbolizing both the "anticipation" and the "fulfillment." Water from Jacob's well stands for a Samaritan tradition of eschatological expectations, which the woman appeals to in her conversation with Jesus (4:15–26). The well and the woman's water jar may be supporting symbols to the Samaritan "water" (4:5, 28). By including this episode of the Samaritan woman, the author of the gospel may be implying that the Samaritan tradition is also preparatory to eschatological fulfillment.[83]

Thus, the water symbol plays a "double role" in the total significance

---

83 The Samaritan's messianic expectation was defined not by the prophetic books but by the Pentateuch, notably Deut 18:15–18. See J. Macdonald, *Theology of the Samaritans* (Philadelphia: Westminster Press, 1964), 359–79.

of the episode, symbolizing the preparatory aspect as well as the fulfillment aspect of eschatological salvation. It also plays a "prime role," being directly used by Jesus. Whereas its use elsewhere is limited or subsidiary, its use here is dominant and indispensable.

When we look into the overall literary development of the gospel, this prime use and double role in John 4 forecast a change. Looking back, the Samaritan discourse is in line with chapters 1 to 5 in presenting a juxtaposition, with "water from the well" symbolizing anticipation. Looking forward to subsequent chapters, "the living water" is the first in a series of metaphorical symbols that stands for eschatological fulfillment. These symbols, "bread," "light," "shepherd," "gate," appear in the central portion of the gospel, and they represent the eschatological Christ, giving expression to the nature of his gifts.[84] Here, in the longer discourses between chapters 6 and 12, these metaphorical symbols bring into sharp focus the polemical question of "who Jesus is." The juxtaposition in the earlier chapters fades into the background. So Jesus stands out as the "protagonist" and polemic figure, and the traditional feasts form the background. Prominent now is the frequently used ἐγώ εἰμι formula, with which Jesus reveals his identity as the eschatological Christ. "Water" is never used with this formula, but is used in apposition with "bread" as a symbol, which signifies the life that Jesus gives (6:35). Thus Jesus, as "the source of living water of life," is "the water of life." Such a use, as symbolic of the eschatological fulfillment, begins actually in 4:1–30 with the Samaritan discourse.

7:37–39. Water symbolism is prominent in the central portion not because the symbol of water appears frequently. Quite the contrary, it looks as if John has ceased using the symbol here. Its prominence is established historically in the background of the feast of Tabernacles, with its daily water pouring ceremony, and literally in the striking statement Jesus made on the last and great day of the feast: Ἐάν τις διψᾷ ἐρχέσθω πρός με καὶ πινέτω . . . ποταμοὶ ἐκ τῆς κοιλίας αὐτοῦ ῥεύσουσιν ὕδατος ζῶντος (7:37–38). Both of these give the air of a "protagonist" to the water motif.

In our previous discussion on the episode of the healing of the blind (9:1–12), we have assumed that the water pouring ceremony was practiced at the Feast of Tabernacles, and that the Pool of Σιλωάμ was the source of

84 Cf. Schnackenburg, *John*, 1:427.

water for that ceremony.[85] This is important as the background to Jesus' discourse in chapter 7 and is helpful towards setting up a consistent theological framework for the gospel narrative. Carson points out rightly, "although the words [7:37] inevitably call to mind Isaiah 55:1 . . . the particular association of the water rite with this Feast demands that we seek more focused significance."[86] The significance is that in Israelite history there had been an ongoing longing for fertility and fruitfulness that only rain could bring. This culminated in the setting up of this water ceremony in the Feast of Tabernacles which, as Zech 14:16–17 implies, had to do with rainfall. Although the practice of the rite began as late as about two centuries before Christ, it serves to summarize the OT anticipation of God's promises to pour out rain in the messianic age. In Jewish traditions, therefore, the water miracle in the wilderness (Exod 17:1–7; Num 20:8–13; cf. Ps 78:16–20) is a "forerunner" of this water rite, which is "a foretaste of the eschatological rivers of living water foreseen by Ezekiel (47:1–9) and Zechariah (13:1)."[87]

The time and manner of Jesus' "cry" indicated an intended impact: Ἐν δὲ τῇ ἐσχάτῃ ἡμέρᾳ τῇ μεγάλῃ τῆς ἑορτῆς εἱστήκει ὁ Ἰησοῦς καὶ ἔκραξεν λέγων (7:37a).[88] I would assume with most commentators that this took place on the seventh day on which the last and most elaborate of the daily water ceremonies was conducted.[89] While the poured water was still flooding artificially out of the ground at the altar, and the priest's hand lifted up to signify the completion of the ceremony, Jesus told his people that "if anyone thirsty would come to him and drink . . . streams of living water will be flowing from within. . . ."

The Greek text of this statement of Jesus can be construed in two different ways. The traditional interpretation punctuates the text in such a

---

85 E. C. Hoskyns is one of the few who disagree with associating the passage with such a rite. See Hoskyns, *The Fourth Gospel*, ed. F. N. Davey (London: Faber and Faber, 1954), 320–21.

86 Carson, *John*, 322.

87 B. H. Grigsby, "'If Any Man Thirst . . .': Observation on the Rabbinic Background of John 7,37–39," *Bib* 67 (1986): 101–8. Carson works out a historical background of the feast from Neh 8:1–15; see Carson, *John*, 326–27.

88 "Like a thunderclap from heaven," as Beasley-Murray portrays it (*John*, 114).

89 The eighth day, the sabbath which ended the whole feast, would have also been a day with an opportunity for Jesus to make this open statement. See Beasley-Murray's delineation of both possibilities, ibid.

way that the believer is portrayed as the source of living water: ἐάν τις διψᾷ ἐρχέσθω πρός με καὶ πινέτω. ὁ πιστεύων εἰς ἐμέ, καθὼς εἶπεν ἡ γραφή, ποταμοὶ ἐκ τῆς κοιλίας αὐτοῦ ῥεύσουσιν ὕδατος ζῶντος. The other way is to place the period after εἰς ἐμέ, so that Jesus' statement forms a chiastic parallel typical of Semitic languages: ἐάν τις διψᾷ / ἐρχέσθω πρός με / καὶ πινέτω / ὁ πιστεύων εἰς ἐμέ, an "A/B/B′/A′" parallel. The effect of this is that the next clause will begin with a quotation formula: καθὼς εἶπεν ἡ γραφή, ποταμοὶ ἐκ τῆς κοιλίας αὐτοῦ ῥεύσουσιν ὕδατος ζῶντος. The antecedent of αὐτοῦ would then be the one who offers the drink. That is, living water will flow from within Jesus. This is called the christological interpretation.

It is hard to decide which is better.[90] There are two main sets of arguments, one arguing from the grammatical style of the gospel, and the other from the habitual use, whether the author refers more likely to the believer or to Christ as the source, but none of these seems conclusive. Regarding style, the christological interpretation provides a nice poetic parallelism (as shown above) which seems to fit John's style.[91] However, others consider it either peculiar, or imperfect, or uncommon in John.[92] Grammatically, John habitually places a participle such as ὁ πιστεύων at the beginning of a sentence construction, rather than tacking it onto a previous conditional sentence, and this fact favors the traditional interpretation.[93] However, it has been pointed out by G. D. Kilpatrick that it is not John's style to make ὁ πιστεύων the subject of the following scriptural citation either.[94] As for parallel uses, John 4:13–14 is closest to John 7:37 in setting forth the idea of living water flowing out from the believer. J. B. Cortez considers the two passages almost identical.[95] Brown and B.-E. Boismard, however, dismiss this argument because "there is no suggestion

---

90 Some hold mediating views, e.g., putting ὁ πιστεύων εἰς ἐμέ in parenthesis (see Brown, *John*, 1:321), but these views are not influential.

91 Brown, *John*, 1:320.

92 Carson, *John*, 324; M.-E. Boismard, "De son ventre couleront des fleuves d'eau (Jo. 7,38)," *RB* 65 (1958): 523–46; G. Balfour, "The Jewishness of John's Use of the Scriptures in John 6:31 and 7:37–38," *TynBul* 46 (1995):369; cf. Dodd, *Interpretation*, 342.

93 The former construction numbers forty-one times in the gospel, whereas the latter construction hardly appears (Brown, *John*, 1:321).

94 G. D. Kilpatrick, "The Punctuation of John 7:37–38," *JTS* 11 (1960): 340–42.

95 J. B. Cortez, "Yet Another Look at Jn 7,37–38," *CBQ* 29 (1967): 79.

in 4:13–14 that the believer will be a source for others."[96] Carson omits 4:13–14 at this point and says that "in the Fourth Gospel believers are never the source of 'living water,'" and this makes up "the greatest strength of the second view."[97] No doubt, "Christ as the source of living water" is more dominant in the gospel. Explicitly he is the giver of the Spirit (14:15; 20:22). Symbolically he is the giver of the living water (4:13–14), and in the light of OT imagery he is the eschatological rock (cf. 19:34).

If we probe into the Old Testament for a reference of 7:38b (καθὼς εἶπεν ἡ γραφή, ποταμοὶ ἐκ τῆς κοιλίας αὐτου), it is more likely that αὐτοῦ points to Christ. Καθὼς and ἡ γραφή are terms used for OT citations, and John's OT use is typically christological and eschatological. Here the actual citations are omitted, but a series of OT passages underlie the idea that "from the rock God gives his people water": Exod 17:6; Num 20:17; Deut 8:15–16; Neh 9:15; Ps 78:15–16; Isa 43:19; 44:3; Ezek 47:1–12; Zech 14:8–11. These passages come from two lines of OT traditions. One adheres to the Exodus rock imagery, and the other reflects eschatological visions of later prophets. We will explore these more fully in chapter four of this book.

Thus interpreted, the presentation of Jesus in 7:37–39 fits perfectly into the scene of the Tabernacle. By identifying Jesus as the source of living water, fulfillment is proclaimed in him as the eschatological Christ. As G. R. Beasley-Murray rightly points out, the sayings or episodes in the gospel often "embody memory of the great deeds of God in the past and anticipation of the saving acts of God in the future, both united in an affirmation of their fulfillment in Jesus in the here and now."[98] The saying of 7:37–38 is an outstanding example of this. From a literary point of view, 7:37–39 places the fulfillment of Jesus at the focus of the scene, the giver of water, and in the background is the feast of Tabernacle with all its water rites, the anticipation. So there is again a double role for the water symbol. In chapter 7 now as in chapter 4 earlier, it stands on the anticipatory side as well as the fulfillment side. It is ceremonial water as well as the water Jesus gives.

---

96 Boismard, "De son ventre couleront," 535; Brown, *John*, 1:321; cf. Cortes, "Another Look," 79.

97 Carson, *John*, 323.

98 Beasley-Murray, *John*, 113.

It is hard to overstate the significance of 7:37–39 in the use of water symbolism in John. It stands at the climax of the narrative development of water symbolism in the gospel. It discloses to us that one prime meaning of the symbol is "the Spirit," an eschatological gift to be given at Jesus' glorification. Because of this disclosure it stands in close connection with the previous juxtaposition of "water" and "spirit" in 3:5 and with Jesus' subsequent promise of the Spirit in chapters 14 to 16. It is at this point that the prime reference of "water" to "the Spirit" is made clear to us. From here onwards Jesus' revelation about the Spirit becomes more explicit. Instead of symbolic references we have, in chapters 14 to 16, long and explicit statements given by Jesus on the sending and receiving of the "Paraclete."

Its Subtle Use in the Later Chapters

In the subsequent chapters, allusion to water becomes very infrequent. It is like the final section of the course of a river, in which the river is not always visible, not being more evident than the delta. Even so it is quietly present and can be seen here and there.

Water symbolism is very subtle in this section. As we draw close to Jesus' death and glorification in the passion narrative, the fulfillment theme overpowers the anticipation theme. So there is no more juxtaposition. In the few incidents in which the symbol appears, it refers exclusively to Jesus or his salvation.

The water at Siloam, 9:1–12, discussed above, is the first of these subtle uses of water in John. Just two more are now to be discussed.

13:1–17. The footwashing episode is commonly agreed to be symbolic, but its interpretation has been controversial. Traditionally the episode is connected with at least a double meaning: Jesus' humility as the primary meaning and water baptism as the secondary. Some connect the meal with the eucharist and read full sacramentalism in it, but this view is generally rejected.[99] A broader meaning of water baptism would be the "salvific bath" of believers in "the fountain of cleansing water at Calvary," an interpretation applicable also to 9:1–12. A double meaning, or alternative meanings, has

---

99 Cullmann, *Early Christian Worship*, 105–9, quoted in Brown, "The Johannine Sacramentary Reconsidered," *TS* 23 (1962): 194.

also been suggested, namely, Christ's once-for-all cleansing on the one hand and Christ's progressive cleansing on the other.[100] Some connect this passage with 15:3, considering Jesus' word to be the means of this cleansing.[101] Then, almost all see an implication of the death of Jesus in the footwashing. Brown says, "If the footwashing is a symbol of water baptism, it may first have been a symbol of Jesus' death."[102] Schnackenburg, opposing the sacramental view, says, "The washing . . . is interpreted in the christological and soteriological sense as a symbolic action in which Jesus makes his offering of himself in death graphic and effective."[103]

The outstanding symbol here seems to be Jesus' action rather than "water," but water symbolism can be established.[104] If we see it in 9:1–12 where not even the word ὕδωρ is mentioned, we should be able to establish it here where Jesus lowered himself and βάλλει ὕδωρ εἰς τὸν νιπτῆρα καὶ ἤρξατο νίπτειν τοὺς πόδας τῶν μαθητῶν καὶ ἐκμάσσειν τῷ λεντίῳ ᾧ ἦν διεζωσμένος (13:5). Early church fathers consistently linked this water symbol with either baptism or spiritual cleansing, which means that water symbolism here had caught their attention.[105] Dodd considers this episode one of the two main examples of Johannine water symbolism.[106] Becerra, who does not find water symbolism in the healing of the invalid at the pool (5:1–15), nor in the healing of the blind at Siloam (9:1–12), finds it here in the footwashing.[107] It is significant that Jesus' dialogue with Peter in this passage focuses on the need of purification, and water is indispensable in Jewish purification. We should note that water cleansing constitutes an important theme in John, and baptism is reiterated in the initial chapters of this gospel more than in the Synoptics. If it is a water rite that Jesus intended

---

100 The phrase εἰ μὴ τοὺς πόδας (13:10) is omitted in Codex Sinaiticus and the texts of early fathers such as Origen and Tatian. Most modern scholars accept the shorter reading as original, and subsequently interpret the footwashing as a symbol of the complete washing.

101 Cf. Bultmann, *John*, 470.

102 Brown, *John*, 1:559.

103 Schnackenburg, *John*, 3:19.

104 Koester deals with this under "symbolic action" but not under "water" (*Symbolism in the Fourth Gospel*, 115–18).

105 Sciberras, "Water According to Greek Fathers," 89–96.

106 Dodd, *Interpretation*, 138.

107 Becerra, "Le symbolisme," 161–77.

to perform on his disciples' feet, it is eschatological blessing that he had in mind: Ἐὰν μὴ νίψω σε, οὐκ ἔχεις μέρος μετ' ἐμοῦ (13:8).[108] From a literary perspective, whereas Jesus appears as a superior baptist in the initial chapter of the gospel, he now appears as a lowly, humbled baptist. The footwashing foreshadows the ignominy of the cross, which is the basis for true, effective cleansing. The symbolic role of water here is subtle but sure.

As we approach the Passion account in the gospel, we see Jesus approach his death and glorification. Here the "water cleansing" theme takes on a new form: footwashing instead of baptism. In this episode, therefore, we perceive a merging of the water theme and the theme of the cross. Water as being symbolic of purification is now drawn close to Jesus' approaching death.

19:31–37. In this episode of the piercing of Jesus' side, we witness the most subtle and yet most significant use of water symbolism in the gospel. If the passage has been edited by redactors from a source and the exposition of the event in 19:35–37 has been inserted, none of these editorial notes brings to light what "water" could have meant. So the recorded phenomenon remains awkward: ἐξῆλθεν εὐθὺς αἷμα καὶ ὕδωρ (19:34b). Bultmann considers this an ecclesiastical redaction to bring in a sacramental sense.[109] But Schnackenburg is more correct in saying, "apart from the fact that the interpretation of 'blood and water' as referring to the two sacraments is not certain, without 34b, something would be missing from the report about the spear-thrust."[110] In any case, the reference of water to baptism in this passage is hard to demonstrate, even though it has been demonstrated in 9:1–12 and 13:1–17, where water is more directly involved with washing.

Physiological explanations have been proposed to prove that such a phenomenon is possible and thus historically trustworthy, but the question remains as to what is implied by this peculiar mention of "blood and water." Two probabilities are commonly accepted. First, "blood and water" indicate that Jesus was, contrary to docetic views, truly human. So the sense of

---

108 Godet says, "Jesus is here thinking of the baptism of water, the symbol of general purification" (*John*, 810). Carson says, "The notion of 'having a part (*meros*) in' something is regularly used with respect to inheritance (e.g., Lk. 15:12), and, in Jewish thought, can refer to participation in eschatological blessings" (Carson, *John*, 464).

109 Bultmann, *John*, 678.

110 Yet, later on, Schnackenburg admits that the possibility of a sacramental meaning may not be ruled out (*John*, 3:286–87, 291).

19:34b is polemic, as in 1 John 5:6–8.[111] Second, a symbolic sense is intended, as Dodd explains, "From the crucified body of Christ flows the life-giving stream: the water which is the Spirit given to believers in Him (vii. 38–9), the water which if a man drink he will never thirst again (iv. 14) and the blood which is ἀληθὴς πόσις (vi. 55)."[112] Dodd assumes that these references to water resemble one another in meaning, which I think is possible. But a clearer delineation of this symbolic sense takes into consideration that "blood" signifies Jesus' atoning death. That significance, initially disclosed in the testimony of John the Baptist, "Ἴδε ὁ ἀμνὸς τοῦ θεοῦ (1:29), can be deduced exegetically from the gospel itself. So, Schnackenburg comments, "The blood is a sign of Jesus' saving death (cf. 1 John 1:7) and the water is symbolic of Spirit and life (cf. John 4:14; 7:38)."[113] Along the same line, a theological connection is made by Carson, "[Christ's] sacrificial and redemptive death is the basis of eternal life . . . "[114]

Thus, these symbolic uses of water in the later chapters of John all refer "subtly" to the death of Christ. In 9:1–12 the reference is still unclear, but a connection can already be worked out.[115] In 13:1–17 the reference is reinforced by Jesus' symbolic action, though it is still allusive. In 19:31–37 the reference is spelled out by the scene on the cross. There has been a growing overlap of the two themes: the water motif and the death of Christ.

Few have commented on the locale of the flow of the blood and water, but our picture would not be complete without looking at it. In patristic and medieval exegesis "Christ's side" is allegorized as the fountainhead of the church. This interpretation lacks evident support from the text and is rejected by modern interpreters. Some scholars point out that there is an allusion in this episode to Exodus: "Strike the rock, and water will come out of it for the people to drink" (Exod 17:6; cf. Num 20:11).[116] The long-suffering Yahweh can indeed be called "the rock" in providing water for his people,

---

111 In Jewish and Hellenistic thinking human life consists of blood and water. Cf. G. Richter, "Blut und Wasser aus der durchbohrten Seite Jesu (Joh 19,34b)," in *Studien zum Johannesevangelium*, ed. J. Hainz (Regensburg: Pustet, 1977), 120–42.

112 Dodd, *Interpretation*, 428.

113 Schnackenburg, *John*, 3:294.

114 Carson, *John*, 624.

115 See Grigsby, "Washing in the Pool of Siloam," 227–35.

116 Cf. Carson, *John*, 624–25.

and now the Christ, pierced on the cross, is the eschatological rock who provides the water of eternal blessings. This symbolic interpretation finds significant support from Jesus' discourse in chapters 6 and 7. The most significant reference is, however, the symbolic reference of Jesus' body to the tabernacle, and vice versa. Notably chapters 6 and 7 also provide a foundation to this interpretation, because Jesus' open pronouncement on living water is made at the Tabernacles, at the temple, where water flows out of the locale which symbolizes Yahweh's presence. The scene is prophetic of the death of Jesus and the piercing of his side. In return, the scene of the cross, with blood and water flowing from Jesus' side, symbolizes the giving of life and blessing from Yahweh's presence. Thus the water motif is intrinsically connected with the tabernacle image. We will turn to this OT theme again in chapter four of this book. Here, it suffices to point out that the tabernacle is also an important theme. In the episode of the cleansing of the temple (2:13–17), Jesus speaks of his own body as the temple. In the prologue of the gospel, the author alludes to the tabernacle when he describes the incarnation of the Son of God: Καὶ ὁ λόγος σὰρξ ἐγένετο καὶ ἐσκήνωσεν ἐν ἡμῖν . . . (1:14)

Summary: The Three Phases of Its Development

We have studied the significance of the water symbol as it appears in different sections of the episodic narrative of the gospel. It is clear that the use of it varies in these sections, as if it changes along with "the contours" of the literary development of the gospel. We can observe three overlapping phases of its use.

The first phase goes from chapter 1 through chapter 5, and consists of the "water" passages 1:14–34; 2:1–11; 3:1–15; 4:1–30; 5:1–15. A constant juxtaposition is found in these episodes, with Jewish or Samaritan traditions on the one side, which are preparatory and inadequate, and Jesus' gifts and acts on the other side, which are powerful and superb. "Water" invariably plays a part on the side which is preparatory and inadequate: "John's baptism," "the water in the stone jars at Cana," "water baptism as an initiation to the life above," "water from the well of Jacob," and "the water at Bethesda." While it plays a consistent role in this phase as part of the "anticipation" theme, it takes different forms in the various episodes. It is sometimes the object of an action, sometimes the subject of a discourse. Such is the adaptability of the Johannine use of water symbolism.

The second phase begins at chapter 4 and lasts throughout the episodes of the feasts till the approach of the last Passover. In this phase the narrative-discourse complexes in chapters 5 to 12 form the literary background, and the Jewish feasts provide the historical background. The characteristic use of "water" in this phase begins as early as chapter 4 with Jesus' offer of "living water," so there is an overlap of the phases. In these chapters the juxtaposition between anticipation and fulfillment recedes into the background. The feasts give the setting, and Jesus' revelation of himself stands out as the main subject. "Water" is here one of the metaphorical and christological symbols which Jesus uses for this revelation. It appears only infrequently here, its role being shared by other metaphorical symbols in these chapters, but the use of it is definitive. It appears in two significant passages, 4:1–30 and 7:37–44. In both passages Jesus is the one who evokes the use of it, and Jesus uses it to refer to his gifts of life, and to the Holy Spirit. In the Johannine framework of water symbolism these are eschatological blessings.

While the use of the symbol is consistent in the first phase, and definitive in the second phase, it is subtle in the third phase. The "farewell discourse" in chapters 13 to 17 and the passion narrative in chapters 18 to 19 form the background of this phase. However, the subtle use, which is typical in this phase, begins at 9:1–12 with the pool of Siloam, so there is again an overlap of phases. The main significance of the water symbol has already been established in the previous phase. So, in all of these three passages, 9:1–12; 13:1–17; 19:31–37, "water" stands for the eschatological salvation brought about by Jesus. In this last phase there is no more juxtaposition between "anticipation" and "fulfillment." As the passion theme becomes dominant, it overpowers the use of symbolism.[117] Water symbolism, however, remains significant because it comes up subtly in crucial scenes. Last but not least is the scene of the flow of blood and water from Jesus' side. The water symbol here tells us that all the eschatological blessings, symbolized by water, finds fulfillment in the death of Christ.

---

117 However, some literary scholars identify a Passover symbolism. See M. W. G. Stibbe, *John as Storyteller: Narrative Criticism and the Fourth Gospel*, SNTSMS 73 (Cambridge: Cambridge University Press, 1992), 35.

The Theological Significance of Water Symbolism in John

The literary development worked out above provides us with an overview of the use of water symbolism in Johannine theology. In the first phase, "water" stands for old rituals and traditions and gives expression to the characteristic eschatology of the Gospel of John. There is, in the gospel, a consistent "anticipation" of the coming of Christ, which finds "fulfillment" only in Jesus. In the second phase, where Jesus announces that he is the giver of "living water," the symbol further contributes to Johannine christology. It describes the messianic gifts, which are bestowed in the eschatological age, namely, the Holy Spirit and eternal life. In the third phase, where "water" plays a subtle role in the scenes that portray the death of Jesus, Johannine soteriology is brought to a climax. Christ's death fulfills the eschatological hope for salvation. Water symbolism in John is everywhere involved with Johannine theology.

In the following section we will seek further understanding of this relation between water symbolism and Johannine theology. We will approach this by taking into consideration the multiple "theological themes" in the Gospel of John.

Thematic Structures

The literary development of water symbolism, as shown above, corresponds with a more or less tripartite literary outline of the gospel. This tripartite outline may be called a thematic outline, which reflects the narrative or theological development of a certain theme in the gospel. Thematic outlines are helpful in studying John, though they may not satisfy any meticulous search for precision. There may even be an element of subjectivity in them that causes alarm.[118] Yet, the multiple development of themes is characteristic of the Gospel of John, and it makes the study of its literary structure intriguing. Many mutually exclusive outlines of the gospel have been proposed, for the repeated use of themes in John causes

---

118 Ashton rightly points out, "where an author has no interest in underlining the structure, it is largely left to the reader to pick out the emphases and make the necessary connections, and here there is inevitably a large element of subjectivity." See Ashton, "Narrative Criticism," chap. in *Studying John*, 154.

interpreters to “find” all kinds of parallels and chiasms.[119] However, our caution should not be against the study of themes or thematic structures, but, rather, against the exclusive use of any particular one. We should also keep in mind that the gospel’s ultimate purpose is theological rather than literary (20:31) and not lose sight of the themes in any fanatic search for neat structures. G. Mlakuzhyil’s criticism of Brown’s “literary-thematic structure,” as “not being always rigorous or exact,” sounds unfair if we bear in mind that it was not for precision in structure that the gospel was ever written.[120] Thematic outlines are useful if they help us “approximate the flow of the author’s thought.”[121] There can be more than one thematic outline, as there is more than one “emphasis” or “connection” that affects the flow. We may look for, for example, the geographical pattern, the alignment of feasts, the repetition of the ἐγώ εἰμι statements, the apparent alternation of signs and discourses, the change of audience to Jesus’ revelation, the heightening of opposition and conflict, and so on. Some of these connections are literary, and some are theological, but one single outline may not reflect all of the author’s emphases and connections. Westcott’s outline, for example, focuses on the phases of Jesus’ revelation.[122] Dodd has one that reflects the narrative-discourse complex.[123] Brown offers one that describes the gospel’s literary and thematic development.[124] C. H. Giblin’s outline works on the change of place, time, and target of Jesus’ ministry.[125]

---

119 Carson, *John*, 104.

120 G. Mlakuzhyil, “Survey of the Structures of the Fourth Gospel,” chap. in *The Christocentric Literary Structure of the Fourth Gospel*, AnBib 117 (Rome: Editrice Pontificio Istituto Biblico, 1987), 82. Over twenty-four outlines are classified in his exhaustive analysis of the structure, 17–85. At least several more structures have been proposed since Mlakuzhyil’s survey. See Kowalski, “Of Water and Spirit”; E. A. Wyller, “In Solomon’s Porch: A Henological Analysis of the Architectonic of the Fourth Gospel,” *ST* 42 (1988): 151–67; C. H. Giblin, “The Tripartite Narrative Structure of John’s Gospel,” *Bib* 71 (1990): 449–68; G. Østenstad, “The Structure of the Fourth Gospel: Can It Be Defined Objectively,” *ST* 45 (1991): 33–55.

121 M. Silva, “Approaching the Fourth Gospel,” *Criswell Theological Review* 3 (1988): 26; cf. Giblin, “The Tripartite Narrative Structure,” 449.

122 Westcott, *John*, xlii–xliii.

123 Dodd, *Interpretation*, x, 289–443.

124 Brown, *John*, 1:cxxxviii.

125 Giblin, “The Tripartite Narrative Structure,” 455.

To broaden our understanding of water symbolism we will look into some related thematic outlines and see how the "water" theme intersects with other theological themes.

Jesus' Revelation in Symbolic Narratives

Lee, in her work quoted in the last chapter, "The Symbolic Narratives of the Fourth Gospel: The Interplay of Form and Meaning," tries to unravel a "literary form" which is unique to certain parts of John, claiming that "form gives rise to meaning" and that "symbol discloses the transcendent." She calls it the "symbolic narrative" and locates six units of it in the gospel.[126] They are the story of Nicodemus (3:1–36), the story of the Samaritan woman (4:1–42), the healing at the Pool (5:1–47), the feeding of the five thousand (6:1–71), the healing of the man born blind (9:1–41) and the raising of Lazarus (11:1–12:11). It can be demonstrated that there is a common "five-stage" structure to all these symbolic narratives.

Stage 1: Foundational image or 'sign'
Stage 2: Misunderstanding
Stage 3: Struggle for understanding
Stage 4: Attainment or rejection of symbolic understanding
Stage 5: Confession of faith or statement of rejection[127]

It should be noted that this narrative structure depicts a theme, namely, Jesus' revelation of truth. As Lee herself works it out from the form: Jesus first reveals himself either in deeds or words, which, then, leads to either misunderstanding or further revelation, and then the audience respond either in rejection or in faith. In agreement with the form and the theme is the theological intent of the gospel, namely, to bring to light the truth revealed by Jesus and thus bring reader to faith. So we have quite a central theme here, namely, "Jesus' revelation," and "water," as a main symbol used in Jesus' revelation, plays an extensive part. As shown in our work in this chapter, "water" is involved in almost all of these six symbolic narratives proposed by Lee. Only in the raising of Lazarus (11:1–12:11) is it totally absent. In the feeding of the five thousand (6:1–71) the part of "water" is taken by "bread," so it is by inference present. In all the other four narratives

126 Lee, *Symbolic Narratives*, 29, 33.
127 Ibid., 11–15.

"water" is the main symbol. This affirms that the water motif interlocks closely with the revelation theme.

Hearing, Seeing, and Believing

Closely connected with the theme of revelation is the theme of faith as response. Koester studies this theme from a literary approach, focusing on the characters in the gospel narrative and treating them as representatives of various types of faith.[128] Koester discovers that characters are juxtaposed in pairs in the Gospel of John.

John 1:19–51	the Jewish delegation and the disciples
John 2	the disciples at Cana and the people in Jerusalem
John 3:1–4:42	Nicodemus and the Samaritan woman
John 4:46–5:16	the royal official and the invalid
John 6:1–21	the crowd and Peter
John 7–12	Jesus' brothers and the blind man
	believing Jews and unbelieving Jews
	Mary, Martha, and Jews who reported to the Pharisees
John 20:1–31	the other disciples and Thomas[129]

Koester works through these passages to show that, according to the gospel, genuine faith is engendered "through hearing, not seeing."[130] The juxtaposed characters are found to be opposite examples in responding to Jesus' revelation in either deeds or words. Koester observes that some, such as the Samaritans, were led to faith without any attendant miracle. Some were able to "see" miracles as testimony to Jesus, but in those cases (e.g., the royal official, the blind man, and Martha), there was always an initial response of faith that arose from hearing, and that initial faith enabled them to perceive Jesus' sign rightly. Not everyone who heard came to faith, Koester affirms, but "those who did manifest a genuine faith, did so after an initial experience of hearing."[131]

The importance of hearing, as pointed out by Koester, concurs with the significance of water symbolism in John. "Water," as a means of Jesus'

128 C. R. Koester, "Hearing, Seeing, and Believing in the Gospel of John," *Bib* 70 (1989): 327–481.

129 Ibid., 328, 329–47.

130 Ibid., 347.

131 Ibid.

revelation, is intrinsically related to hearing. In the "second phase" of water symbolism in John, there is a "prime use" of the water symbol in referring to eschatological gifts (4:1–30; 7:37–38). Here, though the symbol is infrequently mentioned, Jesus uses it for the "hearing" of faith by the audience, and so it has a definitive use. In Koester's terms this definitive use of the symbol is important because it becomes words of revelation for "hearing," rather than objects in deeds of miracle for "seeing."

In the "first phase" of water symbolism, i.e., in the initial chapters of John, "water" expresses the "anticipation" of eschatological blessings. Sometimes it features in a miracle for "seeing" (e.g., 2:1–11; 5:1–15) and other times it comes up in a discourse for "hearing" (e.g., 1:14–34; 3:1–15; 4:1–30). In either case, it testifies to the "fulfillment" brought about by Jesus. Thus, for example, the water baptism of John goes hand in hand with John's testimony of Jesus in evoking faith. The disciples respond in faith but the Jewish delegation do not. We have made it clear that it is "anticipation" rather than "replacement" that the symbol stands for. As "anticipation" it always serves to testify to Jesus and never to oppose or deny him. Thus the water and the wine go together in testifying the eschatological Christ (2:1–11). So do the ineffective water of Bethesda and the healing power of Jesus (5:1–15). In all these cases, it is always the hearing but not the seeing that engendered faith.

The water motif is intricately tied with the theme of testimony, and faith.

The Passover Theme and the Water Symbol

There is a link between the water motif and the death of Christ, as we have pointed out above more than once. In this respect, highly commendable is S. E. Porter's article on the "examination of the OT fulfillment motif and the Passover theme."[132] A primary aim of this article is to recommend the usefulness of traditional exegesis towards the literary-historical approach in the study of John, and a further aim is to examine the Passover theme as

---

132 S. E. Porter, "Can Traditional Exegesis Enlighten Literary Analysis of the Fourth Gospel? An Examination of the Old Testament Fulfillment Motif and the Passover Theme," in *The Gospels and the Scriptures of Israel*, ed. C. A. Evans and W. R. Stegner, JSNTSup 104, Studies in Scripture in Early Judaism and Christianity 3 (Sheffield: Sheffield Academic Press, 1994), 396–428.

an illustration. The Passover theme in John has previously been underlined by M. W. G. Stibbe and M. Davies, literary-historical analysts.[133] Porter points out, however, that they have failed "to appreciate the theme's significance as one that in conjunction with the OT fulfillment motif binds together the entire Gospel."[134] So Porter himself works out the relation between the fulfillment formula theme and the Passover theme, using the traditional exegetical approach as well as the literary approach. He first goes through the fulfillment theme and shows that the climax of the theme is at 19:36–37. At this climax, (1) a series of OT references introduced by fulfillment formulas come to an end, (2) a group of quotations surrounding the death of Jesus also come to an end, and (3) the references to the Passover theme come to an end.[135] Then he works on the Passover theme, commenting on the six passages that allude to the OT Passover event.

a. John 1:29–36, especially vv. 29, 36 ("the lamb of God")
b. John 2:13–25 (Jesus' cleansing the temple)
c. John 6:1–14, 22–71 (Passover feeding and other allusions to Exodus)
d. John 11:47–12:8 (Caiaphas' words and other additional references)
e. John 13:1–17:26 (the Passover meal related with allusive language)
f. John 19:13–42 (the crucifixion of Jesus)[136]

Though some of these are only allusions to the Passover, which cannot be firmly proven by traditional exegesis, the extensiveness of allusions, considered from a literary point of view, can more than sufficiently establish the theme.

Regarding the relation between water symbolism and the above themes, we may note that the water symbol does not come close to any direct OT citations in John and does not cross paths with the OT fulfillment theme that Porter proposes, even though "water" features in many OT passages.[137] As for the Passover theme, water plays a part in John 6, as both bread and water come from the Exodus motif, but other than that it does not have any

---

133 Stibbe, *John as Storyteller*, 95; M. Davies, *Rhetoric and Reference in the Fourth Gospel*, JSNTSup 69 (Sheffield: JSOT, 1992), 7.

134 Porter, "Can Traditional Exegesis Enlighten Literary Analysis," 397.

135 Ibid., 401–7.

136 Ibid., 407–21.

137 The citation at 1:23 introduces John the Baptist, not water baptism. In 7:38, there is not any actual citation after καθὼς εἶπεν ἡ γραφή, so an allusion is involved rather than a citation.

significant part in the Passover. It is in the Tabernacle theme of John that water plays a dominant role. It is clear that "bread" and "sacrifice" dominate in the Passover theme whereas "water" dominates at the Tabernacle. So, "water" can only be an indirect component of the Passover theme.

It becomes significant to further note that all these themes intersect at 19:31–37. It is to the credit of Porter that we first note a convergence of the Passover theme and the OT fulfillment theme in chapter 19. He draws our attention to the two OT quotations in 19:36–37, and points out that they were cited by the author in "double emphatic fashion" to bring the passion story to a close. At this close, both the Passover theme and the OT fulfillment theme come to a "fitting conclusion." The series of OT quotations ends here in special fashion, and the Passover theme, which signifies at various junctures a reaffirmation of Jesus' role as Passover victim, ends here at Jesus' climactic death. Thus the quotations in 19:36–37 are, as rightly suggested by Porter, "final fulfillment statements that bring the entire course of plot development to a close."[138]

In relation to this, it is noteworthy that water symbolism also ends at the same point of the plot, the death of Jesus on the cross. The last appearance of the water symbol in John occurs at the flow of blood and water from Jesus' pierced side, 19:34. That is the point at which also the Passover theme ends. Although the two themes do not often cross paths, they culminate together in the death of Jesus on the cross.

Summary: An Observable Eschatological Framework

In this chapter we have surveyed the use of water symbolism in various passages in the Gospel of John. As a means of baptism and as an element used in Jesus' miracles, "water" symbolizes the anticipation of Christ. As a symbol used by Jesus himself, "water" symbolizes eternal life and the Holy Spirit. As a medium used by Jesus in healing the blind and in washing the disciples' feet like a servant, "water" plays a role in prefiguring Jesus' atoning death. We have also looked into its theological significance. As a theme, water symbolism interlocks with other themes. It participates in Jesus' revelation, plays a part in evoking faith, and goes parallel with the "bread" or the Passion theme in approaching the death of Jesus on the cross.

---

138 Ibid., 421.

It culminates at the scene of the cross with other themes, to testify to the fulfillment of all eschatological expectations, as hinted by Jesus' saying in 19:30, Τετέλεσται.

There is an eschatological framework that delimits all these and shows that "eschatology," among other theological emphases in the gospel, is the characteristic message of Johannine water symbolism, and that it best describes its theological significance.

As early as in the first "phase" of the use of the symbol, there is eschatological significance in all of its appearances in the episodes. The old rites or traditions anticipate the new blessings, and the new blessings are to be brought in by Jesus, the Christ. So the message is eschatological as well as christological. This message can be diagrammed as a three-way structure, with Christ on the top of a triangle or in the middle of a linear line, and with the old anticipatory rites on the one side and the new eschatological blessings on the other. In the initial chapters the note is strong on the anticipation because the old is so often juxtaposed with the new. The frequent appearance of "water" on the side of the old adds to this strong note (1:14–34; 2:1–11; 3:1–15; 4:1–30; 5:1–15).

This structure remains fundamental in the second phase as well as throughout the gospel, as various theological themes develop. Other emphases arise to replace the strong note on anticipation, but the same eschatological message remains. In the long discourses that revolve around the feasts, the christological note is strong, but the anticipatory rites stays in the background to remind us of eschatology. In this phase, "water" represents the new blessings rather than the old rites. Together with other symbols of OT origins, such as "bread" and "light," it depicts the eschatology that looks forward to christology and finds fulfillment in Jesus. "Eternal life" is highlighted among these blessings in chapter 4, and so "the Holy Spirit" in chapter 7. Both of these are given expression in the water symbol.

In the third phase of its use, the death of Christ is the climax of all themes. As the passion narratives begin to take over the stage and the Passover theme makes the stronger note, the water symbol plays a more subtle part and appear only in significant scenes (9:1–12; 13:1–17; 19:31–37). The most significant is the scene of Jesus' death on the cross, in which blood and water flow from his side (19:34). Here also is the culminating point of the OT fulfillment theme in John, with final citations at 19:36–37. The water symbol is an allusive OT reference which accompanies the citations, and it speaks of the truth that God himself and his abode, the tabernacle, is the source of life and blessings. The message is that by being the source of blood and water, Jesus brings these blessings to fulfillment in his death. Thus "water" signifies the final fulfillment accomplished by the death of Jesus.

In the three-way structure of the overall eschatological message of John, the versatile water symbol has switched from one parameter to another as it moves along in the gospel narrative. It plays the part of "old anticipatory rites" in the first phase and "new eschatological blessings" in the second phase. In the climax of the final phase, it participates in declaring the final fulfillment of Christ's salvation on the cross.

As a metaphorical symbol "water" never directly symbolizes Christ, so it plays a comparatively small part in christology. Its part in soteriology is more obvious, being the means of Jesus' healing or cleansing. In Johannine pneumatology it plays a much more significant part, standing for the Holy Spirit, but it is not mentioned at all in Jesus' farewell discourse in which the Spirit is promised. It is only with eschatology that water symbolism in John continuously interacts. It is in Johannine eschatology that the water symbol, with its significance rooted in the Old Testament, plays a most versatile and outstanding role.

CHAPTER THREE

ESCHATOLOGY AND THE SYMBOLIC MEANING OF "WATER" IN JOHN 4

It follows from our previous discussions that the water symbol should not be interpreted with a single referent or described with a simplistic statement. We should, rather, interpret the symbol in its multiple contexts and expound its multifold meanings. "Water" in John 4, for instance, symbolizes not only one's physical need but also one's dependence on earthly resources. Likewise it does not just symbolize a personal eternal life given by Jesus but points to the eschatology profoundly developed in John. This will be my thesis in this chapter as I interpret John 4 and the use of water symbolism in the passage. Instead of delimiting its meaning with a couple of referents that match its use, I will look for its full significance and, subsequently, interpret the message with eschatology in view. In doing so I will exegete the passage both historico-grammatically and with a literary approach. I will also keep in view Léon-Dufour's concept of "double symbolism in the Fourth Gospel" recommended earlier in chapter one. Thus the symbol will be interpreted in light of two historical settings, "the Jewish cultural milieu in which Jesus Himself lived, and the Christian cultural milieu which inspires John's interpretation of the past."[1]

Historicity and the Historical Background of John 4

As a ground for subsequent exegesis we will clarify some of the preconceptions held here with regard to the backgrounds of the Gospel of John. We will not fully reconstruct the original historical settings, but we will try to establish the relevance of a Samaritan theology in the interpretation of water symbolism.

---

1 Léon-Dufour, "Symbolic Reading," 440–42.

Historicity and Inner Coherence of the Episode

Brown says, commenting on John 4:4–42, "Either we are dealing with a master of fiction, or else the stories have a basis in fact."[2] There are four main positions on the historical truthfulness of this account. It is held that the episode is fictitious (e.g., Haenchen), or that it is historically accurate (most former scholars), or that it is basically historical but has undergone literary modifications (e.g., Cullmann), or that it is created theologically with reliable items of information (e.g., Schnackenburg).[3] What a spectrum! We should note that the main arguments against historical trustworthiness are made up of form critical problems. Bultmann finds difficulties in the transitions of the narrative as evidence of the author's clumsy combination of traditional and personal materials, none of which is considered by him historical. These difficulties bolster distrust of historicity.[4] However, a narrative style like John's should not be expected to be always smooth and without awkward transitions. Earlier in the century H. Windisch wrote on "John's Narrative Style," in which he used John 4:1–42 as one of the best examples to illustrate the characteristic "dramatic" style of John:

> The narrative is almost exclusively conversation in lively exchange; the speaking characters come and go. The jumps in the sequence of thought become understandable. Only in the middle (Scene 4 and the end) does the narrator content himself with brief indications: a purely dramatic representation would have given more color here too.[5]

Those who appreciate the gospel from a literary point of view tend to regard the account in John 4 a coherent whole. Recent commentators such as Brown, Schnackenburg, B. Lindars, and Beasley-Murray perceive a coherent

---

2 Brown, *John*, 1:14.

3 E. Haenchen, *A Commentary on the Gospel of John Chapters 1–6*, Hermeneia, trans. R. W. Funk, ed. R. W. Funk and U. Busse (Philadelphia: Fortress, 1984), 226; O. Cullmann, *The Johannine Circle*, trans. J. Bowden (Philadelphia: Westminster Press, 1976), 20–25; Schnackenburg, *John*, 1:21, 420–21.

4 Bultmann, *John*, 175.

5 Note that H. Windisch illustrates by translating the text as a drama in seven scenes, "Der Johanneische Erzählungsstil," in *EYXAPISTHPION: Studien zur Religion und Literatur des Alten und Neuen Testaments, Hermann Gunkel zum 60. Geburtstags*, ed. H. Schmidt (Göttingen: Vandenhoeck & Ruprecht, 1923), 174–213; English translation taken from *The Gospel of John as Literature: An Anthology of Twentieth-century Perspectives*, ed. M. W. G. Stibbe (New York: Brill, 1993), 25–64.

structure and continuity within the text, though it is never denied that there is use of traditions behind the composition.[6] Modern literary theorists attempt to elucidate that inner coherence by applying literary reading (G. R. O'Day), speech act reading (J. E. Botha), and semiotic analysis (H. Boers) to the text, and they all claim to see literary connections in what form critics consider difficult transitions.[7]

Literary coherence is not a "proof" of historical trustworthiness. To the skeptical it means that the account was flawlessly made up. However, just as difficulties bolster distrust, the coherence of an account should strengthen confidence in its historical reliability, so that we may expect to find in John 4 a literary presentation of historical facts.

Here I will also try to show that the Samaritan background in the text is reflected with a coherence that speaks for historicity. In the past few decades there have been important studies made on Samaritanism that inform us about the theology and religious practices of Samaritans in New Testament times.[8] A number of proposals have been made regarding the relation between Samaritanism and the Gospel of John, all targeted on the origins of either the gospel or Samaritanism, the focus of interest being

---

6 Brown, *John*, 1:xxiv, 176; Schnackenburg, *John*, 1:44–48, 420; B. Lindars, *The Gospel of John*, New Century Bible, ed. R. E. Clement and M. Black (Grand Rapids: Eerdmans, 1981 [1972]), 46; Beasley-Murray, *John*, 59.

7 G. R. O'Day, "Revelation in Context (John 4:4–42)," chap. in *Revelation in the Fourth Gospel: Narrative Mode and Theological Claim* (Philadelphia: Fortress, 1986), 49–50; J. E. Botha, *Jesus and the Samaritan Woman: A Speech Act Reading of John 4:1–42*, NovTSup 65 (Leiden: E. J. Brill, 1991), 188–200; H. Boers, *Neither on This Mountain Nor in Jerusalem: A Study of John 4*, SBLMS 35 (Atlanta, GA: Scholars Press, 1988), 77–78.

8 J. Montgomery, *The Samaritans: The Earliest Jewish Sect; Their History, Theology, and Literature* (Philadelphia: The John C. Winston Co., 1907); M. Gaster, *The Samaritans: Their History, Doctrines and Literature* (London: Oxford University Press, 1925); J. Bowman, "Early Samaritan Eschatology," *JJS* 6 (1955): 63–72; Macdonald, *Theology of the Samaritans*; J. Bowman, *Samaritanische Probleme: Studien zum Verhältnis von Samaritanertum, Judentum und Urchristentum* (Stuttgart: W. Kohlhammer GmbH., 1967); H. G. Kippenberg, *Gerizim und Synagoge: Traditionsgeschichtliche Untersuchungen zur samaritanischer Religion der aramäischen Periode* (Berlin: de Gruyter, 1971); R. J. Coggins, *Samaritans and Jews* (Oxford: Blackwell, 1975); A. D. Crown, ed., *The Samaritans* (Tübingen: Mohr, 1989).

how one might have influenced the other.[9] Yet, little is said in regard to the display of Samaritanism in John 4 itself. Nor has the Samaritan background been sufficiently noted in discussions on the historical context of the gospel, though there is a growing tendency today to take seriously the historical, social and geographical details uniquely found in the narratives of the gospel. Brown is among the few who note that in John 4 "the references to the Samaritans, their theology, their practice of worshipping on Gerizim and the location of Jacob's well all seem to be accurate."[10] He also commends the Evangelist for a cogent handling of the Samaritan scene.

> The 'mise en scene' is one of the most detailed in John, and the evangelist betrays a knowledge of local color and Samaritan beliefs that is impressive. . . the well at the foot of Gerizim; the question of legal purity in vs. 9; the spirited defense of the patriarchal well in vs. 12; the Samaritan belief in Gerizim and the Prophet-like-Moses. And if we analyze the repartee at the well, we find quite true-to-life the characterization of the woman as mincing and coy, with a certain light grace.[11]

It is also noted that the woman seems to understand Jesus' claims against the background of the Samaritan expectation of the "Taheb" (4:19–25), and so even in the conversation we may have echoes of a historical tradition of an incident in Jesus' ministry. Thus, in interpreting John 4, we are dealing with a master of narration rather than fiction, and looking into an account that has a basis in fact. My confidence is that, if the tradition had not been historical, this awkwardly edited passage could not have presented these coherent facts for the Samaritan background. The obstinately Samaritan ethos of the woman's response, which seems crude in her dialogue with Jesus, well indicates that the episode is unfeigned.

---

9 J. Bowman, "The Fourth Gospel and the Samaritans," section in "Samaritan Studies," *BJRL* 40 (1958): 298–327; W. A. Meeks, *The Prophet-King: Moses Traditions and the Johannine Christology* (Leiden: E. J. Brill, 1967); G. W. Buchanan, "The Samaritan Origin of the Gospel of John," in *Religions in Antiquity: Essays in Memory of E. R. Goodenough*, ed. J. Neusner (Leiden: E. J. Brill, 1968); E. D. Freed, "Samaritan Influence in the Gospel of John," *CBQ* 30 (1968): 580–97; "Did John Write His Gospel Partly to Win Samaritan Converts?" *NovT* 12 (1970): 241–56; C. H. H. Scobie, "The Origins and Development of Samaritan Christianity," *NTS* 19 (1972–73): 390–414; M. Pamment, "Is There Convincing Evidence of Samaritan Influence on the Fourth Gospel?" *ZNW* 73 (1982): 221–30.

10 Brown, *John*, 1:xlii.

11 Ibid., 175.

Thus there is genuineness of Palestinian life during Jesus' time reflected in John 4. The subjects central to the dialogues, the living water, the true worship, the food of doing God's will, and the hope in the coming of the Messiah, are all Jewish and Samaritan in character. The coherence of these subjects and their somewhat crude allusions to Judaistic eschatology support the view that an original historical setting has been involved.

The Conceptual Background

Now that Hellenism is no longer the most obvious conceptual background for the gospel, two other options open up. One is to locate the gospel in the Judaistic milieu, considering it closer to Essene writings than Gnostic writings, interpreting its dualism as "monotheistic," "ethical" and "eschatological" like that of Qumran.[12] The other option is to ascribe it to mixed influences. Since similarities exist among different conceptual backgrounds, and there seemed to be a crossover between Judaistic and Hellenistic worlds, most are comfortable with the view that there was a rich diversity of influences incorporated into the very substance of the gospel. In most introductions today we can find long lists of more or less the same influences: Gnosticism, Hellenistic thoughts, Hellenistic Judaism, and Palestinian Judaism of various sorts.

We should note, however, that the message of the gospel is distinguishable from its conceptual backgrounds. The gospel is, conceptually speaking, a christological interpretation of the Old Testament which is not found in other "backgrounds." Because of this allegiance to the Old Testament the gospel bears affinity to the various sects of contemporary Judaism. Nonetheless Johannine theology is distinct from them because of its Christian witness. Another distinction to be made has to do with the cause of similarity between the gospel and non-Christian documents. Granted that there are parallels, can we jump to the conclusion that the Gospel of John was acquiring influences rather than influencing others? Regarding this I am in agreement with Beasley-Murray's discussion on the

12 W. F. Albright, "Recent Discoveries in Palestine and the Gospel of St. John," in *The Background of the New Testament and Its Eschatology*, ed. W. D. Davies and D. Daube (Cambridge: Cambridge University Press, 1956), 153–71; R. E. Brown, "The Qumran Scrolls and the Johannine Gospel and Epistles," *CBQ* 17 (1955): 403–19, 559–74.

subject, which he titles "The Religious Relations of the Fourth Gospel."

> The term "relations" is preferable to "background," since it is likely that the Evangelist may have wished to relate the Gospel to groups with religious concepts and traditions other than his own. . . .
>
> . . . John's employment of the [Logos] concept to introduce the story of Jesus was a master-stroke of communication to the world of his day. What he achieved in the prologue to the Gospel he did in the body of the Gospel . . . to ring out the message with a multitude of associations that helped to commend and interpret the good news he sought to convey.[13]

The key word here is "communication." The gospel is not a synthesis of other philosophies but draws upon non-Christian terms and concepts to communicate its own faith in Jesus Christ (20:30–31).

The discovery and study of Samaritan literature began as early as the sixteenth century and is still in process, though it has not aroused as much attention as the discoveries at Qumran and at Nag Hammadi in recent times. We encounter the same confusion of "who influences whom" in this discussion. Among the works written on the subject, Meeks's study of the traditions of Moses as the "prophet-king" proves influential, and it assumes the aforementioned view, that a rich diversity of influences has been incorporated into the essence of the gospel. In his investigation of the "overlapping traditions" in Palestine he studied the Samaritan sources alongside with Rabbinic and non-Rabbinic Jewish sources as well as Mandaean sources. His conclusion is as follows:

> The Johannine traditions were shaped, at least in part, by interaction between a Christian community and a hostile Jewish community whose piety accorded very great importance to Moses and the Sinai theophany . . . the Johannine church had drawn members from that Jewish group as well as from the Samaritan circles which held very similar beliefs, and it has been demonstrated to a high degree of probability that the depiction of Jesus as prophet and king in the Fourth Gospel owes much to traditions which the church inherited from the Moses piety.[14]

Quite contrary to Meeks's view there is the former view of J. Macdonald's, "The Samaritans, at least in later times, were closely influenced by the New Testament. . . it was Johannine literature in particular that was to exercise a lasting influence on the way some Samaritan doctrines

13 Beasley-Murray, *John*, liii–lxvi; cf. Carson, *John*, 61.

14 Meeks, *The Prophet-King*, 318–19.

developed."[15] Macdonald does not ascribe the characteristics of Johannine christology to Samaritan sources as some other scholars do, because extant Samaritan sources are actually later documents than the New Testament.[16] However, evidence is not available to prove Macdonald's point for the situation during New Testament times.[17] Most scholars would be satisfied with a reconstruction and agree that the development of a Samaritan theology was well under way by Jesus' time, and that includes beliefs in the coming of a Moses-like prophet ("Taheb"), referred to in John 4:25 as the Messiah awaited by the Samaritan woman.[18] It only remains controversial whether Johannine christology, which emphasizes the importance of Moses, has been informed by "traditions directly inherited from the Samaritan circles" as Meeks suggests.[19] There are at least three reasons to challenge that this was what happened. First, even though Mosaic christology shares the common root of OT eschatology with Judaistic and Samaritan beliefs in Moses, it was not essentially informed by these beliefs. Second, it is Jesus' superiority to Moses that the gospel seeks to demonstrate, and in that sense the gospel is distinct from Judaistic and Samaritan traditions.[20] Third, though Mosaic christology may be significant, it is but one ingredient of the Johannine message, and it is part of the Exodus motif that the gospel takes over from OT traditions. Furthermore, as Beasley-Murray points out, "Johannine Christology cannot be wholly comprehended under the Moses traditions. . . . the key elements are the Son of Man and Son of God

---

15 Macdonald, *Theology of the Samaritans*, 33.

16 Cf. Bowman, *Samaritanische Probleme*, 55–61, and "Samaritan Studies," 302, n. 2, quoted in Scobie, "Origins and Development," 401, 405.

17 Note Meeks's refutation of Macdonald's view in *The Prophet-King*, 239, 240, 257. Note also Freed's argument for the same position: "We can hardly attribute the lack of a conception of an earthly kingdom of God in the earliest Samaritan literature to influence from Christianity" ("Did John Write to Win?" 251).

18 E.g., J. D. Purvis, "The Fourth Gospel and the Samaritans," *NovT* 17 (1975): 166–68; Scobie, "Origins and Development," 405–6; Beasley-Murray, *John*, lxiv. Note also that the most comprehensive study of early Aramaic Samaritan traditions was contributed by Kippenberg, *Gerizim und Synagoge*.

19 Meeks's thesis is that John's presentation of Jesus has been largely determined by the conviction that Jesus is the one of whom Moses speaks—the ultimate Prophet and Messianic King (*The Prophet-King*, 286–319); cf. Beasley-Murray, *John*, lxv; contra. Pamment, "Samaritan Influence?" 222–23.

20 Beasley-Murray, *John*, lxv; Purvis, "The Fourth Gospel and the Samaritans," 187.

concepts."[21] How then do we evaluate the appearance of Mosaic christology in the gospel? What exactly is the relation between the gospel and Samaritan (and Jewish) beliefs? Again, it should be noted that Johannine theology is distinctly a Christian interpretation of OT traditions. The similarities between the gospel and Samaritan beliefs are explained by the common root they share, rather than by the influence of the latter upon the former.

What is the bearing of this upon Johannine water symbolism and eschatology? They are likewise pronouncements of John's distinct Christian message in a Judaistic and Samaritan conceptual milieu. In studying John 4 we will see that both "water" and "the messianic hope" were common concerns for Jews and Samaritans alike, and they are part of the conceptual background for the gospel. The distinctiveness of the gospel lies in its christology, i.e., its presentation of Jesus' discourses on these issues.

The next relevant question would be, regarding the relation between the gospel and Samaritan beliefs: what was the setting that prompted the presentation of Mosaic christology in the gospel? Were there Samaritans among the audience, with whom the author tried to communicate the gospel? Is it not true that even Meeks, after all that comparison of traditions, conjures up a situation for the Johannine church which would account for the gospel's own characteristic?

The Setting and the Purpose

In Brown's reconstruction ("The Community of the Beloved Disciple") the entrance of Samaritans into the scene is estimated with some reserve. It was only "Jews of anti-Temple views who converted Samaritans and picked up some elements of Samaritan thoughts" who came in, and "it is unlikely" that the community "had permanent contacts with Samaria or lived there."[22] Brown's evidence for this is that "the Samaritan converts are never mentioned after chap. 4."[23] Brown commits a grave mistake here in treating the gospel not as literature but as a history of the Johannine community, postulating that the disciples mentioned in John 1 comprised the first group,

21 Beasley-Murray, *John*, lxv.

22 R. E. Brown. *The Community of the Beloved Disciple: The Life, Loves, and Hates of an Individual Church in New Testament Times* (New York: Paulist Press, 1979), 37–39.

23 Ibid., 39.

the higher christology in John 2 to 4 reflects the admission of a second group, and so on.[24] Of course the Samaritans are not mentioned all through the gospel! Why should they be if the author composed the gospel differently from how Brown conjectures? On the other hand Brown is to be commended for taking the Samaritans into consideration in the construction of a community theory. He is the only one who does so among other theorists. Notably, those who work on Samaritanism together with the Fourth Gospel always hold that Samaritans were directly involved in the composition of the gospel.[25] J. Bowman's suggestion is most frequently quoted.

> Is it not possible that the Gospel writer while not giving up the Jewish claim that salvation is of the Jews, is showing that Jesus is the fulfillment of all Israel's hope, the hope of Judah and also of the Samaritans who claimed to be the descendants of Northern Israel? . . . Is it not possible that the author of John is trying to make a bridge between Samaritans and Jews in Christ?[26]

The first and main part of Bowman's suggestion, that Jesus is the fulfillment of all Israel's eschatological hope, including the Samaritans', is what I have already affirmed in the last chapter. That is, the very symbol of "water" and its double meaning intricately speak for anticipation and fulfillment. It will be the aim of the present chapter to further show that the elements of Samaritan history and theology included in John 4 support precisely such an eschatological interpretation.

The second part of Bowman's suggestion, that the author of John is trying to make a bridge between Samaritans and Jews in Christ, has to do with the purpose of the gospel, and it will call for the explicit working out of a life setting to sustain. Again, I have previously affirmed that the purpose, as stated in the gospel itself (20:31), is to convince readers that Jesus is the eschatological figure who will bring in salvation. There is no doubt that the gospel speaks for the inclusion of the Samaritans in this salvation, though it is not so clear whether it tries to "make a bridge" between Samaritans and Jews in Christ. Here let me summarize the more compelling reasons for

---

24 He even says that there should not be a hostility between the groups because "Jesus reconciles his disciples of chap. 1 to the Samaritan converts of chap. 4" (ibid., 37).

25 Odeberg was among the earliest who contended so, "On the basis of Gaster's work on the Samaritans . . . it may be admissible to urge that the controversial issue of Jn 4 is with a circle of Samaritans that are wholly within the bounds of what we have termed the Samaritan community" (*The Fourth Gospel*, 185).

26 Bowman, "The Fourth Gospel and the Samaritans," 302.

ascertaining the presence of Samaritans in the gospel setting. First, the significance reckoned to Moses in the gospel should have made it appealing to Samaritan readers, because Moses as "prophet-king" is central in Samaritan theology. Likewise the reference of Jesus as prophet reminds them of their eschatological figure "Taheb," which they associate with the divine promise to Moses in Deut 18:18–22.[27] This is exactly what Meeks's thesis has pointed out.[28] Yet, Meeks has also pointed out that this view of Moses is not exclusively Samaritanism, but is shared by Jewish sources in general. What Meeks does not stress enough is that the gospel is distinct from them in demonstrating Jesus' superiority to Moses. As Beasley-Murray expresses it, "The Fourth Gospel appears to relate both positively and negatively to Samaritan views of Moses."[29] The king-prophet theme, therefore, speaks of a corrective purpose of the gospel, but not so much a "bridge" between Jews and Samaritans. Second, the Samaritans are mentioned favorably in the gospel, in John 4 specifically.[30] They were the only non-Jewish group whom Jesus met, whereas "the Jews" are presented as antagonistic.[31] At one point Jesus was despised by "the Jews" as "a Samaritan and demon-possessed."[32] We note that in John, as Meeks

---

27 M. Gaster, *Samaritan Oral Law and Ancient Traditions*, vol. 1, *Samaritan Eschatology* (London: The Search Publishing Co., 1932), 221–77; also *The Samaritans*, 90–91; quoted in Purvis, "The Fourth Gospel and the Samaritans," 182.

28 Freed stresses the similarity between Moses' "convicting and admonishing" function with that of the παράκλητος, but that seems far-fetched ("Samaritan Influence," 585, citing Meeks, *The Prophet-King*, 122, n. 2); Pamment disagrees ("Samaritan Influence," 227).

29 Beasley-Murray, *John*, lxv; cf. Purvis, "The Fourth Gospel and Samaritans," 187.

30 This is especially evident when compared with the way Samaritans are mentioned in the Synoptics. Mark is silent about them. Matthew stresses rather on Jewish particularism (Mt 10:5). Luke is sympathetic towards the Samaritans but shows no special interest (Lk 9:51–55).

31 Bowman, "The Fourth Gospel and the Samaritans," 300; Freed, "Did John Write to Win?" 244.

32 John 8:48; The charge "Samaritan" may be interpreted in several ways: that Jesus was associated with Samaritan heretics such as Simon the Magus or Dositheus (Purvis, "The Fourth Gospel and the Samaritans," 195–96), that he was demon-possessed as some of these heretics might have been accused of (cf. views of church fathers such as Justin and Origen), that his teaching sounded like those of Samaritans (Bowman, "Samaritan Studies," 298–308, Cullmann, *The Johannine Circle*, 50, 90), or that his attitude was like the Samaritans' in challenging the Jews' exclusive right to the Abrahamic promise (Scobie, "Origins and Development," 404).

suggests, there is a thematic preference towards Galilee and Samaria over against Judea.[33] This apparent favoritism towards Samaritans hints at the polemic between hostile Jews and Jesus' believers, rather than the author's attempt to bridge Christian Jews and Samaritans. Third, in the gospel Jesus says that ἄλλα πρόβατα ἔχω ἃ οὐκ ἔστιν ἐκ τῆς αὐλῆς ταύτης (10:16), which alludes to Ezek 34:1–24, God's promise of a David shepherd to take care of his flock. Advocates of Samaritan influence refer Jesus' saying also to Ezek 37:15–23, a prophetic symbol of God's gathering Judah and Ephraim into one nation.[34] An appropriate interpretation of John 10:16 is, rather, that the gospel has a missionary character that originates from Jesus, who once preached to Samaritans (John 4) but actually had the nations in mind. Therefore the gospel proclaims Jesus as Christ and ὁ σωτὴρ τοῦ κόσμου (John 4:42) to both Jews and non-Jews.[35] This emphasis on the universal does not necessarily entail any attempt to "bridge" Jews and Samaritans. On the basis of these arguments we may conjecture that Samaritans were among the audience of the gospel, but we may not know how actively the Samaritans were involved in the life setting of the church.[36] Any suggestion like Brown's, that "Jews who converted Samaritans had come in," or Bowman's, that "the author was trying to bridge Jews and Samaritans in Christ," are speculative.[37] We can only say that the author had Samaritans

---

33 Meeks, "Galilee and Judea," 165–67.

34 Bowman, "Samaritan Studies," 301; Freed, "Samaritan Influence," 580; Scobie, "Origins and Development," 404.

35 Pamment argues effectively on this point. See Pamment, "Samaritan Influence," 228.

36 Less convincing arguments include the connection of all the place names in John with Samaria (Freed, "Samaritan Influence," 580); the use of term and phrases such as τόπος, "our father(s)," even ἐγώ εἰμι, as being particular Samaritan usages (Scobie, "Origins and Development," 406; Freed, "Did John Write to Win?" 251); and allusions to Samaritan beliefs, such as four out of the five points of the Samaritan creed in John 5:42, 46, 47, 37–38: Belief in God, in Moses, in the Law and in the Taheb (Bowman, "Samaritan Studies," 313–14).

37 Brown, *Community*, 38; Bowman, "Samaritan Studies," 302; other interesting suggestions include: that the writer of the Samaritan discourse was a Samaritan (Freed, "Did John Write to Win?" 243); that Jesus and his disciples, or even John the Baptist, were Samaritans (Purvis, "The Fourth Gospel and Samaritans," 169); that the author of the gospel was a Samaritan Christian from a North Israelite Diaspora, and the "beloved disciple" was the Apostle John who was assigned Samaria as his territory of ministry (Buchanan, "The Samaritan Origin," 173–75); that the Johannine traditions originate from a community or communities which stemmed from the mission of Stephen or Philip recorded in Acts (Scobie, "Origin and Development, 407).

in mind as either historical witnesses or targets of persuasion, or both, of the faith that Jesus was the eschatological Christ, who has brought in salvation for all who believe (John 20:30–31). To reiterate, Johannine eschatology is characterized by its christology rather than the inclusion of a Samaritan interest. And the full significance of water symbolism in John 4 has to be established in terms of John's eschatology, not just its historical setting.

Relation between the Event and the Composition

Therefore we give up speculating about settings behind the formation of the gospel, and center on the theological meanings of the historical event presented in the final composition.[38] We have already consulted, in the first chapter of this book, Léon-Dufour's approach of "double symbolism in the Fourth Gospel," which looks for symbolic significance in both settings: the Jewish milieu of the event, and the Christian milieu of John's interpretation of the past. A first principle of interpretation would be to recover the coherence and relevance of the speeches and dialogues by placing them in the Jewish context of the first century. A further principle would be to develop a deeper understanding of the present in light of the past, for the Evangelist does not only present Jesus in contact with his contemporaries but projects upon them the situations of those who encounter Jesus in post-Easter times. The development of this deeper understanding, Léon-Dufour advises, is indispensable for every Christian.[39]

The gist of Léon-Dufour's interpretation lies in his handling of the misunderstanding of Jesus' "interlocutors" such as Nicodemus, the Samaritan woman, and the Galileans. Jesus' revelation often consists initially in an invitation to conversion by unveiling a higher realization of Jewish expectation. When the interlocutor misunderstands or ridicules it, or doubts its possibility, Jesus continues to uphold it in a way that points ultimately to the Easter event. Thus Léon-Dufour sucessfully points out the double

38 I believe that the congregation in which the gospel was formed came from a diversified background but consisted mainly of Hellenistic Jews. The authenticity of the gospel came from the Apostle John himself, no matter who penned the final composition. The place of writing could be anywhere in the diaspora, and the traditional location of Ephesus might well be it.

39 Léon-Dufour, "Symbolic Reading," 444–46.

reference of Jesus' dialogue with his contemporaries. First, Jesus made an appeal to them through their common language, "that of the promises of Israel."[40] Second, while they generally fail to comprehend or believe that he is the "fulfillment" of promises, Jesus goes on with the deeper level revelation of his "paschal death," which is the Christian or Easter faith of the gospel.[41] Thus there are two levels of reference in line with the eschatological interpretation of Johannine water symbolism proposed in this book. In the early sections of the gospel there is a juxtaposition of promise and fulfillment, but towards the end the expression for "fulfillment," which is of the first level, becomes more implicit, and the expression for "passion," which is of the second level, becomes emphatic.

In the account of the Samaritan woman in John 4 we can easily detect these two levels of revelation. In this case, Jesus' dialogue with her does not really end in a failure, but a "digression," which is Jesus' dialogue with his disciples, and thereafter the positive response of the Samaritans from the woman's town. When Jesus mentioned "the gift of God" and "living water" (4:10), he was using the common language of the promises of Israel, which was to be understood in the Jewish milieu. When Jesus said, "a time is coming" (4:21, 23), he was referring to the approaching fulfillment of these promises by himself on the cross, and that fulfillment became clear only later on in the Christian milieu.

Even in the "digression" of this account, i.e., Jesus' dialogue with the disciples (4:31–38), there are two levels of revelation. Jesus began the dialogue with talking about "food," a common language in the Jewish milieu and a language of promises. Then, while the disciples did not understand, Jesus went on to reveal a further truth, that of reaping and sowing, and with that he spoke of the future missionary activity of the church. So there are two levels involved.

Cullmann's interpretation of the passage also points at this two-level significance of the symbolic language.[42] Following are his comments:

> one of the many interests of the author of the fourth Gospel is . . . to show that the Christ of the Church corresponds to the Jesus of history, . . . And in this

---

40 Ibid., 444.

41 Ibid., 445.

42 O. Cullmann, "Samaria and Origins of the Christian Mission," in *The Early Church*, ed. A. J. B. Higgins (London: SCM, 1956), 185–92; cf. *The Johannine Circle*, 15–16.

> manner of recording the life of Jesus the fourth Gospel betrays a special interest in the missionary task. . . .
>
> But his chief interest is in the actual origin of the preaching of the gospel beyond the Jewish people in the mission in Samaria. His aim is to prove that it was begun by Jesus himself even though, during his life, he counseled his followers to avoid the Samaritan towns.[43]

Here Cullmann is making a specific point about the setting of the gospel, not only that Samaritans were targets of evangelism in the author's mind, but that the author, by citing the Samaritan event from the life of Jesus, was providing grounds to the Samaritan mission. Cullmann is known for his assessment of the gospel as a source book for all ecclesiastic activities, with which we may not agree. Yet, mission understood as the proclamation of the eschatological Christ to all people is no doubt a purpose of the gospel, no matter how major a target was Samaria in the gospel setting.

Léon-Dufour's two-level interpretation of the symbol and Cullmann's similar approach to John 4 set up a model for our work here. As we study John 4 in this chapter we will keep both the historical event and the final composition in mind. Our goal is to interpret Johannine water symbolism at two different levels of Jesus' revelation, to know its significance in the Jewish milieu as well as in the Christian milieu. It should be noted that there exists a certain symbolic relationship between these two levels of meaning in the Gospel of John. In theological terms this is essentially an eschatological relationship. While "water" and "food" are OT themes that symbolize "the promises of Israel," in the Gospel of John they become symbols of christological salvation and eschatological blessings. The two symbolic functions are eschatologically related. So, in John 4, we have the account of a historical event in which these symbols function at two levels. They are first used as eschatological promises understood by Jesus and his contemporaries in the Jewish milieu, then as eschatological fulfillment in Christ revealed by Jesus in reference to the accomplishment of his death and resurrection. The post-Easter church brought the two together in the composition of the Johannine gospel. The result is a symbolism that relates OT themes with christological salvation. In this way Johannine symbolism is eschatological in character.

---

43 Ibid., 186–87.

Structure and Thematic Connections

Taken as a whole, the passage John 4:1–42 is well structured. Outlines proposed are quite similar to one another. Introduced below are representative ones. A study on them will shed light on connections between the water symbol and other significant ideas and themes in the passage.

The "Dialogue" Structure

The passage is quite commonly perceived as two successive dialogues. Jesus' two sets of exchanges, with the Samaritan woman and then with the disciples, form two of the main sections. This "common sense" approach is reflected in the works of many commentators and literary scholars. O'Day's outline is a typical example.

vv. 4–6	Introduction: the setting of the narrative[44]	
vv. 7–26	First dialogue: Jesus and the woman	
	A. vv. 7–15	"give me a drink"
	B. vv. 16–26	"Go, call your husband"
vv. 27–30	Transition scene	
vv. 31–38	Second dialogue: Jesus and the disciples	
vv. 39–42	Conclusion: Jesus and the Samaritans[45]	

Supplementary to this bipartite division, we have T. L. Brodie's tripartite structure, which divides Jesus' nine utterances in John 4 into three sections, each with utterances of increasing lengths: (1) 4:7b, 10, 13–15; (2) 4:16, 17b–18, 21–24; (3) 4:26, 32, 34–38.[46] This is a neat but artificial outline, which does not really indicate how the event proceeds. Botha's "speech act" reading of John 4:1–42 comes up with more or less the same units, though extra effort is made to study temporal and spatial settings as well as the change of partners in the dialogue structure.[47] Among literary analyses written on John 4:1–42 there is also Olsson's extensive "text-linguistic" analysis. Olsson divides the narrative into thirty-two "event units," but, as

---

44 O'Day considers John 4:1–3 a section of the central Judea-Samaria itinerary, and considers John 4:4 a diversion from it rather than a part of it (*Revelation in the Fourth Gospel*, 51–52).

45 Ibid., 54.

46 T. L. Brodie, *The Gospel According to John: A Literary and Theological Commentary* (Oxford: Oxford University Press, 1993), 215.

47 Botha, *Speech Act Reading*, vii; 96.

expected, he has to leave the two dialogues (vv. 7–26 and vv. 31–38) intact and treat them separately as speeches instead of events.[48] Boers, on the other hand, studies speeches and events together as "sequences" in his semiotic analysis of John 4, but his division of units are similarly guided by the development of dialogues. Thus he calls the two dialogues "the sequence with the woman" and "the sequence with the disciples."[49]

A further elaboration of this dialogue structure may be found in T. Okure's outline, in which "narration" and "exposition" are the prominent sections. Okure is noteworthy for not only seeing them as two structures of equal importance, but relating them logically as "thesis" and "consequential argument."

> vv 1–26 (27) deals with this [Jesus'] mission dialogically from the standpoint of the non-believer, the Samaritan woman . . . vv 31–38 deals with it didactically from the standpoint of the disciples . . . and vv 28–30, 39–42 deals with it dramatically and conclusively by illustrating . . .
>
> . . . On a different level, the structural relationship between vv 1–26 and 28–42 can be compared to that which exists elsewhere in the gospel between the *Semeion* and its relevant explanatory discourse.[50]

Thus, in Okure's outline, the passage consists of two parts. The first part is Jesus' missionary act, which she calls the thesis, and it mainly consists of the first dialogue. The second part is the explanation of that act, which consists of the rest of the passage including the second dialogue. "Mission" is the emphasis and unifying theme of the entire pericope.[51]

vv. 1–26	Thesis or "Narratio"[52]	
	vv. 1–6	Introduction
	vv. 7–26	The Missionary Dialogue
vv. 28–42	Consequential Argument:	
	vv. (27) 28–30	"Demonstratio"
	vv. 31–38	"Expositio" (an instructional dialogue)
	vv. 39–42	"Demonstratio"

---

48 Olsson, *Structure and Meaning*, 173, 218; elsewhere he says also that the text reveals a "two scene composition" (ibid., 161).

49 Boers, *Neither on This Mountain*, viii.

50 T. Okure, *The Johannine Approach to Mission: A Contextual Study of John 4:1–42*, WUNT 31 (Tübingen: Mohr, 1988), 76–77.

51 Ibid., 77.

52 Okure considers vv. 8, 27 points of intersection (ibid., 133–36).

Very similar to this bipartite structure of Okure's is the tripartite structure proposed by M. Girard ["une introduction narrative (v. 1–6), l'entretien de Jésus avec une femme (v. 7–26), puis l'entretien de Jésus avec ses disciples encadré par l'entretien de la femme avec ses concitoyens (v. 27–42)"].[53] The unifying theme Girard perceives, however, has nothing to do with mission. Instead, he claims to see an extensive use of chiasm, tidy structures and multiple concatenations throughout the passage: "un ensemble organique on ne peut plus cohérent."[54]

The "Drama" Structure

Windisch was the first one who proposed for the passage a "drama" structure. He translates the text as a drama in seven "scenes":

> (1) At the well, Jesus comes to the well with his disciples . . .
> (2) At the well, a Samaritan woman comes and Jesus talks with her . . .
> (3) At the well, the disciples return and the woman leaves
> (4) In the city, the woman testifies and the people go with her . . .
> (5) At the well, the disciples have brought food and Jesus talks . . .
> (6) At the well, the Samaritans have come and Jesus goes with them . . .
> (7) In the city, the Samaritans gather around the woman to say . . .[55]

Though it brings out the lively exchange of conversation and movement of characters and demonstrates the coherence of the passage, Windisch's dramatic structure did not attract attention. For the seven "scenes" do not satisfactorily describe the structure. They at best outline a drama made out of the text. Later on, however, Dodd's observation of the dramatic technique of the dialogues became well known, and has been frequently quoted. Note that Dodd also holds a bipartite dialogue structure.

> The discourse takes the form of a highly wrought dramatic dialogue . . .

---

53 M. Girard, "Jésus en Samarie (Jean 4,1–42): Analyse des structures stylistiques et du processus de symbolisation," *Église et Théologie* 17 (1986): 275–310.

54 Ibid., 290–96. Another "chiastic" view on the structure has been proposed by P. J. Cahill, "Narrative Art in John IV," *Religious Studies Bulletin* 2 (1982): 41–48.
Meeting at the well (5–9)
Dialogue on living water (10–15)
Dialogue on true worship (16–26)
Dialogue on true food (27–28)
Meeting of Samaritans and Jesus (39–42)

55 Paraphrased from Windisch, "John as Literature," 29–32.

> The main dialogue runs from iv. 7 to 27 . . .
> . . . the [next] dialogue . . . forms the conclusion of the whole scene.
> This concluding dialogue exhibits in a rudimentary form a dramatic technique . . . The action takes place on two stages, a front stage and a back stage . . . The return of the disciples and the departure of the woman (27a–8a) divide the dramatis personae into two groups. On the front stage Jesus converses with His disciples (31–8). Meanwhile (ἐν τῷ μεταξύ) on the back stage the woman converses with her fellow-townsmen and induces them to accompany her to the place where she left Jesus (28b–30, 39). The two groups then converge, and move together . . . The scene is thus at an end . . .[56]

Along the same line, Brown proposes a structure of "two scenes," with the two dialogues respectively encompassed.

Scene One (iv 4–26)
  Scene 1a: The Living Water (vss. 6–15)
  Scene 1b: True Worship of the Father (vss. 16–26)
Scene Two (iv 27–38)
  embedding: the use of two proverbs
Conclusion (vss. 39–42)[57]

Lee, instead, separates the passage into three scenes, each with a central image: ὕδωρ ζῶν (vv. 7–15), τόπος (vv. 16–29[30]), and βρῶσις, βρῶμα/θερισμός (vv. [30]31–42). Her outline ends up quite similar to Brown's, bringing out more or less the same themes.[58]

Inner Thematic Connections

The passage is composed of not only dialogues and scenes, but with themes. Bultmann, in extracting "revelation-discourses" from the passage, finds in it the coherent theme of "witness," namely, Jesus' self-witness (vv. 1–30) and the believer's witness (vv. 31–42).[59] We should note that the unity or coherence of a passage cannot be argued for from a purely literary point of view, because there is always some ultimate concerns that are theological rather than literary. Just as symbolism may be a way to speak of eschatology, scenes and dialogues are vehicles that convey theological ideas, often as themes. In this respect, O'Day argues that the so-called "clumsy

56 Dodd, *Interpretation*, 311–15.
57 Brown, *John*, 1:177–85.
58 Lee, *Symbolic Narratives*, 66.
59 Bultmann, *John*, 175–76.

seams" in vv. 8 and 27 should be viewed as signs of careful and intentional crafting, as a thematic unity can be recognized as drawing the episodes together into a whole. O'Day believes that a growing consensus regarding the theme of John 4 is the question of Jesus' identity or self-revelation.[60]

I think there are at least three unifying themes in the passage, in addition to the divisional themes such as the "living water," the "true worship," and "sowing and harvesting."

First, the christological theme of "who Jesus is," as O'Day points out, seems to be the most obvious and significant. It is noted among commentators that there is a "crescendo" of the three confessions made about Jesus: the Prophet (4:19), the Christ (4:29) and the Savior of the World (4:42).[61] Schnackenburg further notes that the increasing strength of the impact of Jesus' revelation, and the leading upward of faith, can be seen in the series of key words used: Ἰουδαῖος (4:9); κύριε (4:11); μείζων τοῦ πατρὸς ἡμῶν Ἰακώβ; (4:12); προφήτης (4:19); ὁ χριστός (4:26, 29); ὁ σωτὴρ τοῦ κόσμου (4:42).[62] These key words or confessions indicate that the revelation of "who Jesus is" remains a central and continual concern throughout the passage, in spite of an apparent digression in the second dialogue. It is thus confirmed that the passage shares the overall emphasis of the gospel, to reveal that Jesus is the Christ and that faith in him will bring about salvation (John 20:30–31).

Second, there is a mission emphasis that binds the whole passage together. The final confession οὗτός ἐστιν ἀληθῶς ὁ σωτὴρ τοῦ κόσμου (v. 42) is a climax to this mission theme. Okure's bipartite structure of John 4:1–42, described above, is an interpretation of the passage from this mission perspective. Cullmann, also mentioned above, would have agreed with this overall mission emphasis of the passage, although he is far more preoccupied with early Samaritan missions.[63] Okure's study has been regarded as

---

60 O'Day, *Revelation in the Fourth Gospel*, 50.

61 Beasley-Murray, *John*, 66; Okure, *The Johannine Approach*, 131; J. Becker, *Das Evangelium des Johannes Kapitel 1–10*, Ökumenischer Taschenbuch-Kommentar zum Neuen Testament (Würzburg: Echter-Verlag, 1979), 165.

62 Schnackenburg, *John*, 1:420; cf. L. Schmid, "Die Komposition der Samaria-Szene John 4:1–42," *ZNW* 28 (1929): 148–58, quoted in O'Day, *Revelation in the Fourth Gospel*, 128, n. 5.

63 For example, Cullmann understands ἄλλοι (v. 37) as Hellenistic missionaries who evangelized Samaria before the apostles did, but Okure interprets it as Jesus and the Father.

excellent.[64] It suffices here to just refer to her views on vv. 8 and 27. Form critical scholars consider vv. 8 and 27 disruptive, but Okure points out that they are necessary "intersections whose purpose is to prepare for the major insertion of vv. 31–38."[65] Γάρ in v. 8 (οἱ γὰρ μαθηταὶ αὐτοῦ ἀπεληλύθεισαν . . .) is explanatory of the fact that Jesus was able to proceed with his missionary dialogue with the woman because the disciples, who were not ready for it, were away. The disciples' later reaction, " ἐθαύμαζον to see Jesus talking with the woman," confirms that they had not been ready and that they needed Jesus' teaching (vv. 31–38) to make sense of the "mission" Jesus was accomplishing and to learn to do likewise. The apparent "insertion" of the second dialogue, therefore, is unified with the total passage under the theme of "mission."

Close to this notion of mission is the emphasis on ἔργον in John 4:1–42, suggested by Olsson in his text-linguistic study. The word "mission" may not be located in the text, but the word ἔργον can be significant. It is not a wonder, therefore, that Olsson finds "Jesus' ergon and the Samaritans" a more precise definition of the theme of the narrative. "Jesus' ergon," he specifies, involves a revelation of Christ to the Samaritans and an incorporation of the Samaritans in the new people of God.[66]

Third, a subtle and yet very important inner thematic connection should be found in the use of symbolism throughout the passage, specifically, the water and food imagery and the harvest imagery. Most scholars have agreed that there is a literary parallel between the two dialogues in terms of "misunderstanding," first of the woman and then of Jesus' disciples.[67] Some further point out that between the two there is even a natural transition from the use of "water" to the use of "food," as symbolic of the need and satisfaction of life.[68] Boers, applying semiotic analysis to the passage, claims that "water" and "food" are figures that make up the semantic level of the discourse structure.[69] Same are the "sower" and the "reaper" in the harvest

---

64 Carson, *John*, 214.

65 Okure, *The Johannine Approach*, 133.

66 Olsson, *Structure and Meaning*, 251–52.

67 See, e.g., Okure, *The Johannine Approach*, 183; Beasley-Murray, *John*, 63; Carson, *John*, 228.

68 Dodd, *Interpretation*, 315; Lee, *Symbolic Narratives*, 87–88.

69 Boers, *Neither on This Mountain*, 79.

imagery.[70] These figures bring to expression themes such as "nourishment" and "disclosure of the identity of Jesus," and they are interconnected with one another at the deepest or most abstract level of the text.[71] Thus Boers affirms the thematic unity between the two. Furthermore, it should be noted that "water" and "food" are OT themes that speak of the needs of Israel, symbolizing God's promise in providing for them. In this passage they become symbols of eschatological fulfillment as well. So there is a fulfillment theme that unifies them.

External Connections of Themes

The three unifying themes proposed above are, also, overall themes of the gospel, verifiable by external connections.

The christological theme repeats itself throughout the gospel in various pericopes composed of either signs or discourses. It is spelled out at the end by the purpose statement, "that you may believe that Jesus is the Christ, the Son of God . . ."(20:31). Many of the literary patterns used in the gospel show a christological interest. The "misunderstandings," or "symbolic narratives" as named by Lee, have to do with faith in Jesus as Christ.[72] The "dialogues," written apparently with a characteristic Johannine style, are often christological in content.[73] In a dissertation written on "Jesu Gespräch mit der Samaritanerin," E. Leidig demonstrates that a number of dialogues in John exhibits a pattern of four steps: "Weckung des Interesses für das Heil"; "Angebot des heils"; "Zeichen oder Erleben des Heils"; and "Bekenntnis zum Messias."[74]

The mission theme can be seen in the universalism that permeates the

---

70 Ibid., 82.

71 Ibid., 85–104.

72 Lee, *Symbolic Narratives*, 11–15; cf. Leroy who views differently (*Rätsel und Missverständnis*, 45–46).

73 Olsson, *Structure and Meaning*, 116, citing C. M. Connick, "The Dramatic Character of the Fourth Gospel," *JBL* 67 (1948): 167–69; and C. H. Dodd, "The Dialogue Form in the Gospel," *BJRL* 37 (1954–55): 60.

74 According to E. Leidig this pattern can be found in John 1:35–42; 1:45–51; 3:1–21; 4:1–42; 5:1–16; 6:1–71; 9:1–41; 11:1–45; 12:20–36; 18:33–38; 20:11–18; 20:24–29 (*Jesu Gespräch mit der Samaritanerin und weitere Gespräche im Johannesevangelium*, Band XV der theologischen Dissertationen, herausgegeben von B. Reicke [Basel: Friedrich Reinhardt Kommissionsverlag, 1979]).

gospel: Οὕτως γὰρ ἠγάπησεν ὁ θεὸς τὸν κόσμον . . . (3:16–17), ἄλλα πρόβατα ἔχω (10:16), οὐ περὶ τούτων δὲ ἐρωτῶ μόνον, ἀλλὰ καὶ περὶ τῶν πιστευόντων διὰ τοῦ λόγου αὐτῶν εἰς ἐμέ (17:20) . . . Even the overall purpose, ταῦτα δὲ γέγραπται ἵνα πιστεύητε (20:30–31), discloses a missionary intent. John 4 contributes to this theme in its own explicit way, with the Samaritan outreach it records. For further thoughts on its connections with the whole I commend Okure's work.[75]

The fulfillment theme prevails throughout the gospel, as there is repeated use of Johannine symbols and allusions to the Old Testament. In John 4 we have "water," "food," "harvest," most of which recur in other passages. These external connections are well reckoned. As Barrett points out, "this section is linked with the preceding sections in two ways: (a) by their common theme that in Jesus Judaism and the Old Testament find their fulfillment . . . (b) by the use of the term 'water.'"[76] J. Bligh's specific comment on the symbol of "food" is also worth noting: "Just as the water theme in Scene 1 looks back to the Nicodemus and John the Baptist episodes in ch. iii, so the food theme of Scene 2 points forward to the bread/food symbolism of ch. vi."[77] These external connections are indicative of an overall fulfillment theme crafted intentionally by the author.

Symbolism in the Second Dialogue

We will study John 4 by going through the symbols used in the two dialogues. I will show that the symbols used in these dialogues are all related to the theme of "living water" in one way or anther, so that they bear significance to the overall use of Johannine water symbolism. To do so I will begin with the second dialogue, so that the symbol of "water," which features mainly in the first dialogue, will come up at a more conclusive stage of the discussion.

The Leaving of the Water Jar

The woman's action, ἀφῆκεν οὖν τὴν ὑδρίαν αὐτῆς ἡ γυνὴ . . . (4:28),

---

75 Okure, "John 4:1–42 in Its Gospel Context" and "The Social Context," chaps. in *The Johannine Approach*, 192–284.

76 Barrett, *John*, 228.

77 Brown, *John*, 1:181, citing J. Bligh, "Jesus in Samaria," *HeyJ* 3 (1962): 334.

calls for attention as one of the very few details in the course of events here. Historico-grammatical exegetes tend to take it as a natural reaction and deny its symbolic meaning, which literary scholars tend to affirm.[78] By symbolic meaning we are referring to the woman's acceptance of or awakening to the revelation of Jesus, given in the first dialogue. The leading idea of that dialogue, of course, is represented by the symbolic language of the living water.

Our interpretation of this is twofold, in reference to the two historical settings. At the historical level of the episode, it was natural that the woman left her water jar behind. She was in a hurry to go, or planning to return, or leaving it for Jesus to use, but the most likely reason was that she was eager to go back to town to spread the news. Thus her action was "psychologically" motivated, as Okure puts it.[79] At the Johannine level, it is also likely that the author makes a significant point of the woman's action, though the meaning is unsaid. Botha, with his speech act analysis, asserts that this action of the woman has literary significance. If the author, Botha argues, is merely being informative, then it is strange that he mentions only this piece of detail but not others. If, on the other hand, the author means to signal that "something else is being communicated by this purely informative utterance," then we must take serious its meaning.[80] What then is the author trying to communicate? There are two possibilities. The author is either creating a literary or dramatic effect, or he is speaking symbolically of a theological conversion. I believe he is doing both. The obvious literary effect is that the woman's eagerness of response is accented.[81] The subtle effect is a contrast between the woman's excitement about Jesus, expressed in her jar-abandoning action at the end of the first dialogue, and the disciples' misunderstanding of him, expressed in their concern about food at the

---

78 Barrett, *John*, 240; Schnackenburg, *John*, 1:443; Carson, *John*, 227–28; Beasley-Murray, *John*, 63; cf. Boers, *Neither on This Mountain*, 192; Botha, *Speech Act Reading*, 162–63; Lee, *Symbolic Narratives*, 84–85; also Brown, *John*, 1:173.

79 Okure, *The Johannine Approach*, 169.

80 Botha continues to speak for a "non-literal reading of the text" (*Speech Act Reading*, 163), with which I disagree.

81 Scholars who offer literary explanations of this detail include Okure, *The Johannine Approach*, 169–70; and O'Day, *Revelation in the Fourth Gospel*, 75.

beginning of the second dialogue.[82] This contrast can be interpreted as the author's theological perception of the woman's action as a renunciation of her old Samaritan religion. It is, admittedly, unclear whether John means to say so much, because "unlike the water jars of 2:6ff., this one has no ritual purification tied up with it ."[83] Yet, we note that the jar in John 4:1–42 is tied up with all that the woman has to boast in her Samaritan tradition, specifically, the well of her father Jacob. Thus the water jar symbolizes all that she held to prior to her conversion to Jesus. The extensive use of symbols in the gospel supports such an interpretation.

The "Food" Imagery

How is the food symbol here related to the water symbol, and how is Jesus' explanation of the symbol, ἵνα ποιήσω τὸ θέλημα τοῦ πέμψαντός με καὶ τελειώσω αὐτοῦ τὸ ἔργον (John 4:34), related to his other discourse in John 6, ἀλλὰ τὴν βρῶσιν τὴν μένουσαν εἰς ζωὴν αἰώνιον (6:27)? I will argue that these related concepts are parallel but at the same time dissimilar.

In a literary sense Jesus' discourse on βρῶσις is closely connected with his preceding discourse on ὕδωρ.[84] There is, in this discourse as in the previous one, a similar pattern of misunderstanding, a similar use of life sustenance as a symbol, and similar dominance of a theme that leads to other interests outside the immediate situation.[85] The question is, does this

---

82 O'Day's literary explanation is also worth noting: "the function of v. 28 is identical with that of v. 8: the details about going for food and leaving the water jar both indicate that the character who is moving off-stage is not disappearing forever. Both details prepare the reader for the character's return" (*Revelation in the Fourth Gospel*, 75).

83 Carson, *John*, 227–28.

84 Some have suggested that the discourse is also parallel to Jesus' answer to the first temptation recorded in Matt 4:4 (e.g., Beasley-Murray, *John*, 63), but this view is not well accepted. Schnackenburg points out that in Matt 4:4 there is no similar antithesis between earthly bread and the word of God (*John*, 1:445). It is clear, however, that in both passages there is an allusion to Deut 8:3, ". . . man does not live on bread alone but on every word that comes from the mouth of the Lord." Even in this case there is no straight parallel because in Matt 4:4 there is a direct quotation whereas in John the allusion is more remote.

85 Cf. L. Morris, *The Gospel According to John: The English Text with Introduction, Exposition and Notes*, ed. F. F. Bruce, NICNT (Grand Rapids: Eerdmans, 1971), 245; Schnackenburg, *John*, 1:445; Lee, *Symbolic Narratives*, 88. Note, however, that the

literary affinity suggest a synonymous relation between "food" and "water"? Bultmann reminds us of the difference, "Clearly one cannot show any close connection. . . . For there the ὕδωρ was a gift which he gives to men; here he himself lives from the βρῶμα."[86] When we compare this discourse with the other one in John 6, we see the same difference. Here βρῶμα refers to Jesus' execution of God's will to its completion, but there it refers to the gift of eternal life, which Jesus gives to believers. Among all the "symbols" used in John, which so often stand for eschatological blessings for humankind, the "food" here distinguishes itself as being a blessing for Jesus himself.

Should we then ignore the long-reckoned bond between "food" and "water" in the Old Testament and in Judaistic understanding, which are the main conceptual backgrounds? In Odeberg's commentary on John, which he claims to have composed "in its relation to contemporaneous religious currents," a synonymous relation is drawn between "water" and "food" in John 4:1–42, and between the concept of food in John 4:31–34 and that in 6:25–29. The fact that ἐργάζεσθαι τὰ ἔργα τοῦ θεοῦ is mentioned together with βρῶσις in both passages provides a ground for Odeberg to say, "The significance of 4:32, 34 immediately becomes clear, when read in the light of 6:27–29 . . ."[87] Thus Odeberg refers to 4:32, 34 on commenting 6:27–29:

> The conception of the 'Bread from Heaven' is to be understood as parallel to that of the 'Water', i.e., it falls under the category of the conceptions of the Divine, spiritual efflux. . .
>
> It is also apparent that the 'Manna of Moses' is the exact parallel of the 'Water of the well of Jacob' of 4:7–15 . . .
>
> The expressions 'Bread from Heaven', the 'Imperishable Food' correspond to current ideas and expressions . . . are in the mystical language further connected with the terms 'water', 'rain' etc. The parallelism between 'celestial bread' and 'spiritual water' is thus not confined to Jn.[88]

Odeberg tends to overestimate Hellenistic influences upon the gospel, and thus he speaks of a "mystic" origin of the concepts with which I do not agree, but the juxtaposition of "food" and "water" in Jewish thinking is

---

two are not all identical. Olsson sees more of their differences with his text-linguistic analysis, *Structure and Meaning*, 220.

86 Bultmann, *John*, 195; cf. Beasley-Murray, *John*, 63.

87 Odeberg, *The Fourth Gospel*, 187–88.

88 Ibid., 238–40.

sound. This is supported by the many quotations that Odeberg lists in support of his view, taken mostly from Jewish literature.[89] It is evident, from the comments made on the Old Testament by the Jewish people, that "manna from heaven," along with "water," stood for Jewish eschatological and messianic expectations.[90] The following words from Midr. Qoh. demonstrate this conception.

> just as the First Savior [Moses] caused the manna to descend, as it is written (Exod 16:4) . . . the Last Savior will cause the manna to descend, as it is written (Ps 72:16) . . . Just as the First Savior brought up the well, so the Last Savior will bring up the water, as it is written (Joel 3:18) . . .[91]

This quotation is also significant in that Moses is saluted in it as the giver of "the manna from heaven," an idea that John 6:32 refutes, and that "the well," "water," and "the manna" are juxtaposed in a style that coincides with the parallelism found in John 4 and 6.

There is no doubt that "the bread of life" in John 6 should be understood in the light of the aforementioned Judaistic background, but can we interpret the "food" symbol in John 4 in exactly the same way? To answer this we must take seriously both the similarity and the dissimilarity between the two passages. The dissimilarity is definite. We have just noted how the referents differ: John 4:31–34 points to a blessing given to Jesus, but John 6:25–29 points to the blessing of eternal life given to believers. The similarity is also definite. In both cases the idea of ἔργον is central to the meaning of the symbol. In both cases there is an antithesis between earthly food and food coming from the Father (note 6:27b, ἐργάζεσθε . . . τὴν βρῶσιν . . . ἣν ὁ υἱὸς τοῦ ἀνθρώπου ὑμῖν δώσει· τοῦτον γὰρ ὁ πατὴρ ἐσφράγισεν ὁ θεός). In both cases the word βρῶσις or βρῶμα is used, instead of ἄρτος.[92] This last point of similarity, in my analysis, is crucial to a right assessment of the relationship between "water" and "food" in John 4:1–42, and the relationship between the "food" discourses in 4:31–34 and 6:25–29. We should note that the words, βρῶσις and βρῶμα, are rarely used in either the Synoptics or

---

89 He lists only a couple of Mandaean sources (ibid., 247–48) to argue for an existing idea of "sacramental bread" in the Mandaean religion, but the evidence is meager.

90 Cf. J. Behm, "ἄρτος," *TDNT*, 1:447.

91 Midr. Qoh 1:28.

92 The two words were used interchangeably, though; according to BAGD, βρῶσις is applied more broadly to actions of eating, etc. BAGD, 147; cf. *TDNT*, 1:642–45. In our present context they can safely be treated as synonymous.

the Gospel of John.[93] They appear more frequently in the Pauline epistles and the book of Hebrews, referring to pagan food or "food and drink" in general. When food is talked about in a Palestinian setting, the word ἄρτος would normally be used. In the Septuagint, unleavened bread, showbread, and bread used for feasts and offerings are all translated ἄρτος, and the manna is generally called ἄρτος (ἄρτοι) οὐρανοῦ.[94] It follows that in the New Testament the sacramental bread is referred to as ἄρτος. That, precisely, is Paul's use of the word as well: ἄρτος refers to the sacramental bread, and βρῶσις and βρῶμα to food and drink that have no theological connotation. Characteristic of the Gospel of John is the symbolic use of the word ἄρτος: ἄρτος ἐκ τοῦ οὐρανοῦ, ἄρτος τῆς ζωῆς, etc., which is rather unique in the New Testament.[95] Furthermore, between the two, ἄρτος is predominantly used in John twenty-four times while βρῶσις is used four times and βρῶμα just once.[96] It is significant, therefore, that in this gospel βρῶσις and βρῶμα are almost exclusively used in 4:32, 34 and 6:27.[97] They are used here in exclusive reference to ἔργον, and outside this gospel we can hardly find them used with such a sense.[98] In John 6, in which ἄρτος is used twenty times throughout and constitutes a "bread" theme, the word βρῶσις is peculiarly used in 6:25–29, the embedded "food" discourse (instead of "bread"). I would contend that in both John 4 and John 6 βρῶσις and βρῶμα are deliberately used in place of ἄρτος, to effect a meaning related to "work."

We can say with certainty that there is a close connection between John 4:31–34 and 6:25–29, first in referring to the concept of "work," second in the symbolic use of "food," and third in the peculiar choice of the words βρῶσις and βρῶμα. It is, therefore, reasonable to interpret the two passages together as Odeberg does, though Odeberg never sorts out the reasons.

---

93 Neither word appears in Acts.

94 In the LXX the many occurrences of לֶחֶם and מַצָּה are translated ἄρτος. Words referring to the general idea of food and drink, such as אָכְלָה and לְחֶם are translated βρῶμα or βρῶσις. See E. Hatch and H. A. Redpath, *A Concordance to the Septuagint and the Other Versions of the Old Testament*, vol. 1 (Grand Rapids: Baker, 1983 [1897]), 161–62, 231–32.

95 Cf. Behm, "ἄρτος," 477.

96 The less common word τροφή is used in John only once, 4:8.

97 The only exception being in 6:55, ἡ γὰρ σάρξ μου ἀληθής ἐστιν βρῶσις, καὶ τὸ αἷμά μου ἀληθής ἐστιν πόσις.

98 The only exception being in 1 Cor 10:3, καὶ πάντες τὸ αὐτὸ πνευματικὸν βρῶμα ἔφαγον.

Indeed, the importance of conceptual backgrounds that Odeberg points out is already a reason for interpreting the passages together. The respective emphasis on "water" as well as "bread" in both John 4 and John 6 reveals that the author has this Judaistic juxtaposition of the two in mind.

Furthermore, both 4:31–34 and 6:25–29 are shorter discourses on βρῶσις and ἔργον, embedded in the longer discourses of "water" and "bread" in John 4 and John 6. In other words, within the "water" and "bread" chapters of the gospel, we encounter these two peculiar little pockets on βρῶσις and ἔργον, 4:31–34 and 6:25–29. How then do we understand the relation between them? The similarity is established, that both "specialize" in βρῶσις and ἔργον, but the difference is also undeniable, that in 4:31–34 Jesus talks about his own food whereas in 6:25–29 he talks about the believers'. O'Day suggests that the shift of βρῶσις in 4:32 to βρῶμα in 4:34 (occurring only here in John) shows that Jesus was introducing a new category: Jesus' own food.[99] So βρῶμα is a crystallization of Johannine christology![100] I totally disagree with this interpretation. The shift of word cannot possibly indicate such a special meaning, for βρῶσις and βρῶμα are largely synonymous. There is a distinction in these little pockets themselves that calls for a different interpretation. We should note that both of these two "pockets" are didactic in nature. In them are the records of Jesus' teaching on "work." In 4:31–34 Jesus teaches with his own example ('Εγὼ βρῶσιν ἔχω...), whereas in 6:25–29 he rebukes and instructs (ζητεῖτέ με οὐχ ὅτι εἴδετε σημεῖα ἀλλ' ὅτι ἐφάγετε . . . ἐγράζεσθε μὴ τὴν βρῶσιν τὴν ἀπολλυμένην ἀλλὰ τὴν βρῶσιν τὴν μένουσαν εἰς ζωὴν αἰῶνιον). Note that in both cases Jesus gives a clear definition of "food" and "work": 'Εμὸν βρῶμά ἐστιν ἵνα ποιήσω τὸ θέλημα τοῦ πέμψαντός με καὶ τελειώσω αὐτοῦ τὸ ἔργον (4:34); Τοῦτό ἐστιν τὸ ἔργον τοῦ θεοῦ, ἵνα πιστεύητε εἰς ὃν ἀπέστειλεν ἐκεῖνος (6:29). Since these words are not mainly christological, what Jesus says about his own food in 4:34 should have a double reference. On the one hand Jesus is implying that he has a work to complete, on the other he is teaching his disciples to do the will of God. The rest of the dialogue, which features the "harvest" theme (4:35–38), will show that Jesus at this point is more concerned about the disciples'

---

99 I.e., to be distinguished from the disciples' food, βρῶσις; O'Day, *Revelation in the Fourth Gospel*, 79.

100 Ibid.

mission than his own self-revelation.

This distinct emphasis in 4:31–34 does not necessarily disqualify the "food" symbol from being a counterpart of the "water" symbol. Just as the shorter "food" discourse is an integral part of the longer "bread" discourse" in John 6, we must treat 4:31–34 as an integral part of the "living water" discourse. It helps to remember the two levels of setting, the plain history and the Johannine composition. At the time of the event Jesus was teaching disciples during the course of his preaching to the Samaritans. He had to switch his attention from the woman to the disciples who were no longer acquiring initial faith as the woman was but had to learn about that faith in a different application. Thus a different idea seems to have emerged: ἔργον! However, is ἔργον so incongruous with the acquiring of ὕδωρ . . . εἰς ζωήν αἰώνιον? Let us now look at John 6, in which case Jesus' audience did not change, and so the congruity between ἔργον and ἄρτος can be more easily seen: by doing the work of God and thus believing in his Sent One (6:29), one will acquire salvation and eternal life (6:35–40). That is equivalent to saying: by seeking the right βρῶσις (6:27) one will get ὁ ἄρτος τῆς ζωῆς (6:35). The question then is whether there is a similar connection in John 4. Can we say that by doing God's work of harvesting (also βρῶσις) one will acquire salvation and eternal life (ὕδωρ . . . εἰς ζωήν αἰώνιον)? This connection is hard to draw at the level of plain history, as the disciples were preoccupied with the earthly food they bought and could not have learned about Jesus' previous discourse instantaneously. At the level of the Johannine composition, however, this connection can more than reasonably be drawn. What Jesus had said was understood in retrospect and put into a way of writing that reflects a theological relation between βρῶσις and ὕδωρ, "work" and "eternal life." At this level the author and readers were no longer preoccupied with food and drink (βρῶσις) as the first disciples were, but were more influenced by the Old Testament and Judaistic concepts that constituted the background of their understanding. In this context ἄρτος and ὕδωρ stood for messianic and eschatological blessings, and the Johannine conviction was that they were given by Jesus Christ. Βρῶσις, then, was the term symbolizing ἔργον, the obedience and cooperation on the part of believers and disciples who acquired those blessings. In the Johannine perspective, ἔργον in working for the harvest (4:38) is as much a prerequisite for salvation and blessing as is ἔργον in believing in the One God has sent (6:29). The common context of ἄρτος and ὕδωρ in John 4 and 6 supports this interpretation. The woman, notably, participated in the work of the harvest instantaneously as she believed in Jesus, expressing her faith in terms of her ἔργον. Moreover, Jesus spoke of the harvest as an eschatological blessing: ὁ θερίζων μισθὸν λαμβάνει καὶ συνάγει καρπὸν εἰς ζωὴν αἰώνιον, as if "harvest work" has the same effect as the "living water." It can be maintained, therefore, that βρῶσις, with a slightly different nuance, is a counterpart of ὕδωρ and ἄρτος symbolizing eschatological blessings. They are related like two sides of a coin. Ἄρτος and ὕδωρ are counterparts on the same side of the coin symbolizing Jesus' gift of salvation and blessings. Βρῶσις is a counterpart on the other side symbolizing the believers' work of faith and obedience.

No doubt, when Jesus instructed the disciples, he had in mind "God's eschatological work" to finish. At the Johannine level, this eschatological sense remains, even though the work has become a current mission (cf. 20:31). It is along this line that the harvest imagery immediately follows.

The "Harvest" Imagery

Jesus' subsequent discourse on the "harvest" is a further proof that the focus of the discourse was not on "work" per se alone but on the coming of the eschaton and the disciples' participation in gathering people into eternal life.[101] The discourse is marked by two apparently quoted sayings (4:35, 37) which introduce two main points: the time of the harvest (4:35–36) and the laborers for the harvest (4:37–38). The passage is also marked with a combination of related ideas, ὁ θερισμὸς, ὁ σπείρων, ὁ θερίζων, and ὁ πέμψας, all symbolic of either participants or events in Jesus' eschatological mission. They are also connected with the previous "food" symbol, forming an integral whole.

Many have tried to recover the meaning of a possible "proverb" behind the first saying, Ἔτι τετράμηνός ἐστιν καὶ ὁ θερισμὸς ἔρχεται (v. 35a), while others are content to think that the saying was only a previous remark

101 Here Okure makes a remark on 4:34 that aptly annotates this transition from Jesus' work to the disciples' work, "the verbs 'to do' and 'to complete' . . . underline Jesus' unique role in the Father's work. . . . Only upon its completion do the disciples come in as active participants and beneficiaries" (*The Johannine Approach*, 145).

made by the disciples on the journey.[102] As regards θεάσασθε τὰς χώρας ὅτι λευκαί εἰσιν πρὸς θερισμόν (v. 35b), most suggest that Jesus was referring to the approaching Samaritans in their white garments. None of these are significant towards the main point of Jesus' speech. Jesus at this juncture is simply pointing out that "by ordinary reckoning there are four months remaining until harvest, but in the salvation-historical plane the harvest has already begun."[103] A symbolic relationship between the earthly harvest and the heavenly harvest is unquestionable here, as the harvest is a common eschatological symbol used in the Old Testament, the apocalyptic, the New Testament, and the rabbinical writings.[104] Jesus himself confirms this eschatological sense by further defining the harvest work in 4:36: ὁ θερίζων μισθὸν λαμβάνει καὶ συνάγει καρπὸν εἰς ζωὴν αἰώνιον.[105] An additional confirmation can be found in 4:36b, ἵνα ὁ σπείρων ὁμοῦ χαίρῃ καὶ ὁ θερίζων, for joy of the harvest is an early OT saying (Ps 126:5) which later became associated with the messianic hope (Isa 9:3). The rejoicing together indicates that sowing has taken place and the anticipated harvest has now come, which is "the critical nature of the present."[106] A distinctly

---

102 The former view are held by many: Brown, *John*, 1:182; Bligh, "Jesus in Samaria," 343; A. W. Argyle, "A Note on John 4:35," *ExpTim* 82 (1971): 247–78. For the latter view see Hoskyns, *The Fourth Gospel*, 271; also Okure, who argues that ὑμεῖς (οὐχ ὑμεῖς λέγετε ὅτι) should refer consistently to the disciples (cf. vv. 32, 35b, 38a, b) and therefore the saying was theirs, *The Johannine Approach*, 149. Some have even worked out a chronology for the event or a liturgical calendar behind the gospel: A. Guilding, *The Fourth Gospel and Jewish Worship: A Study of the Relation of John to the Ancient Jewish Lectionary System* (Oxford: Clarendon Press, 1960), 206–11.

103 Carson, *John*, 230.

104 Joel 4:13; Isa 27:12; 2 Esdr 4:28–32; 7:113; Syriac *Apoc. Bar.* 27: 15; 70:2; *As. Mos.* 1:17; 12:4; Matt 9:37–38; 13:37–43; Mark 4:26–29; Luke 10:1–4; Rev 14:14–20; *Tg. Onq.* Gen 49:1; *Tg. Yer. I* Gen 49:1; *Der. Er. Jose* 150; quoted in Schnackenburg, *John*, 1:450, n. 93, and P. Billerbeck, *Kommentar zum Neuen Testament aus Talmud und Midrasch*, 4 vols. (München: Beck, 1922–28), 1:671.

105 As Schnackenburg comments, "The eschatological perspective is also displayed in the concept of 'eternal life.' The believers whom Jesus gains in Samaria are a harvest or fruit 'for eternal life.' This means that Jesus imparts to them eternal life (cf. 3:16, 36; 5:24 etc.) and thus leads them to eternal life (cf. 12:25). Hence the εἰς is final, possibly also local (in conjunction with συνάγειν), cf. Mt 3:12; 13:30" (*John*, 1:450–51).

106 Beasley-Murray, *John*, 63; cf. Brown, *John*, 1:182. Bultmann's idea that "seedtime and harvest coincide in eschatological events" is not the point here (*John*, 197).

present eschatology is presented here in the gospel by recording Jesus' announcement of the coming of the harvest, . . . λευκαί εἰσιν πρὸς θερισμόν ἤδη ὁ θερίζων μισθὸν λαμβάνει . . . (4:35–36). Whether ἤδη connects backward, . . . πρὸς θερισμόν ἤδη, or forward as most exegetes construe, ἤδη ὁ θερίζων μισθὸν λαμβάνει . . . , the main point remains that the eschatological harvest has already come and is now present. The connection of ἤδη forward, however, gives a clearer clue that Jesus was referring to himself as the one already receiving μισθὸν and to the Samaritans as καρπὸν εἰς ζωὴν αἰώνιον. We should interpret the food imagery and the harvest imagery as a coherent whole, so that the βρῶμα that Jesus earlier talked about (4:34) is one and the same as the μισθὸν he now said he was receiving (4:36), and that the harvest he now engaged in (συνάγει, 4:36) is "part and parcel of the work the Father gave him to do (4:34)."[107] Thus βρῶμα parallels μισθὸν, and ἔργον parallels the gathering of καρπὸν εἰς ζωὴν αἰώνιον, and so the two discourses form a continuous whole.

Who is the sower and who is the reaper? This becomes an issue all because of the next two verses, 4:37–38, which introduces a distinct emphasis on their different roles: ἐν γὰρ τούτῳ ὁ λόγος ἐστὶν ἀληθινὸς ὅτι Ἄλλος ἐστὶν ὁ σπείρων καὶ ἄλλος ὁ θερίζων (4:37). No matter what the origin of this saying is, the sense is that during the eschatological harvest the role of sower and that of reaper will be filled by different people.[108] There are two debated issues involved here: the identity of the laborers (ἄλλοι) and the nature of the sending (ἐγὼ ἀπέστειλα ὑμᾶς). The interpretation of ἄλλοι has been controversial.[109] I will just summarize the solutions that have been proposed. First, in the very immediate context, assuming that the Samaritans were approaching as Jesus talked, the Samaritan woman may be the sower and Jesus the reaper.[110] Second, in a wider literary and geographical context, John the Baptist and his followers may be the sower, and Jesus and his disciples the reapers.[111] Third, in a theological context, Jesus might be

---

107 Cf. Carson, *John*, 230.

108 For an estimate on the orgin of the "proverb," see Brown, *John*, 1:182–83, and Beasley-Murray, *John*, 63–64.

109 See Okure's long discussion on this issue, *The Johannine Approach*, 153–64.

110 Johannes von Neugebauer, "Die Textbezüge von Joh 4,1–42 und die Geschichte der johanneischen Gruppe," *ZNW* 84 (1993): 139.

111 J. A. T. Robinson speaks strongly for this position ("The 'Others' of John 4,38: A Test of Exegetical Method," *SE* 1 [1959]: 510–15), and Beasley-Murray agrees with him (*John*, 64).

referring to the traditional Samaritan faith as "the work of a Divine sowing" and his own coming as the Messiah as "a harvest which he can reap."[112] An alternative of this theological connection is to identify John the Baptist as "the last in the succession of prophets and of others who sowed the seed but did not live long enough to participate in the harvest."[113] Fourth, in the life setting of the New Testament church, the author might have applied Jesus' words to a Samaritan mission that involved different groups of people as sowers and reapers. Cullmann suggested that the Hellenists in the early church, such as Philip, were the ἄλλοι who had sowed in Samaria, and the apostles, Peter and John, were the reapers who came later.[114] Finally, in the so-called "structural" context suggested by Okure, only the Father and Jesus are seen as the sowers (ἄλλοι), and disciples of all times (in both v. 36 and v. 38) are the reapers.[115] This is sound except that the role of θερίζων cannot be limited to disciples only. The disciples could not have "already" harvested at the time of the discourse, and Jesus, as already pointed out in v. 36, was the θερίζων himself.[116] We should consider the rendering that these roles are variously filled at different stages of redemptive history. Scholars who hold strong views on the issue are often concerned with different levels of history, the plain history and the gospel setting, and at different settings the two roles have to be filled differently. J. A. T. Robinson, for example, takes the plain history seriously, but he does not deny that the passage also validates the church's later mission in Samaria , for he says that ἄλλοι refers to the Baptist and his disciples only "in the first instance."[117] Cullmann emphasizes the concern of the Johannine church with the Samaritan mission, but he also considers the episode a historical event and interprets v. 36, συνάγει καρπὸν εἰς ζωὴν αἰώνιον, as Jesus' Samaritan mission.[118] Disputes arise only when details of the settings are conjectured. Robinson's idea that the Baptist himself had worked in Sychar to make way for Jesus seems

112 Odeberg, *The Fourth Gospel*, 190.

113 Carson, *John*, 231.

114 Cullmann, "Samaria and Origins." His view has attracted followers: Bligh, "Jesus in Samaria"; Brown, *John*, 1:184; Schnackenburg, *John*, 1:453.

115 Okure, *The Johannine Approach*, 160–64.

116 Okure supports her interpretation with a highly complicated structural analysis, which is hardly convincing (ibid., 162).

117 J. A. T. Robinson, "'Others,'" 515.

118 Cullmann, "Samaria and Origins," 188.

conjectural.[119] Cullmann's idea that ἄλλοι refers specifically to Philip's kind of Hellenists is also conjectural. Cullmann also treats vv. 35–36 and vv. 37–38 diachronically, so that the former applies only to Jesus' level of history and the latter to the Johannine level. Johannes von Neugebauer, in a recently published article, points out this flaw.[120] He argues that the syntax of v. 37 (ἐν γὰρ τούτῳ ὁ λόγος ἐστὶν ἀληθινὸς ὅτι Ἄλλος . . .) is not epexegetical as often claimed, but that ἐν τούτῳ links the saying to the preceding or ensuing sentences, so that the discourse remains an integral whole.[121] Based on this he proposes that at the time Jesus spoke, i.e., at the historical level of the event, the Father was the sender (v. 34), the woman was the sower (v. 39), Jesus was the reaper (v. 41) and the Samaritans were the harvest field (v. 42).[122] Thus he reckons four roles: the sender, the sower, the reaper and the harvest, instead of just two. I suggest we even optimize their symbolic references. In v. 36, Jesus was referring to himself as the reaper who was gathering the woman as καρπός into eternal life. So the sower must have been someone who had worked before Jesus, rather than the woman herself. The sower here may refer to the Father (Okure) or to the Baptist (J. A. T. Robinson). In v. 37, Jesus went on to remark, with a saying (λόγος), how different (ἄλλος) people had participated in this, and so ἐν τούτῳ here points both backward to v. 37 and forward to v. 38. In v. 38, Jesus was telling the disciples that they would also be "reapers of what others had labored," like himself. Thus the harvest discourse moves on from one set of referents to another. As for the identity of the ἄλλοι, who κεκοπιάκασιν before the disciples, they may include Jesus, and perhaps the woman, and all those who had worked even before Jesus himself. I would not exclude the possibility that even the traditional Samaritan faith is referred here in 4:38 as one of the ἄλλοι who had labored, to build up an anticipation

---

119 J. A. T. Robinson, "'Others,'" 513–14.

120 Neugebauer, "Die Textbezüge," 135; cf. G. Van Belle, "Johannine Style Characteristics," appendix 2 in *The Sign Source in the Fourth Gospel: Historical Survey and Critical Evaluation of the Semeia Hypothesis*, BETL 116 (Leuven: Leuven University Press, 1994), 410.

121 Ibid., 136–37. O'Day also contends for the transitional function of v. 37, "The 'for' (*gar*) with which the verse opens indicates that the proverb . . . is connected with what preceded it, but the proverb can also be understood as introducing a new topic which is then expanded in v. 38. Verse 37 therefore has a transitional function in the series of harvest sayings" (*Revelation in the Fourth Gospel*, 83).

122 Ibid., 139.

of the messiah. Jesus was saying that various efforts had gone into making the field ready for the disciples to harvest. This optimal interpretation agrees with the fact that 4:31–34 is a didactic section, in which Jesus instructs the disciples about eschatological ἔργον, using his own work in Samaria as an example. In such a context, Jesus calls himself the "reaper" (4:35–36) but at the same time commissions the disciples to be "reapers" also, and that precisely is the meaning of 4:38, ἐγὼ ἀπέστειλα ὑμᾶς θερίζειν ὃ οὐχ ὑμεῖς κεκοπιάκατε· ἄλλοι κεκοπιάκασιν . . . The aorist here seems to cause a problem because in the gospel the disciples are formally sent only after Jesus' resurrection (20:21), so many scholars interpret 4:38 as proleptic or prophetic, or as if written from a post-Easter perspective. However, the disciples had been, from the beginning, called for a mission to participate in Jesus' ministry. Even some of their first activities were already to lead people to Jesus (1:40–42, 45–46).[123] The disciples must have already had a sense of being sent to make sense of Jesus' charge at 4:38. Based on this, the symbols in the harvest metaphor should be interpreted with multiple references. Both the Father and Jesus were senders: the Father sent Jesus and Jesus sent the disciples. Both Jesus and the woman were sowers: they made the Samaritans ready for harvest. Both the woman and the Samaritans were the harvest: the woman was the first crop and the Samaritans were the next. Both the disciples and Jesus were reapers: Jesus the Messiah was the eschatological reaper, and he was also the teacher and usher of subsequent reapers, his disciples.[124]

At the Johannine level, there is a "mission" emphasis in this "harvest" discourse. As Schnackenburg points out, words like κοπιάω and κόπος (4:38), signifying "toil" or "labor," are typical Pauline terms for missionary work (cf. 1 Thess 3:5; 1 Cor 3:8; 15:10; Col 1:29 etc.).[125] They indicate

---

123 Note that the individual missions they had been sent for might not have even been fully recorded, although the Synoptics make more mention of them (Luke 9:2; 10:1–2). See Dodd's argument in *Historical Tradition in the Fourth Gospel* (Cambridge: Cambridge University Press, 1965 [1963]), 403–4; cf. Brown, *John*, 1:183; Okure, *The Johannine Approach*, 158–59.

124 Olsson approaches this passage with a "temporal frame with Jesus' 'hour' in the centre," i.e., the sowing and the laboring belong to the time before Jesus' "hour," the harvest and the rejoicing to the time after. He also comes up with "multiple references" for the harvest symbols (*Structure and Meaning*, 249–56).

125 They are used also for activity in the community (cf. 1 Thess 5:12; 1 Cor 16:16; Acts 20:35; 1 Tim 4:10; 5:17); See Schnackenburg, *John*, 1:453.

that in the Johannine church the harvest imagery was consciously applied to missionary activities. Many agree on this missionary emphasis of the Johannine church, and various attempts have been made in recovering a situation of Samaritan mission in the Johannine church. Cullmann suggests that the Johannine church was using Jesus' episode to authenticate missionary work in Samaria, and that "others" who had labored referred to the Hellenist Christians who had gone ahead of the apostles themselves. His view is accepted as well as opposed by many. Bligh, who agrees, further conjectures that the "eirenical" saying in v. 36, ὁ σπείρων ὁμοῦ χαίρῃ καὶ ὁ θερίζων, was an appeal to Christ's authority to resolve "a dispute in the Jerusalem church as to who deserved the credit for the conversion of Samaria," i.e., Hellenist or Hebrew-speaking Christians.[126] Neugebauer, who disagrees with Cullmann, makes a different conjecture that a distinct Samaritan group had already been formed in the Johannine church as a result of earlier Samaritan mission and it caused dissension in theological thinking. So in John 4 Jesus appears as the speaker of the Johannine group against the Samaritan group.[127] However, the consensus is that mission activities must have been going on in the Johannine church. It is probable that the gospel was composed in a mission minded community in which Samaritans were involved as witnesses or targets of gospel preaching. As Okure says, "that the Evangelist himself was interested in mission seems hardly questionable."[128]

The centrality of Jesus is one of the salient features of the gospel's mission emphasis, as pointed out by Okure.[129] Eschatology is just as basic to this mission emphasis. The very inclusion of the Samaritan episode in John 4, with Jesus' disclosure of his ἔργον as "the harvest ἤδη," is an important contribution to the present eschatology of the gospel, as well as to its christology. At the level of the Johannine composition, therefore, the harvest imagery indicates that Christian mission is part and parcel of the eschatological coming of Christ. It speaks specifically of the joy and

---

126 Bligh, "Jesus in Samaria," 344.

127 Neugebauer suggests, therefore, that regarding the mission charge in 4:38 the Johannine group considered themselves sowers of the Samaritan harvest field, and Jesus the sender of the post-Easter church to labor in that field ("Die Textbezüge," 139–41).

128 See Okure for an overall evaluation of "The Missionary Situation from the Gospel Evidence" (*The Johannine Approach*, 231; 230–34).

129 Ibid., 226–27; or 192–227.

satisfaction of gathering people to Christ's kingdom. We may conclude, therefore, that the "harvest" is related to "living water" just as "work" and "food" are related to "water" and "bread." They are counterparts in symbolizing eschatological joy: the joy of being gathered into the kingdom, and the joy of gathering people into the kingdom.[130]

Symbolism in the First Dialogue

We will now examine the references in the first dialogue that might be symbolic in meaning. Besides "living water," which is the leading symbol, the others are "Jacob's well," the woman's "five husbands," and "this mountain or Jerusalem."

Arrival at Jacob's Well

One may wonder if there is any significance in the transitional notes made in John 4:1–9. A note is given in 4:1–4 to clarify that Jesus and his disciples were travelling into Samaria. In 4:5–7a, the specific location of Sychar is described and the scene of Jesus' encounter with the woman is set. Further in 4:8, the isolation of their conversation is pointed out, οἱ γὰρ μαθηταὶ αὐτοῦ ἀπεληλύθεισαν εἰς τὴν πόλιν ἵνα τροφὰς ἀγοράσωσιν, and, in 9b, the peculiarity, οὐ γὰρ συγχρῶνται Ἰουδαῖοι Σαμαρίταις.

For some, these are notes that clarify the background, and they are geographically truthful.[131] For others, the point may be that there is racial prejudice between Jews and Samaritans, or that a women-and-men issue current in the Johannine church is kept in view.[132] None of these finds confirmation in the context, though the barrier between Jews and Samaritans

130 Cf. Odeberg's comment on 4:35–38, "In its deepest sense the 'labour' [for the harvest] perhaps means the longing for the 'living water'" (*The Fourth Gospel*, 190).

131 Cf. Olsson, "Spatial Features," section in *Structure and Meaning*, 138–47, and R. J. Bull, "An Archaeological Context for Understanding John 4:20," *BA* 38 (1975): 54–59.

132 D. Daube, "Jesus and the Samaritan Woman: The Meaning of συγχράομαι," *JBL* 69 (1950): 137–47; G. D. Kilpatrick, "John 4:9," *JBL* (1968): 327–28; D. R. Hall, "The Meaning of *synchraomai* in John 4:9," *ExpTim* 83 (1971): 56–57; M. C. de Boer, "John 4:27—Women (and Men) in the Gospel and Community of John," in *Women in the Biblical Tradition*, ed. G. J. Brooke (Lewiston, NY: The Edwin Mellen Press, 1992), 208–30.

may hint at the need of mission and the conversion of the woman hint at equality between disciples of different sexes.[133] The significance of these notes, besides setting the background, is that the Samaritans were among those who anticipated the Messiah, and Jesus as the eschatological Christ met their need for salvation as well. The account is placed next to the Cana episode, which occurred in Galilee, and the cleansing of the temple and the Nicodemus discourse, which occurred in Jerusalem. It is within a series of episodes revealing Jesus as the eschatological Christ. We may find two symbolic uses in this transitional passage. First, Jesus' moving into Samaria to be met with positive responses can be part of a geographical framework that suggests a preference of Galilee and Samaria over against Judea. This is the thematic symbolism proposed by Meeks, already discussed in chapter one.[134] Second, subtly but unmistakably, Jacob's well stands for Samaritan religious traditions. Our focus here is on the symbolic meaning of Jacob's well.

Jacob's well is not found mentioned in any literature relevant to our text, whether the Old Testament or Jewish or Samaritan writings, although the well itself may be identified as the Jacob's well of today at the foot of Gerizim.[135] This silence, however, may not disprove its significance in John 4. In fact John 4 can be an important piece of evidence for the centrality of Jacob's well in Samaritanism, as well as the importance of other features such as Gerizim, Sychar and Jacob's sons, reflected in many extra-biblical references.[136] Based on these Olsson has worked optimistically on the historical origin of the well: that Jacob gave a field and the well in the field to his son Joseph, and both were passed on to the Samaritans.[137] This well may well have been a monument of Jacob's greatness in Samaria, aside from being the site for the encounter.

---

133 Okure's investigation on some of these details may be legitimate and interesting; see Okure, *The Johannine Approach*, 133–36.

134 Meeks, "Galilee and Judea."

135 It has been pointed out that the trend of some traditions was not to associate Jacob with any particular well but to link him with the traveling well tradition (see 1 Cor 10:4): "Jacob was seventy-seven years old when he went forth from his father's house, and the well went with him," *Pirqe. R. El.* 35, quoted in J. H. Neyrey, "Jacob Traditions and the Interpretation of John 4:10–26," *CBQ* 41 (1979): 419–37.

136 Olsson, *Structure and Meaning*, 140–41.

137 Ibid., 138–42.

At the Johannine level, it has been suggested that the well was used to create a "type scene," hinting at the encounter with the future betrothed at a well.[138] It is also suggested that John 4 exhibits textual similarities to Gen 24, Gen 29 and Exod 2 which were texts used in the Jewish lectionary system, and that the gospel alludes to these Old Testament stories and speaks of the matrimony of Jesus and his believers.[139] Though "type scene" may be an effective language used by John, we do not see any repeated use of this device in the gospel to be sure about this interpretation. If there are allusions to OT scenes, the theological intent is vague, and the proof that there are remains unclear.[140]

I think the significance of the scene lies more at the level of plain history. A straightforward interpretation is that Jacob's well stands for the importance of Jacob in Samaria, and that the well, as a long time provider of life sustenance, symbolizes the trustworthiness of traditional Samaritan doctrines, and to both of these the Samaritan woman gave her allegiance. Thus the arrivals of Jesus and the woman at the well set the scene not only for their physical and social encounter, but for their theological confrontation. The ensuing dialogue on "water," with the repeated use of words such as πηγή and φρέαρ (4:7–15), confirms that Jacob's well is an introductory symbol, introducing Jesus' symbolic use of ὕδωρ. Just as the woman's leaving of her water jar symbolizes renunciation of a former faith, arrivals at the well anticipates a challenge to her allegiance to that faith. Another proof of this is a question raised by the woman later on in the dialogue (4:12): μὴ σὺ μείζων εἶ τοῦ πατρὸς ἡμῶν Ἰακώβ, ὃς ἔδωκεν ἡμῖν τὸ φρέαρ . . . This is an elaboration on the woman's part of what Jacob's well symbolizes for her. Its close parallel to 8:53a, μὴ σὺ μείζων εἶ τοῦ πατρὸς ἡμῶν Ἀβραάμ, which is well recognized, shows that Jacob's well is mentioned at the Johannine level not so much as a "type scene" but as a counterpart of the fatherhood of Abraham (8:12–59). It belongs to "a theme in the gospel which asserts Jesus' superiority to the founding fathers of traditional Jewish religion."[141] The Johannine message is that the Jews

138 R. Alter, *The Art of Biblical Narrative* (New York: Basic Books, 1981), 51–56.

139 N. R. Bonneau, "The Woman at the Well: John 4 and Genesis 24," *The Bible Today* (1973): 1252–59; citing Guilding, *The Fourth Gospel and Jewish Worship*, 231–33; cf. Neyrey, "Jacob Traditions," 425–26.

140 Bonneau, "The Woman at the Well," 1259.

141 Neyrey, "Jacob Traditions," 420.

exalted Abraham and the Samaritans exalted Jacob, but Jesus was able to challenge both, because he is the eschatological Christ.

The "Living Water"

A common approach to the first dialogue is to dissect it into two so that both sections are initiated by a request on Jesus' part: "Give me a drink" (4:7), and, "Go, call your husband" (4:16). The result of this is that "living water" appears to be a theme only in the first section (4:7–15), whereas "worship in spirit and truth" dominates the latter section (4:16–26) as a second theme (see O'Day's outline, discussed above).[142] However, "living water" could well be the major symbol used by Jesus in this dialogue, to reveal to the woman who he is and what he has to give (4:10), and Jesus' revelation to the woman takes the full dialogue to complete. The question τίς ἐστιν ὁ λέγων σοι, Δός μοι πεῖν raised early in the dialogue (4:10) is not answered until the end, Ἐγώ εἰμι [Μεσσίας], ὁ λαλῶν σοι (4:26). Thus the theme of "living water" appears to be central to the whole dialogue. In this case, dissection of the dialogue into sections may obstruct interpretation. Lee's analysis of John 4 as a "symbolic narrative" is an example. She divides the text into three scenes with three respective images: ὕδωρ ζῶν (vv. 7–15), τόπος (vv. 16–29), and βρῶσις, βρῶμα/θερισμός (vv. 31–42), and in each of them she looks for a common pattern: an opening request, a further statement, an initial response, christological revelation, and a faith response.[143] In this way Lee perceives symbolism only in literary patterns. She overlooks the gravity of the water symbol itself, a symbol widely used in the linguistic and theological context of New Testament times. In John 4 the water symbol becomes a theme with an underlying reference to salvation, rather than a mere literary device. It is a vehicle for Jesus' revelation which take the full dialogue to complete, for the "living water" (4:10, 14) cannot be understood without the knowledge of the Messiah (4:25), and Jesus' own identity is key to the understanding of his gifts.

Crucial to interpretation is of course the meaning of ὕδωρ ζῶν, just what Jesus was trying to reveal but the woman misunderstood. I suggest

---

142 That is why commentators tend to enlist three leveled themes for John 4: the "living water," the "true worship," and the "harvest." See, for example, Schnackenburg, *John*, 1:421; Beasley-Murray, *John*, 59; cf. Lee, *Symbolic Narratives*, 66.

143 Lee, *Symbolic Narratives*, 66.

that Jesus' use of ὕδωρ ζῶν should be understood as a double symbolism. First, the earthly symbolizes the heavenly, or the physical symbolizes the metaphysical, for ζῶν can simply mean "fresh" and "running," whereas ζωή means "life." By offering fresh water Jesus was actually talking about the quickening of life (4:10). This may be called the "vertical dimension" of the water symbol, which the woman failed to understand in the early part of the dialogue (4:7–15). Second, there is a horizontal dimension to the water symbol in which the traditional or cultic worship symbolizes the eschatological worship, and the woman was guided by Jesus to grapple with this in the latter part of the dialogue, as she inquired about the place of worship (4:16–26). The latter discourse was not a discrete discussion but an enlightenment on the meaning of ὕδωρ ζῶν, which is both christological and eschatological in this context. It was only at the end of the full dialogue that the meaning of ὕδωρ ζῶν was adequately communicated to the woman. In other words, the exposition of ὕδωρ ζῶν carries on throughout the first dialogue in spite of the apparent shift of topic from "living water" to "true worship."

In the first six exchanges of the dialogue, Jesus attempted two times to bring the conversation up from the earthly level to the heavenly. He first asked for a drink (4:7), and when he was mocked for doing so (4:9) he rebutted by boasting about himself and his "living water" (4:10): Εἰ ᾔδεις τὴν δωρεὰν τοῦ θεοῦ καὶ τίς ἐστιν ὁ λέγων σοι, Δός μοι πεῖν, σὺ ἂν ᾔτησας αὐτὸν καὶ ἔδωκεν ἄν σοι ὕδωρ ζῶν. That was the first attempt. By changing topic from the need of a drink to the offer of ὕδωρ ζῶν, he made it possible for the conversation to move from the earthly level to the metaphysical level. Jesus' disclosure of truth at this juncture involves a double question, "what the gift of God is" and "who he is." The two questions are closely related and equally important, judging from the coordinate structure of the conditional. The chiasm of the sentence, which goes from the "gift of God" to the identity of the speaker and from the speaker back to the "living water," implies that the "gift of God" must also be the "living water" which Jesus offers.[144] In the Judaistic background represented by rabbinic literature, the common semantic domain of these two terms would be one labeled as "Torah." The term "gift," δωρεά, was mainly associated with the Torah by the rabbis, although they were also used to refer to other

144 Schnackenburg, *John*, 1:426; Odeberg, *The Fourth Gospel*, 152.

things bestowed by God such as lights and rain and peace and land.[145] As Odeberg suggests, the general conception of the term δωρεὰ τοῦ θεοῦ must have been familiar to the woman.[146] It is doubtful, however, that she would think of the Torah just as a rabbi would do. If Jesus used the term with the usual sense of his day, so as to communicate with the woman, the term would not have meant only the Torah. It would have included the idea of God's gift of a well, associated with the Israelites' experience recorded in Num 21:16–20. Targumic expansions of this passage confirm the connection of the "gift" idea with the "well."[147] Jesus must have expected the woman to think of Jacob's well in the first place as he mentioned the "gift of God." This is confirmed by the woman's immediate response, μὴ σὺ μείζων εἶ τοῦ πατρὸς ἡμῶν Ἰακώβ, ὃς ἔδωκεν ἡμῖν τὸ φρέαρ (4:12). Jesus was, of course, trying to reveal that he himself was the gift of God, and that is confirmed by his juxtaposition of the other question, τίς ἐστιν, and the Johannine teaching of God's gift as his only begotten Son: Jesus, the giver of gifts, is himself God's gift (3:16).[148] At this point, however, "who Jesus is" might have been harder for the woman to grasp than "what God's gift is," and so, as we will see, the conversation proceeded with "water" as a theme.

In the next two exchanges Jesus attempted again to bring the conversation up from the earthly level to the heavenly. The woman's response in 4:11–12 is a typical Johannine "misunderstanding," responding as if Jesus was talking about earthly water, and as if Jesus was bragging to

---

145 *Gen. Rab.* 6,7; quoted in Odeberg, *The Fourth Gospel*, 149–52, and Schnackenburg, *John*, 1:426.

146 Odeberg, *The Fourth Gospel*, 121, 130, 149–50.

147 The MT on Num 21:18 reads "And [after finding God's well at Beer] from the wilderness they went on to Mattanah (מַתָּנָה)," and the targums interpret the place name as "it was given to them as a gift," on the basis of the perceived root נתן; *Tg. Neof.*, *Tg. Yer. I*, *Tg. Yer. II*, quoted in Neyrey, "Jacob Tradition," 423, and Olsson, *Structure and Meaning*, 165–66.

148 Cf. Odeberg, "The import of the passage . . . is really identical with that of Jn 3:16. It may also be surmised that the discourse on the Divine gift in Jn 3:27–36, attributed to John the Baptist, relates to the present utterance. 'A man (ἄνθρωπος) can receive nothing, except it be given him from heaven (3:21)'; only one man (ἄνθρωπος) , however, has received from heaven, namely Messiah (3:28), the Messenger (3:24), the Son (3:35); and he, on the other hand, has received all gifts: 'The Father loveth the Son, and hath given all things into his hand.' (3:35, cf. 13:3) . . ." (*The Fourth Gospel*, 152).

be greater than Jacob as a giver. She was blind to Jesus' symbolic use of water, and so Jesus differentiated it for her: Πᾶς ὁ πίνων ἐκ τοῦ ὕδατος τούτου διψήσει πάλιν· ὃς δ' ἂν πίῃ ἐκ τοῦ ὕδατος οὗ ἐγὼ δώσω αὐτῷ, οὐ μὴ διψήσει εἰς τὸν αἰῶνα, ἀλλὰ τὸ ὕδωρ ὃ δώσω αὐτῷ γενήσεται ἐν αὐτῷ πηγὴ ὕδατος ἁλλομένου εἰς ζωὴν αἰώνιον (4:13–14). Note that Jesus' differentiation takes the form of two contrastive notes.[149] The first contrast, πᾶς ὁ . . . ἐκ τοῦ ὕδατος τούτου and ὅς ὁ . . . τοῦ ὕδατος οὗ ἐγὼ δώσω, is couched in demonstratives, but symbolically "this water" (that was drawn from Jacob's well) represents "earthly water."[150] The second contrast emerges as an elaboration of the effect of the latter, οὐ μὴ διψήσει εἰς τὸν αἰῶνα but ἀλλὰ τὸ ὕδωρ ὃ δώσω αὐτῷ γενήσεται ἐν αὐτῷ πηγὴ ὕδατος ἁλλομένου εἰς ζωὴν αἰώνιον, with the latter clause explaining the former. The importance of this cannot be overstated. We know that the two kinds of water do not simply differ in the duration of their effects, but they are intrinsically different. What Jesus had to say about ὕδωρ ζῶν in particular is that it "becomes a spring welling up to eternal life." That is how the "living water" works in a person.

How was the symbol used among Jews and Samaritans and how was it understood in the Johannine composition? In the Judaistic background the water symbol has a wider connotation than the "gift of God." In the Old Testament the Lord is called "the spring of living water" (Jer 2:13; Ezek 14:8). Alternatively, "water" stands for the Lord's salvation (Isa 12:3; 49:10). It also signifies cleansing, and along that line it refers to the "Spirit" (Isa 44:3; Ezek 36:25–27). In wisdom and apocalyptic literature it is applied to "wisdom" (Prov 13:14; 18:4; *1 Enoch* 48:1; 49:1).[151] In rabbinic literature "water" is very frequently used to refer to the "Torah," though sometimes also to the "Spirit."[152] Some believe that "wisdom, knowledge and Torah" constitute a triple meaning that was most popularly held for the water symbol

---

149 Schnackenburg comments rightly, "This . . . is couched in very well balanced phrasing," *John*, 1:429.

150 Here is the double use of water symbolism, found in John 4 and 7, as pointed out in the previous chapter.

151 Cf. Bar 3:12; Ecclus 15:3; 24:30; Wis 7:25; Song 4:15; quoted in Schnackenberg, *John*, 1:427. See also Odeberg, *The Fourth Gospel*, 153.

152 Billerbeck, *Kommentar*, 434–35; Odeberg, *The Fourth Gospel*, 154–55; Dodd, *Interpretation*, 312; Barrett, *John*, 233.

in the Judaistic context of New Testament times.[153] Scholarly consensus is that "water" in this context is preeminently either the "Torah" or the "Spirit." It is unclear how the Samaritans used or understood the symbol. With a canon of Scripture restricted to the Pentateuch, they might not have appreciated the prophetic allusions to water, but there is reference to the Taheb's "water" in Samaritan literature.[154] All of these stand at the background of Jesus' use of the symbol.[155]

The use of the symbol must be interpreted in light of its close parallel in 7:37–38, Ἐάν τις διψᾷ ἐρχέσθω πρός με καὶ πινέτω ὁ πιστεύων εἰς ἐμέ, καθὼς εἶπεν ἡ γραφή, ποταμοὶ ἐκ τῆς κοιλίας αὐτοῦ ῥεύσουσιν ὕδατος ζῶντος. The two passages are almost identical in the imagery used: water will be given and will flow out from either the believer or Christ. It may be inferred that "living water" in both passages refers somehow to the Holy Spirit, as is clarified in 7:39.[156] However, this complete meaning is withheld in the early narrative from the wider audience and is disclosed at the later incident.[157] In the previous chapter I have argued for the christological interpretation of "water" in 7:37–38, so it follows that the water imagery respectively depicts, in the two discourses, the situations of the believer and Jesus the giver. The verbs γενήσεται and ἁλλομένου (v. 14b) describe both conceptually and visually the living and life-giving quality of the water, as Okure points out.[158] They may well describe the indwelling and outflowing of the Holy Spirit, or, in New Testament notion, the baptism and gift of the Holy Spirit.[159] The versatile symbol also carries with it a general

153 Olsson, *Structure and Meaning*, 214.

154 According to the Samaritan hymn *Shira Yetima* written by Abisha ben Pinhas of the fourteenth century, "Water shall flow from the buckets of the Taheb." This late document might have been influenced by Christian theology, but it might also reflect early Samaritan eschatology. See Bowman, *Early Samaritan Eschatology*, 64.

155 Significant is F. Manns's comprehensive study on this background, *Le symbole eau-Esprit dans le Judaisme ancien*, Studium Biblicum Franciscanum Analecta 19 (Jerusalem: Franciscan Printing Press, 1983); cf. D. C. Allison, "The Living Water," *St Vladimir's Theological Quarterly* 30 (1986): 143–57.

156 Cf. Burge, *The Anointed Community*, 98.

157 S. D. Moore, *Literary Criticism and the Gospels: The Theoretical Challenge* (New Haven: Yale University Press, 1989), 160.

158 Okure, *The Johannine Approach*, 103.

159 In line with this it has been observed that the Gnostic *Odes of Solomon* speaks of the quenching of thirst in a similar way (11:7; 28:15; 30:4; quoted in Schnackenburg, *John*, 1:430).

sense comparable to that of its neighboring term, the "gift of God," as the juxtaposition of the two implies a degree of synonymy. In this general sense, the "living water" means the gifts of God including Christ himself and all that he bestows, salvation, purification, joy, and eternal life. These gifts are fulfilled in the life of a believer through the Holy Spirit, who is also symbolized by "living water," and has the living life-giving quality symbolized by the constant quenching of thirst.

How much could the woman understand about "living water" in this second discourse? Although Samaritan liturgies such as Memar Markah mention the messianic use of living water, they are too late as sources to prove that a Samaritan theology existed at that time that refers water to "salvation."[160] Nor can it be established that the Samaritans at Jesus' time associated "water" with the "Torah" or the "Spirit." I believe, therefore, that the Samaritan woman held only a general conception of the "gift of God," such as the gift of a well. She could not be perceptive about symbolic sense of the "living water" as the Holy Spirit. It is not surprising that she responded again with a persistence about the earthly water: δός μοι τοῦτο τὸ ὕδωρ, ἵνα μὴ διψῶ μηδὲ διέρχωμαι ἐνθάδε ἀντλεῖν (4:15). It might be for her slowness in understanding that Jesus chose a double-meaning image to communicate with her, namely, πηγὴ ὕδατος ἀλλομένου (4:14). In the targums of Gen 28 and other midrashic accounts we learn of the legendary miracle about Jacob's well: "the well overflowed, and the water rose to the edge of it, and continued to overflow all the time he was in Haran."[161] If the legend was current in Judea at the time of the episode, the woman would have been familiar with it as a descendant of Jacob, and her response would have been natural. Hers would then be a positive response to Jesus' offer, though it is also a misunderstanding of it to be a solution to her need and problem.

The "Five Husbands"

Her need and problem was, on the surface, to have to come to the well for water (4:15). It is commonly assumed that her bad reputation had made

---

160 Macdonald, *Theology of the Samaritans*, 276, 292 and 435, quoted by Burge, *The Anointed Community*, 99, n. 206.

161 *Tg. Yer. I*, *Tg. Yer. II*, and *Tg. Neof.* Gen 28:10; *Pirqe R. El.* 36; *Midr.* Pss 7; 91; quoted in Neyrey, "Jacob Traditions," 423.

it necessary for her to come at noon time (ὥρα ἦν ὡς ἕκτη, 4:6), or walk a long distance to this particular well to avoid crowds.[162] Jesus' sudden summons of her husband at the next exchange of the dialogue implies that her deeper need or problem is of a different kind. Earthly water symbolizes eschatological "living water." The earthly action of coming to a well symbolizes the eschatological action of coming to the Messiah, who says to the woman, Ὕπαγε φώνησον τὸν ἄνδρα σου καὶ ἐλθὲ ἐνθάδε (4:16).[163]

The next exchanges disclose the woman's dubious marital status (4:17–18) and Jesus' omniscience (cf. 4:29). In the history of interpretation Jesus' summons of her husbands was once understood as a challenge to the woman's religion. The five husbands stand for the five books of Moses, which is the Samaritan canon, or the foreign pagan gods introduced to them during the Assyrian conquest of Samarian, by people who came from five cities.[164] The woman, allegorically, would be a symbol of Samaria, but few agree with this nowadays.[165] Most take the plain sense of ἀνήρ as "husband." Was Jesus simply inviting the woman's husband to come for "living water"?[166] Was he exposing the woman's sin in having so many husbands, to lead her to repentance?[167] Was he "disclosing the being of man" as the

---

162 The practice of drawing water at noon was not unknown. See *Ant.* 2.25, quoted by Morris, *John*, 228. If Sychar should be identified as the modern Askar, then it was half a mile from Jacob's well whereas it had its own local or closer by wells. It is then strange that the woman had to walk to Jacob's well at all. Bad reputation is among the best guess at her reason, because there is nothing disclosed about the woman in the text except the fact that she had five husbands.

163 Note the parallel of the verbs (διέρχωμαι, ἐλθὲ) and adverbs (ἐνθάδε) used by the woman and Jesus.

164 2 Kgs 17:24–41; the Hebrew word for "husband," בַּעַל, was also used as a name for a pagan deity. See Brown's explanation of the rationale behind this approach.

165 Olsson is an exception, who argues from the "text-linguistical" point of view that Jesus' repetition of the woman's own words and his changing of the word order (Οὐκ ἔχω ἄνδρα . . . Ἄνδρα οὐκ ἔχω . . .) indicate a transference of meaning from "husbands" to "Samaritan cult" (*Structure and Meaning*, 186). Cf. Neyrey's application of the approach in connection with the type scene of "courtship at a well" ("Jacob's Traditions," 426). Note also Schnackenburg's standard argument against this position (*John*, 1:433).

166 Cf. Godet, *John*, 425; cf. Westcott, *John*, 71.

167 Cf. A. Plummer, *The Gospel According to St John: With Maps, Notes and Introduction* (Cambridge: Cambridge University Press, 1912), 110; Hoskyns, *The Fourth Gospel*, 243; Lindars, *John*, 185; Morris, *John*, 234; Beasley-Murray, *John*, 61; Carson, *John*, 221. For historical notes on marital rules see Billerbeck, *Kommentar*, 437; and Barrett, *John*, 235–36.

existentialist interpretation suggests?[168] The woman's reaction to Jesus (4:19) and her testimony later on (4:29) confirm that the emphasis of the text is actually on Jesus' display of superhuman knowledge as the eschatological Christ. Coherent with this emphasis are the previous question τίς ἐστιν (4:10), and the subsequent remarks: μήτι οὗτος ἐστιν ὁ Χριστός; (4:29) and οὗτος ἐστιν ἀληθῶς ὁ σωτὴρ τοῦ κόσμου (4:42). The identity of Jesus is quite clearly the main issue of the Johannine text. It is the consensus of recent scholars, especially literary scholars, that Jesus is presented as one making a self-revelation to the woman, rather than addressing the problem of her immorality.[169] Some agree, alternatively, that the latter is an issue only as the effect of the revelation.[170] At Jesus' time, however, it could be that Jesus was concerned about the woman's sinfulness in life. While the question of sin is not as relevant as that of faith in the gospel, in the milieu of Jesus' baptism the water symbol acquired a sense of "purification."[171] It was also appropriate that Jesus should invite her husband, the leader of family, to share the salvation he was offering to the woman. In any case, the woman is not symbolic of Samaria, nor her "five husbands" a symbol of pagan cults. Symbolism here remains with the "living water." The need for the "living water" symbolizes the need for the eschatological blessings of Christ: salvation, purification, joy, and eternal life. The necessity of coming to the well symbolizes the necessity of coming to the Messiah, with everything she had done (cf. 4:29). Thus, Jesus' summons of her husband does not introduce a new topic, but is a continuation of the "living water" discourse. This detour in the dialogue effects only in an awareness of Jesus' omniscience, and subsequently his identity. This awareness prepares the woman for seeing the meaning of Jesus' water at a higher

---

168 Bultmann, *John*, 187–88.

169 Okure provides a fair coverage of positions taken by various scholars; see *The Johannine Approach*, 110–12.

170 Barrett, *John*, 236; cf. Okure, *The Johannine Approach*, 110.

171 Okure is not right in saying, "nowhere in the entire gospel tradition does Jesus set out to confront individuals with their sinfulness" (*The Johannine Approach*, 110). The fact is, sin is frequently defined as not believing in Jesus (see 9:41; 15:22, 24; 16:9). This has to do with the Johannine emphasis on grace instead of law (1:17), and on christology.

level, to know who he is, and what he has to give.[172]

Climax: "This Mountain" and "Jerusalem"

This awareness made her say, Κύριε, θεωρῶ ὅτι προφήτης εἶ σύ (4:19)—not a full understanding but a breakthrough in her thinking, a confession coherent with the guiding question brought up in 4:10, "what the gift of God is" and "who he is."[173] A subtopic follows: οἱ πατέρες ἡμῶν ἐν τῷ ὄρει τούτῳ προσεκύνησαν· καὶ ὑμεῖς λέγετε ὅτι ἐν Ἱεροσολύμοις ἐστὶν ὁ τόπος ὅπου προσκυνεῖν δεῖ (4:20). It is unclear what her attitude was in saying so. The respective use of the aorist and present tenses implyies that the authority of her fathers takes precedence over the contemporary Jewish insistence, and the woman meant to confront this "Jewish prophet" now talking to her.[174] At this point she must have become inquisitive, and susceptible to change.

Her question opened up a discourse of Jesus in which the cultic traditional worship "on the mountain" or "in Jerusalem" were only symbols pointing to the eschatological worship: Πίστευέ μοι, γύναι, ὅτι ἔρχεται ὥρα ὅτε οὔτε ἐν τῷ ὄρει τούτῳ οὔτε ἐν Ἱεροσολύμοις προσκυνήσετε τῷ πατρί (4:21). If "living water" symbolizes the gifts of God as argued above, reflecting a vertical dimension of symbolism, I would say that a horizontal dimension of symbolism emerges in Jesus' comments on "this mountain" and "Jerusalem." Since "water," as OT imagery, symbolizes eschagological blessings, in Jesus' use it might well encompass the eschatological, heavenly worship of God now related. In this way a double symbolism of water points both vertically to the heavenly nature of gifts and eschatologically to the

172 My interpretation above opposes Cotterell and Turner's linguistic analysis of John 4, which perceives in the dialogue a kind of random and unconfined topic change which occurs in daily human conversation or general linguistics use. See P. Cotterell and M. Turner, *Linguistics and Biblical Interpretation* (Downers Grove, IL: IVP, 1989), 276–78.

173 The anarthrous προφήτης probably refers to a "Jewish prophet," i.e., a Jewish religious man with prophetic skills. Samaritans themselves did not recognize any prophets, but called the Messiah (Taheb) ὁ προφήτης. A later utterance of the woman, Οἶδα ὅτι Μεσσίας ἔρχεται . . . (4:25), proves that she was not confessing Jesus the Messiah at this point.

174 Okure, *The Johannine Approach*, 115.

new worship.[175] The blessings symbolized by Jesus' water are both heavenly and eschatological.

There should be a natural connection between this statement in 4:21 and its exposition in 4:23–24 because the beginnings are similar, ἀλλὰ ἔρχεται ὥρα καὶ νῦν ἐστιν, ὅτε . . . (4:23).[176] However, a sentence separates them: προσκυνεῖτε ὃ οὐκ οἴδατε· ἡμεῖς προσκυνοῦμεν ὃ οἴδαμεν, ὅτι ἡ σωτηρία ἐκ τῶν Ἰουδαίων ἐστίν (4:22).[177] Jesus did not ratify Jerusalem as the place of worship over against the woman's "mountain," so it was the tradition behind Jerusalem that he ratified as the authentic advancement of salvation. A history is presumed that defines eschatology. It is a history of salvation in the context of which Jesus proclaims eschatological fulfillment of OT promises given to Israel. On this basis Jesus discriminated against Samaritan history and tradition. In the terse way that Carson puts it, "they stand outside the stream of God's revelation, so that what they worship cannot possibly be characterized by truth and knowledge."[178]

The next two verses feature the qualifier ἐν πνεύματι καὶ ἀληθείᾳ, Jesus' counter response to the woman's ἐν τῷ ὄρει τούτῳ . . . καὶ . . . ἐν Ἱεροσολύμοις . . . . With this, Jesus introduced both the worshipers and the God who is worshipped: . . . οἱ ἀληθινοὶ προσκυνηταὶ προσκυνήσουσιν

---

175 Bultmann interprets the concept of "true believers" dualistically (*John*, 181–84). He appeals to *Odes of Solomon* for support of Gnostic influence in John (*John*, 85). My interpretation is different from Bultmann's: John's upper and lower levels of true worship reflect his characteristic present eschatology. Similarity to Gnostic dualism could be a matter of language.

176 The additional καὶ νῦν ἐστιν accentuates the imminence of ἡ ὥρα, which reflects the present eschatology of the gospel. Carson gives the best justification for this oxymoron, that it is a powerful way to assert the proleptical presence of the Easter hour in Jesus' ministry (*John*, 224); cf. Barrett (*John*, 237). Haenchen, alternatively, considers this a Johannine combination of two temporal aspects, the pre- and the pro-Easter aspects (*John*, 222).

177 Many explanations have been proposed: that it is a later ecclesiastical gloss (Haenchen, *John*, 222); that it was intended partly to remove the scandal of the Messiah from Israel (Schnackenburg, *John*, 436); that traditional material had been used that retained a positive attitude towards Judaism (C. J. A. Hickling, "Attitudes to Judaism in the Fourth Gospel," in *L'Évangile de Jean: Sources, redaction, théologie* (Leuven: Leuven University Press, 1977), 347–54; that the statement defines the essentially Jewish character of Jesus' messiahship (Leidig, *Jesu Gespräch*, 157–60); that it affirms the Jewish nationality of "the savior of the world" (Okure, *The Johannine Approach*, 117).

178 Carson, *John*, 223.

τῷ πατρὶ ἐν πνεύματι καὶ ἀληθείᾳ· καὶ γὰρ ὁ πατὴρ τοιούτους ζητεῖ τοὺς προσκυνοῦντας αὐτόν. πνεῦμα ὁ θεός, καὶ τοὺς προσκυνοῦντας αὐτὸν ἐν πνεύματι καὶ ἀληθείᾳ δεῖ προσκυνεῖν (4:23–24). The worshippers are qualified as ἀληθινοί, which means "true" in the sense of "real" rather than "sincere," because Jesus was speaking in response to the woman's concern about the τόπος (4:20–21). The same use is found in John 1:9, ἦν τὸ φῶς τὸ ἀληθιόν, where ἀληθιός marks the heavenly character of light, just as the word ζῶν marks the heavenly character of ὕδωρ. The heavenly character of the worshipers and the worship is thus coined as "in spirit and truth," and a contrast made between ἐν τῷ ὄρει, ἐν Ἱεροσολύμοις and ἐν πνεύματι καὶ ἀληθείᾳ. Thus, the Father seeks heavenly worshipers who worship in the heavenly manner, and that manner is qualified by ἐν πνεύματι καὶ ἀληθείᾳ. I think the discourse assumes a symbolic view of worship: cultic activities on the mountain and in Jerusalem symbolize the eschatological worship in spirit and truth, and only worshipers of the latter kind are called ἀληθινοί. This is in agreement with the Johannine concept of symbolism, found in τὸ φῶς τὸ ἀληθινόν (1:9), ὕδωρ ζῶν (4:10), and now οἱ ἀληθινοὶ προσκυνηται (4:23) and ἐν πνεύματι καὶ ἀληθείᾳ (4:23–24).

The comprehensiveness of Johannine symbolism calls for the next inquiry: is there a personal reference to the Spirit in the phrase ἐν πνεύματι καὶ ἀληθείᾳ? The Spirit is also called τὸ πνεῦμα τῆς ἀληθείας in John 16:13, which can be a parallel to ἐν πνεύματι καὶ ἀληθείᾳ if the latter is taken as a hendiadys. Besides, the giver of the Spirit, Jesus, is explicitly called ἡ ἀληθεία in 14:6, another example of a personal reference of the word. If ἐν πνεύματι καὶ ἀληθείᾳ should at the same time be interpreted with this personal sense, we have a dual reference here. On the one hand it points to the eschatological worship as the true worship, in response to the woman's concern for the place of worship, on the other hand it hints at the Spirit of truth given by Jesus as the agent of true worship.[179]

---

179 O. Betz takes a different approach and suggests that "in spirit and truth" refers specifically to the historical traditions of Joshua's covenant with the people at Sechem (Josh 24) and the subsequent perversion of the Samaritans (2 Kgs 17). The idea is that the woman was reminded of these traditions on hearing the word "truth." See O. Betz, "To Worship God in Spirit and in Truth: Reflections on John 4,20–26" in *Standing before God: Studies on Prayer in Scriptures and in Traditions with Essays in Honor of John M. Oesterreicher*, ed. A. Finkel and L. Frizzell (New York: Ktav Publishing House Inc., 1981), 53–72.

Jesus' remark ends with an explanation for the necessity of heavenly worship: πνεῦμα ὁ θεός, καὶ τοὺς προσκυνοῦντας αὐτὸν ἐν πνεύματι καὶ ἀληθείᾳ δεῖ προσκυνεῖν (4:24). "God is spirit" is a difficult statement because the term πνεῦμα is widely used in pagan as well as Jewish religions to refute anthropomorphic views of God. Consensus is that the OT idea of God's spirituality distinguishes itself in referring not to the nature of God as physical (cf. Stoicism) or metaphysical (cf. Gnosticism) but to the mode of his creative and life-giving activities.[180] Although God is never formally called "spirit" in the Old Testament, he is said to be superior because of the power of his Spirit (Isa 31:3) in creation and redemption. He is said to instruct the chosen people by the Spirit (Neh 9:20), lord over them and save them by the Spirit (Isa 63:10, 14), restore their life by the Spirit (Ezek 36:27) and send them the Spirit in the eschatological age (Ezek 39:29). In comparison with this, as Schnackenburg points out, formal parallels deduced from religions outside Christianity are only superficial, for it is mainly the "eschatological outlook" which links this Johannine passage with the OT prophecy of the last days.[181]

In this sense, it is an eschatological activity of the spirit of God to quicken worship in these last days.[182] On this basis and in line with my analysis above, I interpret this discourse on "true worship" as a component of Jesus' revelation on the "living water." The Holy Spirit, with his living and life-giving quality like the ὕδωρ ζῶν that quenches thirst, fulfills the needs of a believer's life of heavenly worship. This again involves a double symbolism. In the vertical sense the Holy Spirit enables a heavenly worship symbolized by the early one ἐν τῷ ὄρει and ἐν Ἱεροσολύμοις. In salvation historical sense the former traditions of worship are symbols of a future worship brought in by Christ and the Holy Spirit. Thus, with the coming of Christ, the Holy Spirit will make this heavenly and eschatological worship possible.

In this double symbolism, the spirit is the mark of both the heavenly

---

180 Barrett, *John*, 239; Schnackenburg, *John*, 1:440; Beasley-Murray, *John*, 62; Okure, *The Johannine Approach*, 116; Carson, *John*, 225; et. al.

181 Schnackenburg, *John*, 1:440. Cf. Burge, *The Anointed Community*, 192.

182 Okure points out, "In the Johannine perspective, the 'seeking' by the Father signifies, not a passive desire on his part, but his causative action in the individual without which a genuine human response is impossible (cf. 6:44, 65; 15:1–2)" (*The Johannine Approach*, 116).

and the eschatological. With regard to the heavenly, we may agree with Schnackenburg, "In John, πνεῦμα means all that belongs to God and the heavenly world, in contrast to all that is earthly and human."[183] Therefore, "God is spirit" requires that those who worship him must worship in a manner that complies with God's heavenly way (4:24). In this context, ἐν πνεύματι καὶ ἀληθείᾳ means God's heavenly way. In the eschatological sense, πνεῦμα characterizes the revival or fulfillment of life and worship that occurs at the end times. In John this event is imminent with the coming of Christ, as Jesus repeatedly reveals that he will send the Holy Spirit. Temporal references, such as εἰς τὸν αἰῶνα, εἰς ζωὴν αἰώνιον (4:14), ἔρχεται ὥρα, καὶ νῦν ἐστιν, ὅτε . . . (4:21, 23), are indicators of this eschatology. Likewise is Jesus' saying in the dialogue, ὅτι ἡ σωτηρία ἐκ τῶν 'Ιουδαίων ἐστίν (4:22), which presumes a salvation history that anticipates the coming of the Holy Spirit. It is through the eschatological giving of the Spirit that the Father τοιούτους ζητεῖ τοὺς προσκυνοῦντας αὐτόν (4:23). In this context worship ἐν πνεύματι καὶ ἀληθείᾳ is made possible by the gift of the Holy Spirit.[184]

Granted that ἐν πνεύματι signifies the heavenly and eschatological in worship, what does the additional καὶ ἀληθείᾳ say? In the view of some it totally reshapes the meaning of the phrase. Okure and E. D. Freed interpret the phrase with an ethical sense: the life quality of the worshiper, made proper by the Spirit, or right conduct in attitude and action as the essence of worship.[185] Freed argues for this by citing from the Qumran texts, where there is a parallel stress on spirit and truth, speaking of the shaping up of humanity's conduct in preparation for eschatological worship.[186] It is important to see that although there is such a parallel use, Jesus' revelation on the true worship of God goes beyond Qumran. Schnackenburg argues,

---

183 Schnackenburg, *John*, 1:439. For this reason I do not totally agree that "God is spirit" (4:24) is a parallel statement to "God is light" and "God is love" (1 John 1:5; 4:8). Commentators who draw this comparison include Carson (*John*, 225) and Beasley-Murray (*John*, 62).

184 Cf. Burge, "Worship in Spirit," section in *The Anointed Community*, 192–93.

185 Okure, *The Johannine Approach*, 116; E. D. Freed, "The Manner of Worship in John 4:23f," in *Search the Scriptures: NT Studies in Honor of R. T. Stamm*, ed. J. M. Myers, O. Reimherr and H. N. Bream (Leiden: E. J. Brill, 1969), 33–48.

186 1QS 4:20–21, quoted in Freed, "Manner," 40; and in Schnackenburg, *John*, 1:437–38, together with 1QS 3:6 ff.; 8:5–6; 1QH 16:11–12; 17:26; etc.

as follows, that the gospel's concept of worship revolves around Christ.

> This immediate, eschatological gift of the Spirit has come about through Jesus Christ. Hence true adoration in the Spirit is only possible in union with Christ. His glorified body is the holy temple of God (2:21); true worship is performed in him. To this extent, the ἐν πνεύματι of John is akin to the ἐν Χριστῷ of Paul.[187]

More boldly than Schnackenburg, many scholars interpret the phrase as if the second word, ἀληθεία, refers plainly to Christ.[188] For example, Burge considers the effect of it as "drawing in the christological stress." The strongest reason for this view is that ἀληθεία is typically applied to Christ in the gospel: 1:14, 17; 14:6; 15: 17, 26; 16:13; cf. 8:32.[189]

Without denying the definitive role of Christ in the eschatological worship ἐν πνεύματι καὶ ἀληθείᾳ, we must insist that the phrase itself refers mainly to "heavenly reality," with both nouns hinting at the reality of worship made possible by the Holy Spirit. 'Αηθείᾳ, in the Johannine sense, refers to the divine reality which Jesus reveals for his believers in this eschatological age. The two nouns are governed by the same preposition ἐν, and their closeness in meaning is commonly agreed upon. Schnackenburg says, for instance, "The pair of words, in which the emphasis is on πνεύματι, means the same thing in both of its elements."[190]

Furthermore, the construction of this phrase, which occurs twice but only in this passage, is distinct from the other uses of ἀληθεία in the gospel and thus calls for a separate rendering. Elsewhere the word may refer to Christ (1:14, 17; 8:32; 14:6), to the Spirit of Christ (14:17; 15:26; 16:13), or the word of God (17:17). Here it is used as a coordinate to reiterate ἐν πνεύματι. Its sense is therefore close to ἀληθινός which describes the heavenly worshipers (4:23).[191]

In the final exchange of the dialogue the speakers move right to the

---

187 Schnackenburg, *John*, 1:438.

188 Bultmann, *John*, 190–91; Barrett, *John*, 238; Burge, *The Anointed Community*, 193–94. Alternatively the word is linked with "knowledge" or "redemptive revelation," Carson, *John*, 225–26; Beasley-Murray, *John*, 62.

189 Burge argues that the hendiadys "spirit of truth" denotes the Spirit of Christ; see his discussion on this issue (*The Anointed Community*, 193–95).

190 Schnackenburg, *John*, 1:437; cf. Haenchen, *John*, 223.

191 J. P. Louw and E. A. Nida, eds., *Greek-English Lexicon of the New Testament Period: Based on Semantic Domains*, 2d ed., vol. 2, *Introduction and Domains* (New York: UBS, 1989), 667, pars. 70.3 and 70.4.

question of "who Jesus is." It is unsure how much the woman understood what Jesus had said about worship, but she was led to think of the Messiah: Οἶδα ὅτι Μεσσίας ἔρχεται . . . ὅταν ἔλθῃ ἐκεῖνος, ἀναγγελεῖ ἡμῖν ἅπαντα (4:25).[192] The dialogue ends with Jesus' final and personal revelation, Ἐγώ εἰμι, ὁ λαλῶν σοι (4:26). We know from the woman's reactions recorded later on in the account, μήτι οὗτός ἐστιν ὁ Χριστός (4:29), that she was at least partially convinced. The sudden but climactic ending of this dialogue implies that the misunderstanding had dissolved.

Summary and Conclusion

In the above discussion three major theses had been established regarding the interpretation of water symbolism in John 4, namely, the coherence of the first dialogue with "living water" as the main theme, the double dimension of symbolism in John 4, and the comprehensive meaning of the water symbol.

The Coherence of the First Dialogue

Two questions, posted right at the start, direct the rest of the conversation, "If you knew the gift of God and who it is that asks . . . ."(4:10a). The symbol of "living water" is at the same time introduced as a counterpart of the "gift of God" ("you would have asked him and he would have given you living water," 4:10b). This initial disclosure of who Jesus is prompted the woman to challenge the person, "Are you greater than our father Jacob?" (4:11–12)—a misunderstanding of who he is. Jesus then clarified his point by elaborating on the gift: "the water I give him will become in him a spring of water welling up to eternal life" (4:13–14). Another misunderstanding follows. This time, the woman misunderstood the gift ("give me this water, that I may not thirst, nor come here to draw," 4:15). By now Jesus had said all that was explicit about the "living water," but the woman had not understood its real meaning.

The specific mention of "living water" seems to stop here in the

---

192 Faith in Mount Gerizim as the chosen house of God, and faith in the Day of Vengeance and Retribution with the coming of the Taheb (Samaritan Messiah), are two among the five Samaritan creeds. They are also the two more distinctly Samaritan creeds. See Bowman, "Samaritan Studies," 310.

account, but the revelation of the symbolized truth has just begun.

Jesus' summons of her husband (4:16) leads to the disclosure of his omniscience as a divine person (4:17–18), which awakened the woman in thinking once more who Jesus was: "Sir, I can see that you are a prophet" (4:19). With this partial knowledge of Jesus' identity she raised the question of where the place of worship should be, a disputed issue between the Samaritans and the Jews: "on this mountain or in Jerusalem" (4:20).

This is, for Jesus, another way of asking what the "gift of God" is, and Jesus answered by talking about the "eschatological worship" of God, which is not defined by the place of worship (4:21). It is defined by the revelation received in the traditions of the Jews (4:22). This worship is not an earthly but a heavenly worship. The worshipers, called "true worshipers," are sought and enabled to worship by the Father himself (4:23). The manner of worship, "in spirit and truth," calls for the help of the Holy Spirit—part and parcel of God's eschatological gifts. It is here that the question of "what the gift is" gets answered. Our interpretation of "living water," the leading symbol of the passage, would not be complete without referring to the whole dialogue. Jesus' gift of "living water" includes the true worship in spirit, as well as God's creative and life-giving activity as Spirit in seeking for worshippers (4:24).

The woman might not have fully understood this revelation of Jesus', but she was prompted to get back to the other question, "I know that Messiah is coming . . . he will explain everything to us" (4:25). The dialogue ends with Jesus' climactic disclosure of his true identity, "I . . . am he" (4:26).

In this way the first dialogue is continuous and unbroken in relation to the full meaning of "living water."

The Double Dimension of Johannine Symbolism

I have argued in the previous chapter that the water symbol plays a double role in John 4. Water from the well symbolizes tradition, and water offered by Jesus symbolizes eschatological blessings. The structure of water symbolism thus formulated has an eschatological sense, and it extends throughout the gospel. If we represent eschatological symbolism as horizontal, then in our study above, we discovered a vertical dimension of Johannine water symbolism. In this, "living water" is offered as superior to "water from Jacob's well," and "true worshipers" is described as distinct from "worshipers on the mountain or in Jerusalem," just as the "true light" is proclaimed in the gospel over against "the world's darkness." This vertical symbolism can be detected in Jesus' discourse on worship, in which "true worshipers," "God is spirit" and "worship in spirit and truth" refer constantly to a heavenly reality.

This double symbolism is characteristic of John 4, and it characterizes the present eschatology of the gospel. It may in fact be explained by it. In John 4 this present eschatology is seen in Jesus' offering of the "living water" right where Jacob's well was, and in his talking about "heavenly worship" as a present reality in contrast to Gerizim and Jerusalem. Since much of Jesus' revelation was related in symbolic language, this present eschatology brings into our view a vertical dimension of symbolism. Heavenly gifts have now come down because of the incarnation and revelation of the eschatological Christ: the true light (1:9); the new temple (raised in three days, 2:19); the living water (4:10, 13–14); the heavenly bread (6:32–33).[193]

At the same time, in John 4 as elsewhere in the gospel, symbols of former traditions remind us of the promises and hope in salvation history. Jacob's well and the woman's water jar are such symbols, though the eschatology that Jesus endorsed in the episode was a Jewish eschatology (4:22). Thus, the horizontal and vertical dimensions of symbolism come together in John 4. Theological speaking, incarnation and salvation history converge here. The incarnated Son of God is also the eschatological giver of gifts. The Christ formerly anticipated has now come. The one who is heavenly and above is now revealed to us and is with us (cf. 1:18). What glorious truth expressed in Johannine symbolism: light, temple, water and bread, speaking of life and blessings given by Jesus, now and eternal (4:14).

The Comprehensiveness of the Water Symbol

Where salvation and incarnation converge, and Christ comes to bring fulfillment to eschatological hope, the Holy Spirit plays a significant role. It is told to us in John 4 that the Spirit comes at the eschatological hour to quicken life and worship. In Jesus' words, "the hour is coming and now is, when the true worshippers will worship the Father in spirit and truth, . . . God is spirit, and his worshipers must worship in spirit and in truth" (4:24).

193 Cf. Brown's discussion on the "vertical" and the "horizontal" aspects of God's salvific action, under "Eschatology" (*John*, 1:cxv).

This is also expressed symbolically as Jesus' offer of the "living water," which is said to "become a spring of water welling up to eternal life" (4:14; cf. 7:39). With these, "water" stands out as the leading symbol in John 4, and as a prime symbol in the gospel.

By virtue of the eschatological role of the Holy Spirit, the symbol is associated with all the salvific blessings that effectuate the quickening of life: rebirth, purification, joy, satisfaction analogous to the quenching of thirst, heavenly worship, eternal life. This life-giving activity of the Spirit is none other than the eschatological salvation of Christ which brings along multiple life blessings, or God's recreation of the world as if "bringing in a harvest." Therefore, "living water" entails the "eschatological harvest." The symbol gives expression to the work of the Spirit in a believer as "a spring of water welling up to eternal life," meaning, the believer's life in Christ is continuously quickened by the Spirit to live in a manner that complies with God's way—that entails participation in God's harvest of gathering people into his kingdom. Thus the symbols of "food" and "the harvest" point to the believer's obedience and participation in Christian mission, which is also part of the eschatological salvation—symbolized as "living water" in John 4.

CHAPTER FOUR

THE BIBLICAL THEOLOGICAL SIGNIFICANCE OF THE WATER MOTIF

A full interpretation of "water" in John and John 4 has to be sought not only by critical methods, but also by an open search for its canonical significance. In this chapter we will survey its use in the Old and New Testaments, and inspect the part it plays in biblical eschatology. This approach assumes continuity in biblical revelation, and two suppositions, related in earlier chapters, hint at this continuity. First, the foundation of Johannine symbolism lies in the Logos' creation and revelation, and its function is epistemological (see chapter one). The gospel itself, in its use of symbols, looks beyond mere history into theology. Second, the gospel shows an allegiance to the Old Testament and bears witness to the redemptive history recorded in it (see chapter two). In the life and words of Jesus the Christ, the Son of God (20:31), there is a salvation historical relation both backwards and forward. It leads from the incarnation of the Logos to the writing of the Old Testament on the one hand and to the community of the exalted one on the other.[1] This salvation historical relation will be the framework of our search for the theological significance of water symbolism in the Old and New Testaments.

It will be relevant to first look at scriptural references of the Gospel of John itself, to pave way for our biblical theological study of water symbolism.

The Characteristics of John' s Use of the Old Testament

John's use of the Old Testament as "citations" is not as conspicuous as the Synoptics', and that explains why it has not been well explored. There are, however, numerous "allusions" to the Old Testament in John, so

1 Cullmann, "Johanneische Gebrauch," 360.

that there is an overabundance of OT ideas. Barrett, Carson, M. Hengel and A. T. Hanson have given substantial introductions on the subject. To them partially we owe the following observations.[2]

The Arrangement of Citations

The first six of the thirteen direct quotations are generally introduced by γεγραμμένον (in 1:23 by ἔφη; in 2:17; 6;31; 6:45; 10:34; 12:14f. by γεγραμμένον). The latter seven are introduced by ἵνα . . . πληρωθῇ (in 12:38; 13:18; 15:25; 19:24; 19:36 by ἵνα . . . πληρωθῇ ; in 12:39f. and 19:37 the quotation is linked to the previous one πάλιν, forming double quotations). Hanson conjectures that citations introduced by ἵνα . . . πληρωθῇ came from messianic texts of the Old Testament commonly held by Christians, whereas the others were discovered by John himself.[3] More evident is that the clustering of "fulfillment" formulas has to do with the passion of Jesus and the obduracy motif in the double quotation at and following 12:39, which introduced the latter section of quotations.[4] The formula at 19:28, ἵνα τελειωθῇ ἡ γραφή, which does not introduce any quotation, marks the climax of this section.

> Only here in the entire Gospel does the Evangelist speak of a τελειοῦν of the Scriptures, an increase over the previous formulaic πληροῦν, which expresses the 'ultimate fulfillment' of all christological prophecy in the Scriptures, which in turn reach their goal in the death of Jesus. The Evangelist consciously placed this ἵνα τελειωθῇ ἡ γραφή between the twice-occurring τελέλεσται, Jesus' knowledge that the end had come in v. 28, and his death cry in v. 30.[5]

---

2 C. K. Barrett, "The Old Testament in the Fourth Gospel," *JTS* 48 (1947): 155–69; D. A. Carson, "John and the Johannine Epistles," in *It Is Written: Scripture Citing Scripture: Essays in Honour of Barnabas Lindars*, ed. D. A. Carson and H. G. M. Williamson (Cambridge: Cambridge University Press, 1988), 245–64; A. T. Hanson, "John's Use of Scripture," in *The Gospels and the Scriptures of Israel*, ed. C. A. Evans and W. R. Stegner, JSNTSup 104 (Sheffield: Sheffield Academic Press, 1994), 358–79; M. Hengel, "The Old Testament in the Fourth Gospel," in *The Gospels and the Scriptures of Israel*, ed. C. A. Evans and W. R. Stegner, JSNTSup 104 (Sheffield: Sheffield Academic Press, 1994), 380–95.

3 A. T. Hanson, *The Living Utterances of God* (London: Darton, Longman and Todd, 1983), 113ff., quoted in Carson, "John and the Johannine Epistles," 248.

4 C. A. Evans, "On the Quotation Formulas in the Fourth Gospel," *BZ* 26 (1982): 79–83.

5 Hengel, "The Old Testament in the Fourth Gospel," 393.

This has no obvious bearing on water symbolism, but two connections are significant. First, I have shown at the end of chapter two that the use of water symbolism in John ends with the flow of blood and water from Jesus' pierced side at the cross (19:34), and there also are the end points of the Passover theme and the OT fulfillment theme. Thus all these themes converge at the crucifixion of Jesus Christ. Second, it is not only the passion and the fulfillment themes that ends here, but God's work of creation and salvation, which begins with ἐν ἀρχῇ in Gen 1:1 and John 1:1, that comes to be τετέλεσται at this point, i.e., in the death of the Son. We should note, again with Hengel's help, that the gospel begins with ἐν ἀρχῇ, the very beginning, before the six days of creation, and Jesus dies in the evening of the sixth day of the week and thereby finishes God's work.[6] I suggest that these connections reveal the author's theological thinking, that the crucifixion is the climax; the OT scriptures anticipates salvation, and salvation and creation comes from the same source, Jesus Christ the Son. By "eschatology" we refer to the natural framework of all these, and "water," as a frequently used symbol in the formation of these themes, becomes a theme itself woven into the literature and thus contributes to the gospel's eschatology (cf. chapter two).

Therefore, although "water" never appears in any direct quotation in the gospel, we can still be sure of its biblical origin. Just as creation and salvation are biblical themes construed from the fulfillment of OT anticipations, "water" is a biblical theme evoked in the Gospel of John to be symbolic of this eschatology.

The Message

Four of the citations introduced by formulas are attributed to Jesus (6:45; 10:34; 13:18; 15:25), one to John the Baptist (1:23), and one to the crowd (6:31). The other seven are editorial, and two among them (2:17; 12:14f.) refer to the disciples as "remembering" scriptures. The two quotations, which are not introduced by any formula, 1:51 and 12:13, are

---

6 Ibid.; Hengel further substantiates this point with "a widespread Jewish haggadah," according to which "the first human couple was created on the sixth day, and at the tenth hour—about the time of Jesus' death—sinned," and thus "the Son 'finishes' the work of God's creation, which had been upset by human sin" (ibid., 394).

attributed respectively to Jesus and the crowd.[7]

It is significant that the citations are always christological, pointing to Jesus in one way or another. The Evangelist uses the Scriptures to show the identity of Jesus as Christ, to explain his acts as messianic, and to interpret the details of his life and death as being anticipated in the Old Testament. We may note, for example, that in the account of the crying of John the Baptist in the wilderness, "Make straight the way for the Lord!" (1:23), it is not just the action of the Baptist that is clarified, but his role as subservient to Jesus as the Christ. In the full context of the gospel's theology, it is also eschatology and salvation history that is presented in these citations (cf. 1:51). As Carson says, "the christology and eschatology of the Fourth Gospel can both be grounded in the Old Testament." [8]

John's citations of the Old Testament make a more focussed point than the Synoptics'. The point is that Jesus is the Christ and that he has brought in the eschatological age.[9] From the author's manner of composition, we know that he has given us only a sample of known citations. The impression we gather from the gospel is that all of the OT scriptures speak of Christ and ought to be interpreted christologically: "We have found the one Moses wrote about . . . whom the prophets also wrote" (1:45; 2:22; 3:10; 5:39, 45f.; 20:8f.). There are few parallels of these citations in the Synoptics, so Hengel talks about "the originality" of John's christological interpretation of scripture, as well as his scribal knowledge as a user of the Hebrew text and a corrector of Septuagintal formulations.[10]

A distinct feature in John's reference to the Old Testament is the part played by the post-resurrection remembering of events in Jesus' life. Based on this, Hengel suggests that John's christological interpretation is a Spirit-informed christology coming from the "messianic testimony of Scripture," which is a later development in early Christian exegesis, whereas there is a

---

7 See Carson, "John and the Johannine Epistles," 246.

8 Ibid., 246–47.

9 A good case can be made from this for the view that the Gospel was written for a missionary or evangelistic purpose. Carson, in considering John's use of the Old Testament, expresses preference for the theory that the Gospel is "designed primarily to evangelise diaspora Jews" (ibid., 258).

10 Hengel, "The Old Testament in the Fourth Gospel," 395. Regarding John's use of texts see G. Reim, *Studien zum alttestamentlichen Hintergrund des Johannesevangelium*, SNTSMS 22 (Cambridge: Cambridge University Press, 1974), 96; and Hanson, "John's Use of Scripture," 376.

charismatic and atomistic messianic interpretation in Matthew's, which comes from the "traditional Jesus-logia."[11] The divergence between the two gospels may not be as clear cut as Hengel suggests. Nevertheless John's remembrance motif discloses that there was a process of hermeneutical reflection going on during the apostolic age. There is a tension in the gospel, as Carson points out, between the presentation of christological interpretation as a moral obligation (e.g., 5:39f., 45f.) and the recognition that even the disciples came to understand it fully only after the resurrection (e.g., 2:22; 20:8f.).[12] Thus biblical theology was in the making. Jewish exegetical traditions formed the background and Christian apologetics made the breakthrough. In this process the Gospel of John is the most innovative among the gospels. A "Spirit-informed" model can be seen in John's use of the Old Testament for biblical interpretation and theology.

Special Johannine Use: Allusions and Themes

OT allusions and themes in John are countless and more than compensate the scarcity of OT citations. They constitute a significant part of John's OT interpretation, and account for its characteristic. Earlier works on OT allusions and themes in John were done by E. C. Hoskyns, C. K. Barrett and F.-M. Braun.[13] Fascinated by the complexity of the subject, Hoskyns drew many connections between the Old Testament and John's gospel. Barrett is influenced by Hoskyns's work in finding thematic allusions in the gospel to some "Synoptic Testimonia," which "have disappeared as Testimonia but which have been worked into the thematic structure of the Gospel."[14] His suggestion has not proved convincing. Among recent works only Olsson suggests at one point that the gospel may be viewed as a midrash on the gospel tradition, and that also receives very little attention.[15]

---

11 Hengel, "The Old Testament in the Fourth Gospel," 383, 391.

12 Carson, "John and the Johannine Epistles," 257, 259.

13 Hoskyns, *The Fourth Gospel*; Barrett, "The Old Testament in the Fourth Gospel"; F.-M. Braun, *Jean le théologien*, vol. 2, *Les grandes traditions d'Israël et l'accord des écritures selon le quatrième évangile* (Paris: J. Gabalda, 1964).

14 Barrett, "The Old Testament in the Fourth Gospel," 157; and 155, citing Hoskyn, *The Fourth Gospel*, 69–87.

15 Olsson, *Structure and Meaning*, 284–85, quoted in Hanson, "John's Use of Scripture," 361.

Barrett singles out three "allusions," in 1:29; 7:37f. and 19:36, which he calls "cruxes." I think these passages actually represent three different ways in making reference to the Old Testament. First, "the lamb of God" in 1:29 may be called an OT theme.

> Here, a single theme, used in the O.T. several times and in different ways, is brought out once in the special form demanded by its special context in the ministry of Jesus; light as it were, from numerous O.T. sources is brought to a focus on that unique point.[16]

"The lamb of God" (1:29–31) is certainly not the only OT theme in John. Other major ones include "the shepherd" (1:1–16) and "the vine" (15:1–8). The second of the cruxes is found in 7:37f., in which the words of Jesus form an "allusion" to the Old Testament. There is no explicit quotation here, but the introduction formula in 7:38, καθὼς εἶπεν ἡ γραφή, indicates that they refer to the Old Testament. Unspecified quotations such as this are found only in 7:38, 42; 17:12 and 19:28, but allusions can be many more. Since allusions do not match with OT passages as citations are, and one allusion can refer to more than one OT passage at the same time, the boundary of this category is hard to define. Hanson even conjectures that "on the basis of Scripture John may shape his narratives or introduce episodes or pieces of teaching that have no basis in history."[17] The third crux, which Barrett calls an allusion, is found in 19:36, and it is a citation of three OT passages introduced by one fulfillment formula.

Thus, the three cruxes pointed out by Barrett, all of which he calls allusions, actually represent three main categories of John's reference to the Old Testament: citations (19:36), allusions (7:37f.), and the use of OT themes (1:29). "The use of the O.T. in the Fourth Gospel is not a simple matter," Barrett concludes. Later scholars owe it to him to see that "the evangelist does not rely mainly on quotations and proof-texts, but he has, so to speak, absorbed the whole of the Old Testament into his system."[18]

---

16 Barrett, "The Old Testament in the Fourth Gospel," 165.

17 Hanson, "John's Use of Scripture," 367; cf. A. T. Hanson, *The Prophetic Gospel: A Study of John and the Old Testament* (Edinburgh: T. & T. Clark, 1991), 21–233; *The New Testament Interpretation of Scripture* (London: SPCK, 1980), 166–71, quoted in "John's Use of Scripture," 370.

18 T. F. Glasson, *Moses in the Fourth Gospel*, SBT 1/40 (London: SCM, 1963), 36, n. 1, quoted in Hanson, "John's Use of Scripture," 373.

Although "water" never appears in John's explicit citations, it plays a definite role in John's allusions to the Old Testament (cf. 7:37f.), and is itself a dominant OT theme (cf. John 4). It is in line with John's use of the Old Testament, therefore, to pursue the significance of Johannine water symbolism in biblical theology.

Interpretive Method: Salvation History

The next question is on John's method of interpretation: what are John's appropriation techniques and hermeneutical axioms? There are two main approaches to the question, respectively of historian and theologian interests. Historians might be satisfied with locating John's techniques along Jewish exegetical traditions: midrash, midrashic haggada, or targum.[19] Attempts of this sort have not produced impressive results. Even if targumic methods are used in the gospel, "that is not the same thing as saying that the Gospel is a targum," as says Hanson. It is likely that John's appropriation techniques bear similarities to Judaistic methods. John could have re-oriented the text or modified the point of application as Jewish exegetes did, but, it is important to note that John's hermeneutical axioms or interpretive goals remain distinctly Christian.[20] As shown above, his citations have the focussed purpose of witnessing for Jesus and proclaiming the coming of the eschatological age. It is likewise so with John's use of water symbolism. Whenever "water" alludes to the Old Testament, a christological point is made in one way or another, and the perspective is always eschatological. It is John's theological or interpretive goals that are distinctive rather than his appropriation techniques.

The other approach to John's interpretation is that of typology, a theological reading of the Old Testament which treats the account as "salvation history." This has been considered a dominant approach in John,

---

19 R. Bloch, "Midrash," in *Approaches to Ancient Judaism*, ed. W. S. Green (Missoula, MT: Scholars Press, 1978), 29–50; M. Black, *An Aramaic Approach to the Gospels and Acts* (Oxford: Clarendon Press, 1967), 151; quoted in Hanson, "John's Use of Scripture," 358–61.

20 D. J. Moo, *The Old Testament in the Gospel Passion Narratives* (Sheffield: The Almond Press, 1983), 374–81; Carson, "John and the Johannine Epistles," 249; cf. Hanson, "John's Use of Scripture," 364.

and is defined by Carson as follows.

> At the risk of oversimplification . . . typology . . . is itself based on a perception of patterns of continuity across the sweep of salvation history. The Davidic typology that surfaces repeatedly in the NT may well stand behind some of the Psalm quotations in the FG . . . [21]

Salvation history is also a Judaistic understanding. In interpreting "truth" in John 1:17 as a typological term, C. van der Waal comments on a sermon by Melito of Sardes dated back to before A.D. 190.

> Melito frequently mentions the term *aletheia*. But he certainly does not do this in a platonic way. According to Plato the idea is the truth, its earthly shadows being a weak, unreal depiction only. In Melito's sermon things are *totaliter aliter*. He brings the *history of salvation* into account. This history of salvation contains not only the prefiguration, the *tupos*, but also the fulfilment or realization of this *tupos*. Melito, then, calls the latter: *aletheia*.[22]

The concept of salvation history, which contains promises and fulfillment, as well as types and truths, was fundamental to Jewish thinking, and I suggest that it provides the best model for understanding allusions and themes in John. If John's interpretation is not atomistic but "has the whole of the Old Testament absorbed into his system," then the system is found in salvation history, not in midrashic or targumic writing. A theologically minded writer like that of the Gospel of John could not have used allusions and themes without a theological reading of the scriptures. Hanson explains as follows:

> By salvation history I mean the belief that God's dealings with his people . . . should be regarded as a history of salvation; and that therefore one may expect a certain pattern in God's dealings . . . which will be reflected in what happens in the messianic age. In this sense John's exegesis of Scripture is not atomistic: he is not content to cite or echo individual texts from Scripture, isolated from their context. . . . Scripture was being fulfilled . . . against the background of the saving events of the old dispensation . . .[23]

This will be the approach we take as we relate Johannine water symbolism to its canonical context.

---

21 Carson, "John and the Johannine Epistles," 249.

22 C. van der Waal, "The Gospel According to John and the Old Testament," *Neot* 6 (1972): 28–47.

23 Hanson, "John's Use of Scripture," 365.

A "Creational Typology"

Typology can be a fuzzy system that refuses delimitation. Different attempts have been made and some are more restrictive than others. Most of the earlier attempts on the typologies of John, which focus on its Exodus theme, have not won approval.[24] G. Reim, the learned writer on the OT background of John, criticizes a number of them as "over-valuation."[25] The study of typology nevertheless is popular, and Reim himself agrees with the use of a couple of typologies in John.[26] Examples of typological reference can be found in articles written by Carson and Hanson on John's use of the Old Testament.[27]

We will take a further step here to demonstrate the uniqueness of John's typology in relation to creation and incarnation. It is a typology characterized by, so to speak, a vertical dualism. John's association of salvation with creation can be seen right from the start of the Gospel: Ἐν ἀρχῇ in John 1:1 alludes to Gen 1:1, and John 1:3ff., πάντα δι' αὐτοῦ ἐγένετο. . . , declares that ὁ λόγος is the creator. I have shown, in chapter two, that John has intricately made various themes in the gospel converge at a consummation point at crucifixion. Hengel also makes a similar observation, that in John both creation and salvation come from the same source, Jesus Christ the Son, and all was then brought to completion at the cross.[28] This is the basic theological formulation of the gospel reflected also in John's typology.

The uniqueness of this typology may be partially explained by the original style of the gospel. As it is well known, typology is overt in the Book of Hebrews. It is less so in Paul's writings but still explicitly developed. The allusions are concealed in the Synoptics and even more carefully hidden in the Gospel of John. L. Goppelt properly points out, "Rather than balanced

24 H. Sahlin, *Zur Typologie des Johannesevangeliums* (Uppsala: Almquist & Wiksell, 1950), 5; J. J. Enz, "The Book of Exodus as a Literary Type for the Gospel of John," *JBL* 76 (1957): 208–15; G. Ziener, "Weisheitsbuck und Johannesevangelium," *Bib* 38 (1957): 396–418, and 39 (1958): 37–60; R. H. Smith, "Exodus Typology in the Fourth Gospel," *JBL* 81 (1962): 329–42.

25 Reim, *Studien*, 262–66. Cf. Hanson, "John's Use of Scripture," 363–64.

26 Ibid., 266–68.

27 Carson, "John and the Johannine Epistles," 249–50; Hanson, "John's Use of Scripture," 363–64.

28 Hengel, "The Old Testament in the Fourth Gospel," 393.

individual typologies, we find continuous indications of a comprehensive typological approach in terms of creation typology. These types, however, frequently shade over into typological symbolism."[29]

While it is right for Goppelt to associate explicit typology with direct quotations in Hebrews and the writings of Paul, and the allusive typology of John with symbolism, he seems to be too rigid in defining typology as historical, and is, therefore, partial in evaluating the typology in John.

> the typology is diminished in extent and in form. Christ is still compared with the saviors of the OT, but he is presented exclusively as their Lord, and no longer as their antitype . . .
>
> The special character of the typology in John is not the result of any lesser regard for the OT nor of a different theological position on this matter; it is the result of a different point of view.[30]

Goppelt has to say that "typology" is diminished in John because elsewhere in the New Testament typology is monopolized by a horizontal comparison between types and antitypes. In John, the Christ is exalted, and this effects what Goppelt calls "a different point of view" on typology. This point of view is actually a vertical perspective on creation, incarnation and salvation. In this the creator is seen as descending from heaven to earth to become a savior. This vertical perspective sets John free from the traditional typology, which is characterized by a horizontal relationship between types and antitypes and by "balanced individual typologies," as Goppelt describes. In connection with this, let me reiterate that I have previously, in chapter three, expound the idea of "double symbolism" in the use of ὕδωρ ζῶν in John 4, and claimed that in John 4 this double symbolism incurs a vertical contrast between the heavenly worship and the earthly worship. The vertical dimension of this double symbolism is exactly the perspective that accounts for the uniqueness of John's characteristic typology. Just as there is a vertical dimension to John's symbolism, there is a vertical dimension in his typological thinking.

Thus Goppelt is aware of the fact that "types have arisen in two interrelated categories," and that "the basic orientation of this gospel accounts for the fact that Jesus' work moves exclusively on the level of

---

29 L. Goppelt, *Typos: The Typological Interpretation of the Old Testament in the New*, trans. D. H. Madvig (Grand Rapids: Eerdmans, 1982), 181.

30 Ibid., 194.

creation typology."[31] Here I do not totally agree with Goppelt in considering John's creation typology "exclusive" in that Christ is compared with OT saviors only as Lord and not antitype. Goppelt is saying that "water" and "bread" and "light" are types of Christ in John whereas mediators of salvation, such as Abraham and Moses, are not. In Goppelt's thinking there is earthly water and heavenly water, but Christ cannot be a "heavenly Abraham."[32] I think, instead, that we should take a broader view of typology, to see that there is a typological relation between Abraham and Christ that remains horizontal, so that John's typology is not exclusively creational, but both horizontal and vertical. Abraham and Moses are horizontal types of Christ whereas the symbol of water speaks of a type of the creational order.

Goppelt's suggestion of creation typology maps out the vertical dimension of John's typology, which is also a characteristic of the use of water symbolism in the gospel. Furthermore, because symbols are often used in this creation typology, Goppelt also coins the term, "typological symbolism," saying, "these types frequently shade over into typological symbolism."[33]

Thus John's typology opens up avenues for our biblical theological study on the significance of water symbolism.

Old Testament Perspectives

Following is an evaluation of the significance of water in various sections of the Old Testament, beginning with the Pentateuch, then through the Historical Books, the Psalms, the Writings, and the Prophets. Reim's study on John's OT allusions and motifs goes more or less in the same order, except that he groups the Writings with the Apocrypha, where the use of "water" is negligent.[34] Here we will not deal with the Apocrypha,

---

31 Ibid., 181; 180.

32 There is a general failure in appreciating John's vertical and dual perspective. In Hanson's defense for John's use of typology, in response to Reim's denial, "No doubt what he [Reim] means is that John is more likely to represent Jesus as superseding in his own person some person or object in the Old Testament than to present that person or object as a type of Christ" (Hanson, "John's Use of Scripture," 362).

33 Ibid., 181.

34 Reim, *Studien*, vii.

but work only on canonical writings.[35]

The Pentateuch

We can hardly overstate the theological significance of "water" found in the Pentateuch. Most of the later theological use of "water" originates from here.

At creation. In Gen 1:2, "the waters" refers to the primeval waters, representing all that there was in the universe over which the Spirit of God hovered, through the six days of God's work of creation. Here I take the view that Gen 1:1 is a main clause in the Hebrew text describing the first act of creation which resulted in "the heavens" and "the earth," and, that the passage Gen 1:2ff. describes the subsequent phases of creation, the structuring of the earth and the formation of the visible universe. The Gospel of John alludes to the creation account as it begins with 'Εν ἀρχῇ ἦν ὁ λόγος. We must also note that the symbolic reference of "water" to "the Spirit" is well attested in the gospel. Here in Gen 1:2, "God's Spirit hovering over the waters" forms a "water-spirit" imagery which we may refer to in contemplation of the OT connection of the Johannine water symbol. It is not unreasonable to say that in John, because of the way the Old Testament is referred to, imagery like this carries more import than mere citations. We must, from the start, contemplate a creational model for John's typology and symbolism that looks for imagery rather than words, analogy rather than verbal agreement.

On the second day of creation (Gen 1:6–7), "the waters" under and above the expanse were separated, thus the heavenly waters became the sky, the visible heavens, and the earthly waters became the land and the seas which, on the third day of creation (Gen 1:9–10), were further separated. The extensive use of the term "waters" in the creation account is a prelude to the extensive use of "water" in biblical language. It helps us visualize the significance of water in the visible universe: when the land was further made to produce vegetation (Gen 1:11–12), it was "watered" (Gen 2:5–6).

35 F. Manns points out, in his work on "water-spirit," that the non-existence of the symbol in the Apocrypha was caused by an expectation of God's direct intervention, which "excluded all intermediary," thus "wisdom" featured as a theme rather than "water" or "spirit" (*Le symbole*, 299).

This is further carried over to another water imagery, that of Eden: "Now the Lord God had planted a garden in the east, in Eden; . . . made all kinds of trees grow out of the ground. . . . A river watering the garden flowed from Eden; from there it was separated into four headwaters . . ." (Gen 2:8–14). Though the Gospel of John makes no direct mention of this Garden of Eden, the idea of fertility and abundance lies behind some of its use of "water." The water rituals at Tabernacles referred to in John 7 hint at fertility and abundance, as "water coming out of the temple" is analogous to "water coming out of Eden." Further on we will see a similar use in Ezek 47:1–12. The recurrence of this imagery speaks of a "paradise theme," a "temple theme," or a "tabernacle theme" in the biblical literature. John's use of "water" is not customarily related to these creational sayings if we look for only citations, but on the basis of John's reference to Gen 1:1 and his unique use of OT allusions and themes, we should allow for connections between the creation imagery and Johannine symbolism.

After the Fall. After the fall there is no more mention of the "water" in the Edenic picture which flowed out to irrigate the earth cultivated by humankind. Instead, "flood" arose to destroy the land and humankind. In Jewish literature and early Christian literature, the "flood" imagery and God's rescue of Noah are classic illustrations of divine judgement and the deliverance of the righteous. Subsequent to the flood, history of the patriarchs demonstrates a basic need for water as life sustenance (Gen 21:15–19). Settlement began with the digging of wells (Gen 26:18–19, 32–33). Communal life revolved around the drawing of water (cf. the so-called betrothal meetings, Exod 2; Gen 24; Gen 29). As a mundane item in life, "water" is not featured at this point as a promise of salvation, as is "milk and honey" (Exod 3:8, 17). Yet the abundance of water is a mark of blessings (Num 24:7), and the later division of sea waters at Exodus means salvation (Exod 13–14; cf. Josh 3–4).

In the events of the Exodus, the need for water became a test of faith. The rebellion of God's people in the wilderness found expression in the complaint of the lack of water, as of food, e.g., at Marah (Exod 15:22–27), Meribah (Num 20:1–13; cf. 21:4–9) and Rephidim (Exod 17:1–6; Num 33:14). The theological significance of these "water events" is given in Deuteronomy: it is part of salvation to be tested, to be humbled and to be taught to remember the Lord of salvation.

> Remember how the Lord your God led you all the way . . . to humbled you and

> to test you. . . . For the Lord your God is bringing you into a good land—a land with streams and pools of water, with springs flowing in the valleys and hills; a land with wheat and barley . . . he led you through the vast and dreadful desert, that thirsty and waterless land, with its venomous snakes and scorpions. He brought you water out of hard rock. He gave you manna to eat in the desert . . . to humble and to test you so that in the end it might go well with you. . . (Deut 8)

Note how the Deuteronomist describes the land not as a land of "milk and honey," but as one "with streams and pools of water, with springs flowing in the valleys and hills" (Deut 8:7). The wilderness experience has evidently turned "water" into a symbol of divine provision and salvation. Another symbolic use of "water" is about to emerge at this point, namely, the representation of "the word of the Lord." This can be seen in the Deuteronomist's juxtaposition of "bread," the counterpart of "water," with "every word of the Lord" in this instruction for obedience: "He humbled you . . . to teach you that man does not live on bread alone but on every word that comes from the mouth of the Lord" (8:3).

Besides this incipient use of water as a main symbol, there is also formation of OT motifs in these biblical accounts, motifs such as the Exodus, the wilderness, the rebellion of God's people, and the imagery of "the rock," "the manna," "the springs," and "the snake." The way they all reappear in the Gospel of John shows that they are used as biblical theological language in referring to God's salvation.

With the Mosaic law. Water is specified in some of the ritual laws as the element used for ritual washing. It is used in the washing of the inner parts of animals for offering (Lev 1:9, 12; 8:21) and the rinsing of ceremonial vessels (Lev 6:28). In the Mosaic law, there is an initial use of water for personal purification. For Levites specifically, the law says, "To purify them, do this: Sprinkle the water of cleansing on them; then have them shave their whole bodies and wash their clothes, and so purify themselves" (Num 8:7). In another law, the use of "running water" is designated for the cleansing of uncleanness (Lev 15:13). These establish a longstanding association of water with cleansing in the Israelite religion.

Although these cleansing rituals are not specifically mentioned in the Gospel of John, they are significant to John in two ways. First, as part of "the law that was given through Moses," they are juxtaposed with "the grace and truth that came through Jesus Christ" (John 1:17). As I previously pointed out, in the initial chapters of John there is juxtaposition of Jesus' blessings with traditional rites, in which the water symbol repeatedly plays a major role. Traditional rites at Jesus' time included ceremonial cleansing, such as baptism, daily cleansing activities, and cleansing prior to temple worship. These rites had roots in the Mosaic law, but according to the Gospel of John, Jesus was the true fulfillment. Second, there is a subtle but worth noting reference in John to the cleansing rituals recorded in the book of Numbers. In the recording of the flow of blood and water from Jesus' pierced side (John 19:34) there is an allusion to the following passage.

> The Lord said to Moses and Aaron: 'This is a requirement of the law that the Lord has commanded: Tell the Israelites to bring you a red heifer without defect or blemish and that has never been under a yoke. Give it to Eleazar the priest; *it is to be taken outside the camp and slaughtered* in his presence.' Then Eleazar the priest is to take some of its blood on his finger and sprinkle it seven times toward the front of the Tent of Meeting.[36] While he watches, the heifer is *to be burned—its hide, flesh, blood and offal*. . . . gather up the ashes of the heifer and put them in a ceremonially clean place *outside the camp*.[37] They shall be kept . . . *for use in the water of cleansing*; it is for purification from sin. . . . put some ashes from the burned purification offering into a jar and pour fresh water over them . . . (Num 19:1ff., italics mine).

Related to the piercing of Jesus' side there is a fulfillment passage cited in John 19:36, Ὀστοῦν οὐ συντριβήσεται αὐτοῦ, which expressly points to the role of Jesus as the unblemished Passover lamb, the means of salvation. Besides this, there is also a cleansing role of Jesus, comparable and superior to that of a red heifer that is implied in the gospel. In Num 19 "water," together with "blood"—burned to form ashes, is designated the means of purification from sin. The passage is alluded to in two recorded details of

---

36 The blood of a red heifer was considered "the ritual detergent *par excellence*, which will remove impurity from those contaminated by contact with corpses"; see J. Milgrom, *Numbers: The Traditional Hebrew Text with the New JPS Translation*, The JPS Torah Commentary (Philadelphia: The Jewish Publication Society, 1990), 159. For the symbolic meaning of cleanness and uncleanness, see V. S. Poythress, *The Shadow of Christ in the Law of Moses* (New Jersey: Presbyterian and Reformed Publishing Co., 1991), 81–82.

37 Cf. other purification offerings, Exod 29:14; Lev 4:11; 8:17; 16:27. The blood is burnt because it is the primary agent for the cleansing function and can give the ashes a powerful cleansing effect; see T. R. Ashley, *The Books of Numbers*, NICOT (Grand Rapids: Eerdmans, 1993), 365. According to the rabbis, after the sprinkling, the high priest wiped his hands on the carcases to assure that not a single drop of blood was wasted; see Milgrom, *Numbers*, 159.

the crucifixion: Jesus' death "near" but "outside the city" (19:20; cf. 19:17) and the flow of "blood and water" from his body. This "implicit fulfillment" of the Mosaic law tells of the effectiveness of Jesus' death in sin purification.

The Historical Books, the Psalms, and Others

The theme of "water" is meager here in comparison with what we have seen in the Pentateuch. There is nevertheless some connection between the "water" here and the use of "water" in John.

The historical books. Most noteworthy are the "water miracles" that Elisha performed during the time of the divided kingdoms. In 2 Kgs 2:19–22, Elisha is said to have cured the water of the city Jericho. In 2 Kgs 3:9–20 he is said to perform a miracle to provide water for the army of Judah, Israel and Edom. His oracle, which announced the miracle, says, "This is what the Lord says: Make this valley full of ditches. For this is what the Lord says: You will see neither wind nor rain, yet this valley will be filled with water, and you, your cattle and your other animals will drink . . . " (2 Kgs 3:15–17). The well of Jacob, mentioned in John 4 as the well from which "Jacob and his sons and his flocks and herds drank," was traditionally connected to Num 21:16–20, where a well have allegedly been given to God's people through Moses. There might also be an allusion to 2 Kgs 2:9–20 in the presentation of Jesus as the giver of the living water in John 4, and, as the one who promised the flow of "streams of living water" at Tabernacles, at the traditional "rainfall ceremony."

Reim points out an allusion in John 9:7 to 2 Kgs 5:10, which also records a miracle of Elisha's.[38] The washing of Naaman was to be done, seven times, in the Jordan, whereas the blind man that Jesus healed was to wash his eyes in the Pool of Σιλωάμ. The idea is that the waters of Israel have healing power and that power is to be realized in Jesus, "the Sent One."[39]

Finally, the Israelites' drawing and pouring of water before the Lord during the Mizpah repentance signifies ritual cleansing (1 Sam 7:6). It may, alternatively, be an expression of deep repentance.[40]

---

38 Reim, *Studien*, 157.

39 Cf. John 5:2, which may allude to Neh 3:1 as Jewish traditions suggest; see Reim, *Studien*, 159.

40 Manns, *Le symbole*, 48.

The Psalms. Psalms is a major source of John's OT citations, but none of the citations from Psalms has to do with the theme of "water."[41] "Water" is mentioned in various ways in the Psalms, e.g., for figurative use (Ps 1:3; 58:7; 63:1; 109:18), for the description of nature as the powerful presence of God (Ps 18:11; 65:9; 77:17), or being referred to as part of the Exodus history (Pss 78–105; 114).

In the historical psalms the wilderness theme and the "rock" image often appear along with the water symbol.

In Ps 46:4 a river imagery harks back to the paradise imagery of Gen 2:8–14 in which water comes out of Eden: "There is a river whose streams make glad the city of God, the holy place where the Most High dwells."

Most obvious is the allusion of John 4:14 to Ps 36, where "the fountain of life" describes the abundance of the Lord.

> Your love, O Lord, reaches to the heavens, how faithfulness to the skies.
> Your righteousness is like the mighty mountains, your justice like the great deep.
> O Lord, you preserve both man and beast. How priceless is your unfailing love!
> Both high and low among men find refuge in the shadow of your wings.
> They feast on the abundance of your house; you give them drink from your river of delights.
> For in you is the fountain of life; in your light we see light (Ps 36:5–9).

Out of the seventeen allusions that Reim lists this is the only allusion to Psalms in John that has connection with the "water" theme.[42]

Other Writings. In the psalm quoted above, "fountain" is the imagery featured, instead of "water." There are also a good number of passages in Proverbs that feature "fountain" as the major imagery. Examples are found in Prov 10:11, "the mouth of the righteous is a fountain of life, but violence overwhelms the mouth of the wicked"; Prov 13:14, "the teaching of the wise is a fountain of life, turning a man from the snares of death"; Prov 14:27, "the fear of the Lord is a fountain of life, turning a man from the snares of death"; Prov 16:22, "understanding is a fountain of life to those who have it, but folly brings punishment to fools"; and Prov 18:4, "the

---

41 Ps 69:9, quoted in John 2:17; Ps 78:24, quoted in John 6:31; Ps 82:6, quoted in John 10:34; Ps 62:11, quoted in John 12:14f.; Ps 35:19 and 69:5, quoted in John 15:25; Ps 22:18, quoted in John 19:24; Ps 34:21, quoted in John 19:36.

42 Reim, *Studien*, 160.

words of a man's mouth are deep waters, but the fountain of wisdom is a bubbling brook."

This almost massive reference to "wisdom" as "the fountain of life" depicts an outlook found in the wisdom tradition, namely, "water" is related to "God's wisdom."[43] Brown appeals to the wisdom writings in his interpretation of John 4:14 for a confirmation of the idea that "living water" means "God's wisdom that grants life." He specifically cites Sir 24:21, in which "Wisdom" sings her own praises: "He who eats of me will hunger still; he who drinks of me will thirst for more."[44] The text that Brown cites shows literary parallelism to the text in John 4:14, but considering the many OT allusions there are in John, it is an oversimplification to limit the meaning of "water" to "wisdom" just because there might have been literary borrowing from Sir 24:21. It is more appropriate to view "wisdom" as one of the items that constitute the "abundance of the Lord" as Ps 36 depicts.

It is probably in continuity with the wisdom tradition that the rabbinic literature identified "wisdom" with the Torah, and derived a popular allegorical use of "water" that refers to the Torah.[45]

The Prophets

In the prophetic books there is a great advance in the symbolic meaning of "water." The word itself is used more extensively than in the corpuses previously discussed, used either figuratively or as the major component of a vision. It appears most frequently in Isaiah and Ezekiel, though it is not just the frequency of use that make it importance. It is in the prophetic books that the water symbol takes on an eschatological reference to the Spirit.

Rebellion and salvation. The exile is like a wilderness experience repeated. The water imagery, representing the nation's trial in the wilderness and the Lord's gift of salvation, now depicts the nation's rebellion prior to the exile, and afflictions because of the Lord's punishment.

> Your silver has become dross, your choice wine is diluted with water (Isa 1:22).

---

43 Hellenistic Judaism also has a tradition of associating the theme of "water" with wisdom; see Manns, *Le symbole*, 137–74.

44 Brown, *John*, 1:178.

45 Sir 24:23–29 continues to depict how the Torah fills people with wisdom like rivers overflowing their banks, ibid.; cf. Manns, *Le symbole*, 303.

> As a well pours out its water, so she [Jerusalem] pours out her wickedness (Jer 6:7).
>
> See now, the Lord . . . is about to take from Jerusalem and Judah both supply and support: all supplies of food and all supplies of water (Isa 3:1).
>
> By a mere rebuke I dry up the sea, I turn rivers into a desert; their fish rot for lack of water and die of thirst (Isa 50:2).
>
> See, I will make this people eat bitter food and drink poisoned water (Jer 9:15).
>
> The nobles send their servants for water; they go to the cisterns but find no water (Jer 14:3).
>
> Judah's leaders are like those who move boundary stones. I will pour out my wrath on them like a flood of water (Hos 5:10).

In the prophetic books there is also a continuation of the "wisdom" motif, for which "water" stands for the Lord's word, i.e., law, or will. In this respect Jeremiah does use the "fountain" image, though for only a couple of times.

> My people have committed two sins: They have forsaken me, the spring of living water, and have dug their own cisterns, broken cisterns that cannot hold water (Jer 2:13; cf. Jer 17:13).
>
> The days are coming, declares the Sovereign Lord, when I will send a famine through the land—not a famine of food or a thirst for water, but a famine of hearing the words of the Lord (Amos 8:11).

There is also a theme of "thirst" in these writings, as Braun suggests.[46] This theme shows that the prophets go beyond the Deuteronomist in understanding historical events as trials. They are able to see the brighter side of the Lord's discipline and anticipate his salvation. The same metaphor of "garden and water" is thus used in opposite ways.

> You [the rebellious] will be like an oak with fading leaves, like a garden without water (Isa 1:30).
>
> The Lord will guide you [the contrite] always; he will satisfy your needs in a sun-scorched land and will strengthen your frame. You will be like a well-watered garden, like a spring whose waters never fail (Isa 58:11).

Against this background we have "water passages" in the prophetic

46 "Dans la mentalité hébraïque, toute imprégnée des souvenirs du désert, avoir soif est autre chose qu'un malaise passager. . . . Ex 17,1–4; Os 2,5; Am 4,8; Is 5,13; Is 29,8. Il serait aisé d'allonger cette liste. Encore faut-il se rappeler que le symbole importe plus que la réalité physique," F.-M. Braun, "Avoir soif et boire (Jn 4,10–14; 7,37–39)," in *Mélanges bibliques en hommage au R P Béda Rigaux*, ed. A. Descamps and A. Halleux (Gembloux: Duculot, 1970), 247–58.

books which distinctly speak of salvation. It is significant that the "living water" passage in John 4:14 shows affinities with two major passages of this kind, both of them in Isaiah.

> With joy you will draw water from the well of salvation (Isa 12:3).
>
> Come, all you who are thirsty, come to the waters; and you who have no money, come, buy and eat! Come, buy wine and milk without money and without cost (Isa 55:1).[47]

"*The eschatological Spirit.*" Note that in Isa 55:1 all "water," "wine," and "milk" enter the scene. The combined imagery occurs also in Joel in the long oracle which prophesies the coming of the eschatological "day of the Lord," and, specifically, the outpour of the Spirit.

> And afterward, *I will pour out my Spirit on all people.*
>
> Your sons and daughters will prophesy, your old men will dream dreams, your young men will see visions.
>
> Even on my servants, both men and women, I will pour out my Spirit in those days (Joel 2:28–29).
>
> . . . .
>
> Then you will know that I, the Lord your God, dwell in Zion, my holy hill.
>
> Jerusalem will be holy; never again will foreigners invade her.
>
> In that day the mountains will drip new wine, and the hills will flow with milk; all the ravines of Judah will run with water.
>
> *A fountain will flow out of the Lord's house* (3:17–18).

This is one of the prophetic passages in the Old Testament in which the announcing of the eschatological Spirit is placed alongside a "water passage" that depicts the abundant blessings of that eschatological day. Another one of these may be found in Isa 32:15–20.

> *Till the Spirit is poured upon us from on high, and the desert becomes a fertile field*, and the fertile field seems like a forest (v. 15).
>
> Justice will dwell in the desert and righteousness live in the fertile field (v. 16).
>
> The fruit of righteousness will be peace; the effect of righteousness will be quietness and confidence forever (v. 17).
>
> My people will live in peaceful dwelling places, in secure homes, in undisturbed places of rest (v. 18).
>
> Though hail flattens the forest and the city is leveled completely (v. 19),

---

47 In variance to Brown's suggestion of a "wisdom" background, these are two of the passages which are more likely behind John 4:14. Others include Ps 36:9, as mentioned above. See, e.g., Lindars, *John*, 183.

> *How blessed you will be, sowing your seed by every stream*, and letting your cattle and donkeys range free (v. 20).

F. Manns, in his work on *Le symbole eau-Esprit dans le judaisme ancien*, locates the above passage as where the symbol of water might have been first used by a prophet to stand for the Spirit.[48] Convinced or not, one must take note of his argument. The literary structure of both passages, quoted above, can be understood as chiastic. In Joel 2:28–3:18 the chiasm is an ABCB′A′ arrangement.[49]

> Restoration by the Spirit (2:28–29)
> The Day of the Lord (2:30–32)
> Judgment of the Nations (3:1–13)
> The Day of the Lord (3:14–16)
> Restoration with Blessings (3:17–18)

In Isa 32:15–20 the oracle begins and ends with the theme of "fertility" (vv. 15–16, 19–20), and at the center is "justice" and "peace" (vv. 17–18). Manns calls it a concentric structure.[50] In either case, "the Spirit" which appears in the first line of the structure can be said to correspond closely with "water," or "fountain" or "stream," which appears in the last line.

In the above passages the Spirit is presented as just one among other eschatological blessings, though the preeminent one. In Isa 44:3–4, however, it is singled out, and the symbolic reference of "water" to the Spirit becomes evident.

> For I will *pour water* on the thirsty land, and streams on the dry ground;
> I will *pour out my Spirit* on your offspring, and my blessing on your descendants.
> They will spring up like grass in a meadow,
> Like poplar trees by flowing streams (Isa 44:3–4).

This succinct but picturesque presentation of "water" as "God's Spirit" establishes a powerful symbolism that harks back to both God's creation and salvation activities. The dual imagery of water and spirit prompts us to recall the creation scene in Gen 1:2, "the Spirit of God was hovering over the waters." Both passages describe a creator and creature relationship: the Spirit hovers over the waters, as the creator over the land and the people.

---

48 Manns gives this use of the symbol a technical term, "eau-Esprit" (*Le symbole*, 39).
49 Ibid., 54.
50 Ibid., 40.

While water is part of the creature, the Spirit is the creator, God's own spirit. Secondly, the symbol speaks of salvation. Isaiah is announcing God's salvation as a promise. God will restore his chosen people for his own sake (cf. 43:25). That is, just as water blesses the thirsty land with grass in a meadow, the Spirit of God blesses his offspring of his chosen. Manns explains, "La fécondité et la fluidité de l'eau servent de point de comparaison à l'activité de l'Esprit de Dieu; dans le souffle de Dieu sont présentés à la fois la grâce de la fécondation et la subtilité d'un élément qui pénètre partout."[51] Manns interestingly combines the two aspects, namely, God's hovering as creator and restoration as savior, and says, "Les miracles de l'exode s'étendaient au cosmos tout entier"! Surely enough, the prophet Isaiah views the end of the exile as a new exodus, and this restoration as a new creation. It is precisely this combination of creation and salvation that is characteristic of the typology in John. As Goppelt points out, "in Jesus the redemptive gifts of the former salvation come in perfected form, and this signifies that the first creation is being perfected in a new one."[52] This typology is the background against which John's water symbolism should be explored.

The passages quoted so far point at a one-to-one correspondence between "water" and "the Spirit." However, there is something different in the following "water-spirit" passage taken from Ezekiel.

> I will sprinkle clean *water* on you, and you will be clean; I will cleanse you from all your impurities and from all your idols. I will give you a new heart and put a new spirit in you; I will remove from you your heart of stone and give you a heart of flesh. And I will put *my Spirit* in you and move you to follow *my decrees* and be careful to keep *my laws* (Ezek 36:25–27).

Here, "water" is a main figure presented in conjunction with the idea of ceremonial cleansing (note the words "sprinkling" and "impurities"). The Spirit is listed as one among other gifts, given with a focussed purpose, namely, to follow the decree of the Lord. Manns points out, "Plus que le symbole eau-Esprit, c'est le trinôme eau-Esprit-loi qui est repris ici."[53] The relation between the cleansing with water and the giving of the Spirit may be variously understood, depending on how the Hebrew conjunction

---

51 Ibid., 50.
52 Goppelt, *Typos*, 39; 182.
53 Manns, *Le symbole*, 47.

is understood, but there is a symbolic relation between "water" and "the Spirit" in any case. Notably, it is typical of Ezekiel to make emphasis on cleansing and on the decree of the Lord.

To account for this difference, Manns differentiates two series of prophetic passages, and between the two there is a divergence in the use of the water symbol. The first series of passages "ayant recours au symbole eau-Esprit," whereas the second series "associant la purification dans l'eau—parfois l'eau vive—et le don de l'Esprit."[54] Isa 44:3–4 is typical of the first series, which actually outnumbers the second series. Ezek 36:25–27 is an example of the second series, which probably arose during the exile. It is imperative to note that Palestinian and Hellenistic Judaism derived their use of water symbolism exclusively from the latter series, which emphasize ceremonial water cleansing and obedience to the law, "au détriment du symbole eau-Esprit," as Manns puts it.[55] My thesis is, if we interpret the Gospel of John exclusively in terms of Judaistic exegetical traditions, assuming that John had altogether abandoned the earlier prophetic use of water symbolism, we will lose sight of John's broader perspective on creation and salvation. We will also fail to appreciate the transcendent significance of the Spirit in the Johannine water symbol.

The temple or Zion. As we have just seen, Joel prophesied that "a fountain will flow out of the Lord's house" (Joel 3:17–18, quoted above). This includes a composite symbol: the fountain symbolizes salvation, and the house, which is the temple, symbolizes the Lord. This temple motif became significant in prophetic books such as Ezekiel and Zechariah, which were written during or after the exile, a time when temple worship had been abrogated. So the water imagery is compounded with the temple theme, a liturgical element reflecting the hope of the nation for restoration. In Ezek 36:25–27, quoted above, ceremonial cleansing is the liturgical element, in the following quoted passage, Ezek 47:1–12, the temple is the liturgical element.

> The man brought me back to the entrance of the temple, and I saw water coming out from under the south side of the temple, south of the altar. He then brought

---

54 Ibid., 300.

55 Manns proposes two reasons for this development: first, the symbol became closely connected with the Feast of Tabernacle which led people to think of the libation of water as a rite; second, the "eau-Esprit" symbol was harder to conceive than a simple reference of "water" to "law" and "wisdom," ibid., 300.

> me out through the north gate and led me around the outside to the outer gate facing east, and the water was flowing . . . ankle-deep . . . knee-deep . . . up to the waist. . . . He measured off another thousand, but now it was a river . . . (Ezek 47:1–6).

This "water" dominates through Ezek 47:1–12. It becomes a river (vv. 6–7) that heals the sea and the banks (vv. 8, 12) so that fish and trees (vv. 7, 9–10, 12) flourish. *Because the water flows from the sanctuary*, trees bear fruit and the fruit will serve for food and their leaves for healing (v. 12).

Although the "water-temple" imagery is dominant in Ezek 47:1–12, the "water-spirit" imagery is not totally absent from the picture. A grand vision of the temple described in Ezek 40 to 46 precedes the water-temple in 47:1–12, and prior to the issue of water in this vision, this temple was visited by the glory of God, the Spirit, who entered from the east gate.

> Then the man brought me to the gate facing east, and I see the glory of the God of Israel coming from the east. His voice was like the roar of rushing waters, and the land was radiant with his glory. . . . The glory of the Lord entered the temple through the gate facing east. Then the Spirit lifted me up and brought me *into the inner court*, and the glory of the Lord filled the temple . . . (Ezek 43:1–5).

Thus, where the Lord entered, and filled the temple, there issued an abundant stream of water. I think it is a mistake that Manns does not include Ezek 47:1–12 among his list of "eau-Esprit" passages. A liturgical connection does not have to eliminate the symbolic relation between the water and the spirit. Therefore, the importance of this passage in biblical water symbolism should not be overlooked: "water" features as the main figure, but is at the same time tied in with the centrality of the temple, and ultimately with the glory of God (the Spirit) which fills the temple. I think this biblical imagery is in the mind of John when he repeatedly alludes to "water" in his gospel.

Last but not least we should look at Zechariah's oracle on the Day of the Lord, Zech 12 to 14. There are two significant points in our interest. First, the fulfillment citation in John 19:37 draws our attention to Zech 12:10, and there an outpouring of "the Spirit" is indicated: "I will pour out on the house of David and the inhabitants of Jerusalem a spirit of grace and supplication. They will look on me, the one they have pierced, . . ." Although no mention of "water" is made here, the oracle begins with a creation imagery in which "water" is, as always, included.

> An Oracle: This is the word of the Lord concerning Israel. The Lord, who stretches out the heaven, who lays the foundation of the earth, and who forms

> the spirit of man within him, declares: . . . (Zech 12:1).

In this imagery the spirit of the person is highlighted at the expense of "water." Later on in Zech 13:1, however, a mention of "fountain" makes up that absence.

> On that day a fountain will be opened to the house of David and the inhabitants of Jerusalem, to cleanse them from sin and impurity (Zech 13:1).

The second point to be noted about Zechariah's oracle in 12 to 14 is that a "water-Jerusalem" imagery is formed in Zech 14:6–11, its vividness comparable to that of the "water-temple" vision in Ezekiel 47:1–12.

> On that day there will be no light, no cold or frost. It will be a unique day, without daytime or nighttime—a day known to the Lord. When evening comes, there will be light. On that day *living water will flow out from Jerusalem*, half to the eastern sea and half to the western sea, in summer and in winter. The Lord will be king over the whole earth. On that day there will be one Lord, and his name the only name. . . (Zech 14:6–11).

This imagery involves an even broader picture. It covers the whole earth. Whereas in Ezek 47:1–12 "water" comes out of the temple and heals the holy land, in Zech 14:6–11, "living water" comes out of the holy city and heals the whole earth. The Hebrew concept is that the temple is the center of Jerusalem and Jerusalem is the center of the whole earth. The two passages give essentially the same message, that there will be restoration in the day of the Lord, beginning from the temple which symbolizes the Lord's presence, and from there reaching out to all the earth. Furthermore, as it has been suggested, "Zion's role as God's special place on earth meant an identification of the holy city with the Edenic paradigm."[56] These prophecies of Ezekiel and Zechariah hark back on the one hand to the Genesis accounts with their temple-water imagery, and on the other hand speak symbolically of a full eschatological redemption of the present creation.

New Testament Perspectives

In the New Testament, the word "water" occurs most frequently in the Gospel of John (for almost twenty times) and the Book of Revelation (for

---

56 C. L. Meyers and E. M. Meyers, *Zechariah 9–14: A New Translation with Introduction and Commentary*, AB, vol. 25C (Garden City, NY: Doubleday, 1993), 435.

over ten times). In the relatively short First Epistle of John the word occurs only twice, but with heavy theological overtones. It appears only several times in each of the Synoptics and in Acts, and it appears one to three times respectively in Ephesians, Hebrews, James, and the Epistles of Peter.[57] It is reasonable to expect a more extensive role played by "water" in the Johannine writings than in other NT writings.

Books Other Than the Johannine Writings

The mention of "water" is primarily linked with Christian baptism in the New Testament, but there are significant allusions to the Old Testament as well.

The Synoptics and Acts. The meaning of "water" in these books hardly goes beyond that of water baptism. The baptism of John is mentioned in all of the Synoptics (Matt 3:11, 16; Mark 9:22; Luke 3:16) and in John. In Acts, besides the baptism of John (Acts 1:5), Christian baptismal activities is recorded a few times (8:36, 38, 39; 10:47). Subsequent to the Pentecost the issue was whether spiritual baptism had priority over the water ritual (11:16). The issue arose as consequential to the eschatological coming of the Messiah, and was displayed in certain episodes recorded in Acts 8 and 10.

Apart from being an element of baptism, "water" rarely features as a symbolic theme in the Synoptics or Acts. Possible exceptions may be found in Jesus' walking on water (Matt 14:23–33) and Jesus' commanding of the winds and the water to calm down (Luke 8:22–25; cf. Matt 8:23–27 and Mark 4:36–41). Jesus' sovereign power over nature represented here corresponds to the victory of God in the Exodus events, in which "water" is not a blessing but an opposing force.

The limited use of "water" in the Synoptics makes it all the more clear that there is intended meaning in the extensive use of "water" in John.

The Pauline Epistles. The use here is again limited. In Ephesians it is restricted to a liturgical sense: "Husbands should love their wives as Christ loved the church and gave himself up for her to make her holy, cleansing her (καθαρίσας) by the washing (τῷ λουτρῷ) with water (τοῦ ὕδατος) through the word" (Eph 5:26). Ritual cleansing is implied in the words "cleansing"

57 Accidental uses such as "Stop drinking only water . . ." (1 Tim 5:23) are not counted here.

and "washing." While it is possible to translate the aorist participle simply as "cleansing," which indicates a simultaneous action to that of the main verb (ἁγιάσῃ, to make holy), it is more precise to translate it as "having cleansed," rendering it a prior act. "The washing with water" would then be water baptism.[58] The symbolic meaning of "conversion," "rebirth" or "initiation in the faith" may also be the underlying meaning.[59] "The word" (ῥῆμα), grammatically used as instrumental to the washing or the cleansing, may refer to the baptismal formula pronounced over the candidate, or the word of the gospel which has brought about conversion and baptism (cf. Eph 6:17).[60]

A slightly different use can be found in 1 Cor. In 1 Cor 6:11 there is a reference to washing: "But you were washed, you were sanctified, you were justified in the name of the Lord Jesus Christ and by the Spirit of our God." A direct reference to baptism is not so likely here because an ethical issue is sharply in focus (6:9–10). In using the words ἀπελούσασθε, ἡγιάσθητε and ἐδικαιώθητε Paul is stressing the supposedly clean status of the Corinthians in front of God, rather than any cleansing rituals. In the longer epistles of Paul, the emphasis is on the theological significance of baptism, namely, justification and sanctification, rather than baptism itself (cf. 1 Cor 1:14–17).

Another Pauline allusion to "water," found in 1 Cor 10:1–5, proves significant.

> For I do not want you to be ignorant of the fact, brothers, that our forefathers were all under the cloud and that they all passed through the sea. They were all baptized into Moses in the cloud and in the sea. They all ate the same spiritual food and drank the same spiritual drink; for they drank from the spiritual rock that accompanied them, and that rock was Christ. Nevertheless, God was not pleased with most of them; their bodies were scattered over the desert.

Here is a conglomeration of images taken from the Exodus event: the cloud, the sea, the food, the drink, the rock, and the wilderness. In this passage we

---

58 Alternatively, some scholars interpret it as "the bridal bath." Such a notion is not irrelevant to the passage (cf. Ezek 16:8–14), but a direct reference to the ritual is unlikely.

59 Cf. Titus 3:5, "He saved us through the washing of rebirth and renewal by the Holy Spirit."

60 A. T. Lincoln, *Ephesians*, WBC, vol. 42 (Dallas, TX: Word Books Publisher, 1990), 376.

see an affinity of Paul's typological view with John's use of the Exodus themes. First, the Exodus event is a type of Christ's salvation (cf. John 1:29). Second, the images collected from the event correspond typologically to various aspects of the salvation of Christ (cf. John 3:14). Thus the cloud and the sea speak of a "baptism into Moses" which is a type of the baptism into Christ. The spiritual food, manna, and the spiritual drink, water from the rock, are types of Christ's blessings, just as John perceive them (John 4–6). The rebellion of the forefathers effects in Paul a warning against falling into temptation (1 Cor 10:11–13), whereas in John, in the polemic context, and in Jesus' dispute with the Jews, the failure of the fathers effects a christological message (John 6–9; note John 6:49, 58; 8:41). The wilderness speaks of God's displeasure and judgment, in Paul just as in John (cf. 9:41). Last but not least, note Paul's identification of Christ as the spiritual rock. In John this typology is expressed in the giving of "living water" by Jesus (John 4:10), as well as the flow of water (and blood) from the pierced side of the crucified Christ (John 19:34).

This demonstrates the similarities between the typological views of Paul and John, which echo each other in an impressive way, as Goppelt describes.

> When Jesus is portrayed by Paul as the second Adam and by John as God's incarnate Logos these are really two sides of the same figure. It reflects the difference between a Pauline and a Johannine view of salvation and is congruent with the fact that the metaphor of the struggling church is developed in great detail by Paul, but scarcely at all by John. It is very significant that the antithesis [Paul's] . . . is not missing from the figure of the world perfecter that is found in John. Only through his being lifted up does Jesus become the bread of life and giver of the Spirit who brings about the new creation.[61]

Thus there is a unity between the typology of John and that of Paul, although there is also difference between them, the former being more of a vertical, creational type and the latter horizontal and eschatological.

The Book of Hebrews. In Hebrews "water" is linked with sacrifice and cleansing. In Heb 9:19 the discussion is on the sprinkling of blood for the inauguration of the old covenant: "When Moses had proclaimed every commandment of the law to all the people, he took the blood of calves, together with water (μετὰ ὕδατος), scarlet wool and branches of hyssop,

61 Goppelt, *Typos*, 194–95.

and sprinkled the scroll and all the people." The actions mentioned here do not exactly match with the details in the Exodus account, which speak of the division of blood into two parts but do not mention the mixing of the blood with water, or the use of wool and hyssop for sprinkling.[62] The author was not being particular about details here, but was generalizing OT rituals. The mention of water indicates the need of water in the purification of lepers (Lev 14:5–9) and the ceremonially unclean (Num 19:7–10).

In Heb 10:22, there is mention of water cleansing which resembles Paul's use in 1 Cor 6:11.

> Let us draw near to God with a sincere heart in full assurance of faith, having our hearts sprinkled to cleanse us from a guilty conscience and having our bodies washed with pure water. Let us hold unswervingly to the hope we profess . . . (Heb 10:22–24)

Here, liturgical terms, ῥεραντισμένοι and λελουσμένοι, are used to speak of the ethical and religious status of a Christian: "sincere," with "full assurance of faith," and "cleansed from a guilty conscience." Along this line, "pure water" (ὕδωρ καθαρόν, 10:22) should have a reference to Christian baptism, used here as symbolic of Christian purity (cf. 1 Cor 6:11; Eph 5:26; Tit 3:5).[63] The author is using the very terms that stand for the obsolete rituals to depict the effectiveness of Christ's salvation, and thus instruct about perseverance in the new faith.

The Petrine Epistles. Both of these two epistles, which differ considerably from each other, mention the flood: showing how patient God is in withholding judgment, and pointing out from it the significance of "water" in the Noah event.[64]

In First Peter the message is written for Christians who were suffering from the ungodly. Peter urged them to look to Christ who died even for the unrighteous, and to God, who waited patiently for humanity to obey (1 Pet 3:17–20a). "The days of Noah while the ark was being built," is cited as a

---

62 According to some textual witnesses of Hebrews, the blood of both "calves and goats" was sprinkled (cf. 9:12). That would make another point of divergence.

63 P. Ellingworth, *The Epistle to the Hebrews: A Commentary on the Greek Text* (Grand Rapids: Eerdmans, 1993), 524.

64 It should be noted that the flood was a classic illustration in Jewish literature both of divine judgment and the deliverance of the just, and it functions similarly in early Christian literature; see J. R. Michaels, *1 Peter*, WBC, vol. 49 (Waco, TX: Word Books Publisher, 1988), 212.

time "when God waited patiently" (1 Pet 3:20a). However, "in it only a few people, eight in all, were saved through water, and this water symbolizes baptism that now saves you also" (1 Pet 3:20b–21a).[65] We note that, first, "saved through water," διεσώθησαν δι' ὕδατος, expresses the fact that Noah and his family were brought safely through the flood "by means of the flood waters themselves."[66] So the waters are the medium of salvation.[67] Second, the author continues to underscore the significance of this water by saying that it symbolizes baptism. That is, "just as the flood waters saved Noah's family, now what baptism signifies saves you," and that forms a typological relation (ὅ καὶ ὑμᾶς ἀντίτυπον νῦν σῴζει βάπτισμα). The resemblance between the waters of the flood and the water of baptism may be explained further as follows.

> As the flood waters cleansed the earth of man's wickedness, so the water of baptism indicates man's cleansing from sin. As the flood separated Noah and his family from the wicked world of their day, so baptism separates believers from the evil world of our day. Baptism, then, is the counterpart of the flood.[68]

In Second Peter the message is written to warn about judgment. That is, though "the Lord . . . is patient . . . the day of the Lord will come like a thief" (2 Pet 3:8–10). The epistle reminds believers not to forget as the scoffers do. In this passage, "water" is the medium of judgment.

> But they deliberately forget that long ago by God's word the heavens existed and the earth was formed out of water and by water. By these waters also the world of that time was deluged and destroyed. By the same word the present heavens and earth are reserved for fire, being kept for the day of judgment and destruction of ungodly men (2 Pet 3:5–7).

---

65 The passage goes on to explain how baptism saves, "not the removal of dirt from the body but the pledge of a good conscience toward God." The pledge, ἐπερώτημα, signifies the believer's appeal to God for a clear conscience or his request for God's help to make a decision to serve him. In either case it is not just the outward ceremony that effects Christ's salvation.

66 Διά may be either local or instrumental, ibid., 213.

67 Some may argue that they were saved by the ark, rather than by the water, and that the water is just the ordeal through which they were saved. However, as Michaels argues, "Peter is interested in 'water' in the story, not in 'wood,' because there is something he wants to say about Christian baptism" (ibid.).

68 S. J. Kistemaker, *New Testament Commentary: Exposition of the Epistles of Peter and the Epistle of Jude* (Grand Rapids: Baker, 1987), 147.

There are again two points to note here. First, there are "pairs of words" used in the passage which link various aspects of creation with later events, effecting an eschatological outlook. For example, οὐρανοὶ . . . γῆ recalls the creation account in Genesis. Ἐξ ὕδατος καὶ δι' ὕδατος stresses the connection between the waters of creation and the waters of the flood.[69] Τῷ θεοῦ λόγῳ . . . τῷ αὐτῷ λόγῳ points out a typological relation between the creation and the final judgment, both being effected by God's very word. Second, the typological relation is now between the creation and the judgment, as well as between the flood and the judgment. Both the creation and the judgment are effected by God's word, and in both the flood and the judgment the heavens and earth are deluged and destroyed.

From the perspective of these Petrine passages, there is a typological relation drawn through the creation, the flood and the final judgment. Whereas in 1 Pet 3:20 the flood is a type of salvation, in 2 Pet 3:5–6 the flood is a type of judgment. Whereas "water" features as the medium of salvation in 1 Pet 3:20, in 2 Pet 3:5–6 "water" functions as the medium of creation and judgment. Thus divine judgment and deliverance are both viewed as being mediated through "water," just as the world is created out of the waters.

The Johannine Writings

In this section we will first examine the Epistles and the Revelation of John. A recapitulation of water symbolism in the Gospel of John will be done in the next chapter as a conclusion of this book.

The Epistles of John. There is a passage in 1 John 5:6–8 in which "water" is symbolically used twice: first, as one of the ways Jesus came; second, as one of the three "testifiers" of God (cf. 5:9–10).

> This is the one who came by water and blood—Jesus Christ. He did not come by water only, but by water and blood. And it is the Spirit who testifies, because the Spirit is the truth. For there are three that testify: the Spirit, the water and the blood; and the three are in agreement (1 John 5:6–8).

In the first use of the word "water" (5:6), the different prepositions attached

69 The phrase "out of water and by water," for instance, is best understood as a repetition of synonymous prepositional phrases stressing the significance of water in creation; see Kistemaker, *Peter and Jude*, 329.

to "water and blood" are probably used synonymously: διά (δι' ὕδατος καὶ αἵματος) and ἐν (οὐκ ἐν τῷ ὕδατι μόνον ἀλλ' ἐν τῷ ὕδατι καὶ ἐν τῷ αἵματι). The two consecutive clauses contain the same elements of content, but whereas the first clause points demonstratively to Jesus Christ, the second clause stresses the ways Jesus came. That may be part of the reason why articles are used in the second clause. As for the symbolic meaning of water, Jesus' "coming in water and blood" has been variously interpreted, as referring to the sacraments, or the incarnation, or the baptism and the death of Jesus, or the death of Jesus exclusively, and so on. It is unlikely that "water" refers just to the sacrament of baptism or to Jesus' incarnation, for a polemic seems to be in view in the saying, "not by water only," and the polemic does not seem to involve a denial of the sacraments or the incarnation.[70] Nor is it likely that "water and blood" refers exclusively to the death of Jesus, for John 19:34 is the only indirect support of this theory. It is with the baptism of Jesus that association should be made. Brown, who associates the elements exclusively with the death of Jesus, concedes that "the adversaries may be emphasizing a coming in water, i.e., Jesus' baptism."[71] If that is the case, it follows naturally that "water" symbolizes the baptism of Jesus and "blood" symbolizes Jesus' death. In support of this is the fact that the two terms are given their own articles and prepositions in 1 John 5:6b. According to this interpretation, popularly held, the coming of Jesus is not just his entering into the world but also his approach to his mission.[72]

The other use of water in the passage has to do with "testifying," the verification of truth (cf. 4:1–3). Regarding "the Spirit," "the water" and "the blood," i.e., the three that testify (1 John 5:8), a great variety of symbolic interpretations has been suggested.[73] Most of them are based on a shift of

---

70 R. E. Brown points out that the implied theory of the opponents does not involve a direct denial of the incarnation, *The Epistles of John: Translated with Introduction, Notes and Commentary*, AB, vol. 30 (Garden City, NY: Doubleday, 1982), 575–76.

71 Ibid., 578.

72 This view is, also, most defensible if Cerinthus's heresy can be accepted as one of the problems which called the epistle into being. Alternatively, an unbalanced reading of John's Gospel might have resulted in an insufficient view of Jesus' humanity ("neither limited nor salvifically significant," as Smalley puts it), which called for the epistle's dual emphasis on Jesus' true divinity and true humanity. See S. S. Smalley, *1, 2, 3 John*, WBC, vol. 51 (Waco, TX: Word Books Publisher, 1984), 279.

73 See the options listed in Brown, *1 John*, 580.

meaning from 5:6 to 5:7–8. However, if we take into consideration the inner coherence of the passage, we would interpret "the three" in 5:7–8 as the same "spirit," "water" and "blood" in 5:6. As I. H. Marshall suggests, the "water" and the "blood" in this context signify the same thing as in verse 6, namely, "the water of Jesus' baptism and the blood shed at this death."[74] Here, John seems to have personified the "water" and the "blood," considering them witnesses alongside the Spirit. Thus there is a unity in testimony. If one rejects the testimony of the water and the blood and thus denies the true character of Jesus, one is, at the same time, rejecting the witness of the Spirit.

In this way "water" takes on a special meaning in 1 John, namely, Jesus' being baptized in water at the beginning of his ministry on earth.

The Book of Revelation. There are three groups of "water" passages in Revelation, one related to calamities, one to God's promise of salvation, and one to the consummation.

In the calamity passages, water is part of the heavens and earth which suffer from afflictions. At the sounding of the third trumpet, for example, "a third of the waters turned bitter, and many people died from the waters that had become bitter" (Rev 8:10). At the pouring out of the third bowl, "the river and springs of water became blood" (Rev 16:4), and the sixth, "the great river Euphrates, and its water was dried up . . ." (16:12). It is not a coincidence that Euphrates was one of the four headwaters flowing out from the river that watered the garden Eden (Gen 2:10–14). The created world described in the creation accounts of Genesis is depicted in the Apocalypse as the catastrophic universe. The message of this is: "Fear God and give him glory, because the hour of his judgment has come. Worship him who made the heavens, the earth, the sea and the springs of water" (14:7).

For those who worship God, i.e., those "who have come out of the great tribulation," there are promises of salvation issued from the throne, described in Rev 4 to 5 in the heavenly court of worship.

> Never again will they hunger; never again will they thirst. . . . For the lamb at the center of the throne will be their shepherd; he will lead them to springs of living water. And God will wipe away every tear from their eyes (Rev 7:15–17, at the interlude between the seals and the trumpets).

---

74 I. H. Marshall, *The Epistles of John*, NICNT (Grand Rapids: Eerdmans, 1978), 237.

At the coming of the new heaven and earth, and the new Jerusalem (Rev 21:1–6), which is the climax of Revelation, the promises of salvation is restated by a pronouncement issued from the throne, and "water" is the main feature in this pronouncement.[75]

> To him who is thirsty I will give to drink without cost from the spring of the water of life (ἐγὼ τῷ διψῶντι δώσω ἐκ τῆς πηγῆς τοῦ ὕδατος τῆς ζωῆς δωρεάν, Rev 21:6).

This promise is repeated again in the epilogue of Revelation (Rev 22:7–21) as a summons.

> Whoever is thirsty (ὁ διψῶν), let him come; and whoever wishes, let him take the free gift of the water of life (ὕδωρ ζωῆς δωρεάν, Rev 22:17).

It is, again, not a coincidence that the key words in these passages are exactly those that appear in Jesus' offer of living water to the Samaritan woman (John 4:10, 14). The language is that of a biblical language, penned by either the author of the gospel or someone well versed in the gospel.

In the interlude between the trumpets and the bowls there is an episode on "the woman and the dragon," in which water is issued from the mouth of the serpent: "The woman was given . . . out of the serpent's reach. Then from his mouth the serpent spewed water like a river, to overtake the woman and sweep her away with the torrent. . ." (Rev 12:14–15). The correlation is not in the "water," as if the water is promised by God, but in the Exodus typology which is distinct in John, as R. H. Mounce points out:

> The pursuit of the woman is similar to Pharaoh's pursuit of the children of Israel as they fled from Egypt (Ex 14:8). The two wings . . . echo the words of God from Sinai, "I bore you on eagles' wings and brought you to myself" (Ex 19:4). The river of water which flowed from the dragon's mouth may reflect Pharaoh's charge to drown the male children of the Israelites in the Nile (Ex 1:22). The opening of the earth is reminiscent of the destruction of the men of Korah . . . (Num 16:31–33)[76]

---

75 God is the speaker from the throne (cf. Rev 1:8; 16:1, 17). However, considering that some of the words are the same as those from the Son of Man, "I am the Alpha and the Omega" (Rev 1:8; 22:13), Swete is probably right in saying, "the Incarnate Son is in view" here; see H. B. Swete, *Commentary on Revelation: The Greek Text with Introduction, Notes and Indexes* (3d ed., London: Macmillan, 1911; repr., Grand Rapids: Kregel Publications, 1977), 280.

76 R. H. Mounce, *The Book of Revelation*, NICNT (Grand Rapids: Eerdmans, 1977), 245.

The use of Exodus typology in Revelation is different from its use in John. In John, the wilderness items such as "manna," "water," "rock," and "Moses' snake" are singled out in different passages to recall God's salvation. Here, the initial movement of the escape is recaptured. The typology recalls the power struggle between God and Pharaoh and depicts a heavenly, spiritual war, instead of the salvation of humankind on earth by God. The children of God is symbolically represented by the woman, her persecutor by the serpent, and the drowning of male children in the Nile depicted as the serpent's issue of water from the mouth. The passage exemplifies a different emphasis in the use of the Exodus typology, one that is antithetical. Here "water" symbolizes destruction rather than salvation, and it originates from the serpent, the counterfeit god.

The third group of "water" passages occurs at the end of the Book of Revelation, in Rev 21 to 22. The antithetical struggle we saw in Rev 12:14–15 is now over, and "water" features as a flawless item on the consummation scene. I have already noted Rev 21:6 and Rev 22:17 as passages on the promise of salvation. Those are spoken passages. In Rev 21 to 22 we have a picturesque presentation instead, a picture of the new heaven and new earth and the new Jerusalem.

> Then the angel showed me the river of the water of life (ποταμὸς ὕδατος ζωῆς), as clear as crystal, flowing from the throne of God and of the Lamb down the middle of the great street of the city. On each side of the river stood the tree of life (ξύλον ζωῆς), bearing twelve crops of fruit, yielding its fruit every month. And the leaves of the tree are for the healing of the nations. No longer will there be any curse. The throne of God and of the Lamb will be in the city, and his servants will serve him. They will see his face, and his name will be on their foreheads. There will be no more light. They will not need the light of a lamp or the light of the sun, for the Lord God will give them light. And they will reign for ever and ever (Rev 22:1–5).

This passage recaptures some significant scenes one come across in the biblical use of "water." In the pronouncement passages of Rev 21:6 and 22:17, it is the symbolic use of "water" as salvific gifts that is recapitulated—a use originating from the Exodus accounts as life provision, from the writings as wisdom and law, and from the prophets as the Spirit. In the consummation picture of Rev 22:1–5, the role of water in God's creation is recapitulated. Thus the passage harks back to Gen 1 to 2 (cf. Ps 46:4); Joel 3:17–18; Ezek 40 to 48 and Zech 12 to 14, in which we have grand visions of Eden, of Zion, of Jerusalem and the temple, locations of God's presence among humankind. In all these there is always "water," or a river, to symbolize life, the life of humankind in the presence of God.

The significance of the final vision. This final vision in Revelation should be interpreted not just by analysis but with appreciation of its biblical language. We must seek to understand it both as a vision and in light of a unified biblical eschatology.

In the vision of Rev 22:1–5 there is a conglomeration of OT concepts—a point well recognized by commentators. H. B. Swete traces the concept of ὕδωρ ζωῆς to Joel 3:18; Zech 14:8 and Ezek 47:9.[77] Mounce traces the source of "the tree of life" to Gen 2:9; 3:22 and Ezek 47:12, and traces "the lack of need for light" to Isa 60:19–20 and Zech 14:7.[78] This tracing of concepts can be done in great details.[79] However, allusions in the Apocalypse, more so than those in the Gospel of John, must be traced not just by looking for similar words or concepts, but by comparing visions and pictures. W. J. Dumbrell, in his study on Rev 21 to 22, claims to have answered the question, "How did the seer of Revelation arrive at the content of his panoramic final vision."[80] Dumbrell makes use of five themes in Rev 21:1–5, "the New Jerusalem, the New Temple, the New Covenant, the New Israel and the New Creation," and traces "the birth and growth of the idea through the Old Testament, the Gospels, and the Epistles," and finally returns to Rev 21 to 22.[81] This is a commendable approach because there is extensive study on the themes involved in detecting the meaning behind the vision of Rev 21 to 22.

> each of the five themes serves as a window on the entire structure of the Bible. Each works as a single perspective. . . . This is not to say that each perspective is of equal importance nor that each is equally capable of capturing the same breadth of biblical data. *Nor indeed that these are the only possible themes for consideration.* . . . Neither is it to say that each of the themes is independent of the others . . .

---

77 Swete, *Revelation*, 298.

78 Mounce, *Revelation*, 387–88.

79 Cf. R. L. Thomas, *Revelation 8–22: An Exegetical Commentary* (Chicago: Moody, 1995), 481–88.

80 W. J. Dumbrell, *The End of the Beginning: Revelation 21–22 and the Old Testament*, The Moore Theological College Lectures 1983 (Homebush, Australia: Lancer Books, 1985), vii.

81 Ibid., vii–viii.

> . . . Any separation of themes such as we have indulged in is bound to be arbitrary, and this is indicated by overlapping use of some major sections of the OT. This, of course, is also shown from the fact that St John has fused all these details into his one great vision of the end (italics mine).[82]

It is my belief that "water" is another significant theme that contributes to the final vision, and, therefore, another important perspective with which to view biblical data.[83]

The convergence of these themes speaks of the rich diversity of Scripture on the one hand and its profound unity on the other. If there is divine purpose in the progress of biblical revelation and therefore a common goal in the movement of biblical data, I have referred to this movement towards the final goal as "eschatology." Much of this present chapter has been written on the basis of this biblical eschatological presupposition.

---

82 Ibid., viii.

83 On the choice of themes, Dumbrell singles out the five as "distinct and important," partly because, as he explains, they "each has an immediate relevance to the Bible's wider concept of government" (Ibid., ix). I think Dumbrell is too preoccupied with "government" as a superimposed title to the five themes. He fails to proportionately emphasize the role of "water" in the final vision.

CONCLUSION

From what we have studied it is clear that the use of water symbolism in John is far more extensive than in other canonical books. First, the literary skill involved in its use is fascinating. I have pointed out that there can be many definitions for "symbolism" in John, according to how scholars refer to it, and this diversity springs from the elusiveness of symbolism *per se*, as well as the multiple literary skills used in the gospel. So the water symbol plays its part in various ways, as metaphors, as narrative units, as double meaning, as misunderstanding or irony, as themes, and as OT allusions. Only in John can we find such a variety of forms in which the symbol is cast.

Second, the water symbol is dominant in the gospel because of its repeated and thematic use. There is also a progression or development of its use along the flow of the narrative. In the early chapters of the gospel the symbol appears more frequently than others and is closely tied to an "anticipation and fulfillment" theme. It becomes most dominant in John 4 and 7 because of the explicit statements made about "water" in 4:13–14 and 7:37–39. In later chapters, especially in the discourses, it does not appear so frequently but it remains significant in the bread and water theme as a metaphorical representation of Christ. Towards the end of the gospel the use of "water" seems reticent, but in a subtle and profound way the symbol participates in the account of the crucifixion, in "the flow of water and blood from Jesus' side." At that climax it converges with other significant themes, such as the Passion theme. There is consistently an eschatology note in the message spelt out by Johannine water symbolism.

Third, Johannine water symbolism takes root in its historical and conceptual backgrounds. This is evident in John 4 in which "living water" features as a leading symbol. There is multifold reference of "water" to eschatological blessings, the anticipation of which takes root in the Old Testament and was common in Judaistic thinking. The symbol is found closely related to other kinds of imagery in John 4, such as "the harvest" and "this mountain and Jerusalem." There is also a significant reference to Christ and the Holy Spirit in 4:13–14, which becomes clear later on in 7:37–39. It can be shown that just as water from Jacob's well anticipates the water given at the eschatological hour by Christ, the earthly worship "in the mountain and Jerusalem" points to the heavenly worship made possible by the Holy Spirit given by Christ. In this way there is a double dimension in John's use of symbolism, the horizontal and the vertical. In the horizontal dimension the historical anticipates the eschatological. In the vertical dimension the earthly symbolizes the heavenly. This double dimension is also a characteristic of Johannine eschatology.

Therefore, John's use of water symbolism excels in extensiveness and profundity, and there is even further significance of it to be sought in John's use of the Old Testament. At the literary level, symbolism involves implicit allusion rather than explicit citation. So the Gospel of John distinguishes itself from the Synoptics in the form of its OT use. There are allusions and themes in addition to traditional christological citations. Whereas most other NT writers refer only to the sacramental meaning of "water," there is rich symbolic meaning of it found in the Gospel of John, and only in 1 John and Revelation can one see any comparable symbolic use. Behind these Johannine writings there is a mastermind in expounding OT imagery. The writer visualizes a creation typology that is distinct from the typology of the Synoptics, and he expresses it with symbols. Only in 1 Cor 10:1–5 do we see OT eschatology interpreted in a similar way. Within the Johannine corpus, Revelation is likewise filled with OT themes, and the two books unite in the formulation of a typology that harks back to creation. The Gospel of John begins with Ἐν ἀρχῇ ἦν ὁ λόγος, καὶ ὁ λόγος ἦν πρὸς θεόν . . . , alluding to Gen 1:1, and Revelation crowns the use of Johannine water symbolism with the vision of the new heaven and the new earth, and the new Jerusalem, where the river of the water of life flows from the throne of God and the Lamb (Rev 22:1ff.). Redemptive history that ends in consummation is the theological background against which Johannine water symbolism finds its full meaning.

BIBLIOGRAPHY

Albright, W. "Recent Discoveries in Palestine and the Gospel of St. John." In *The Background of the New Testament and Its Eschatology*, edited by W. D. Davies and D. Daube, 153–71. Cambridge: Cambridge University Press, 1956.

Allison, D. C. Jr. "The Living Water—John 4:10–14; 6:35c; 7:37–39." *Saint Vladimir's Theological Quarterly* 30 (1986): 143–57.

Alter, R. *The Art of Biblical Narrative*. New York: Basic Books, 1981.

Argyle, A. W. "A Note on John 4:35." *ExpTim* 82 (1971): 247–48.

Ashley, T. R. *The Books of Numbers*. NICOT. Grand Rapids: Eerdmans, 1993.

Ashton, J. "The Identity and Function of the *Ioudaioi* in the Fourth Gospel." *NovT* 27 (1985): 40–75.

________. *Studying John: Approaches to the Fourth Gospel*. Oxford: Clarendon Press, 1994.

________. *Understanding the Fourth Gospel*. Oxford: Clarendon Press, 1991.

Bacon, B. W. *The Fourth Gospel in Research and Debate*. 2d ed. New Haven: Yale University Press, 1918.

Balfour, G. "The Jewishness of John's Use of the Scripture in John 6:31 and 7:37–38." *TynBul* 46 (1995): 357–80.

Balmforth, H. "The Structure of the Fourth Gospel." *SE* 2 (1961): 25–33.

Banks, R., ed. *Reconciliation and Hope: New Testament Essays on Atonement and Eschatology: Presented to L. L. Morris on His Sixtieth Birthday*. Exeter: Paternoster, 1974.

Barrett, C. K. *The Gospel According to St. John: An Introduction with Commentary and Notes on the Greek Text*. 2d ed. Philadelphia: Westminster Press, 1978.

________. *The Gospel of John and Judaism*. London: SPCK, 1975.

________. *The Holy Spirit and the Gospel Tradition*. London: SPCK, 1966.

________. "The Holy Spirit in the Fourth Gospel." *JTS* 1 (1950): 1–15.

________. "The Old Testament in the Fourth Gospel." *JTS* 48 (1947): 155–69.

________. "The Place of Eschatology in the Fourth Gospel." *ExpTim* 59 (1948): 302–5.

________. "The Theological Vocabulary of the Fourth Gospel and of the Gospel of Truth." In *Current Issues in New Testament Interpretation: Essays in Honor of Otto A. Piper*, edited by W. Klassen and G. F. Snyder, 210–23. London: SCM, 1962.

________, ed. *The Fourth Gospel in Recent Criticism and Interpretation*. London: Epworth, 1955.

Barth, K. *Church Dogmatics*. 4 vols. Edited by G. W. Bromiley and T. F. Torrance. Edinburgh: T. & T. Clark, 1969.

Bartlett, W. "The Coming of the Holy Ghost According to the Fourth Gospel." *ExpTim* 37 (1925): 72–75.

Bates, H. W. "Born of Water (John 3:5)." *BSac* 85 (1928): 230–36.

Bauer, W. *A Greek-English Lexicon of the Greek New Testament*. Revised by F. W. Gingrich and F. W. Danker. 2d ed. Chicago: Chicago

University Press, 1979.

________. *Das Johannesevangelium.* 3d ed. Handbuck zum Neuen Testament. Tübingen: Mohr-Siebeck, 1933.

Beasley-Murray, G. R. *Baptism in the New Testament.* Reprinted edition. Grand Rapids: Eerdmans, 1981.

________. "The Eschatology of the Fourth Gospel." *EvQ* 18 (1946): 97–108.

________. "John 3:3, 5: Baptism, Spirit and the Kingdom." *ExpTim* 97 (1986): 167–70.

________. *John.* Edited by D. A. Hubbard and G. W. Barker. WBC, vol. 36. Waco, TX: Word Books Publisher, 1987.

________. *John.* Word Biblical Themes. Edited by D. A. Hubbard, J. D. W. Watts, and R. P. Martin. Dallas, TX: Word Books Publisher, 1989.

Becerra, E. "Le symbolisme de l'eau dans le Quatrième Évangile." Dissertation, Université des Sciences Humaines de Strasbourg, 1982.

Becker, J. *Das Evangelium des Johannes Kapitel 1–10.* Ökumenischer Taschenbuch-Kommentar zum Neuen Testament. Würzburg: Echter-Verlag, 1979.

Behm, J. "ἄρτος," *TDNT*, 1:447.

Belleville, L. "'Born of Water and Spirit:' John 3:5." *TrinJ* 1 (1980): 125–41.

Bernard, J. H. *A Critical and Exegetical Commentary on the Gospel According to St. John.* 2 vols. Edited by A. H. McNeile. ICC. New York: Charles Scribner's Sons, 1929.

Best, E. "Spirit Baptism." *NovT* 4 (1960): 236–43.

Betz, O. "Early Christian Cult in the Light of Qumran." *Religious Studies Bulletin* 2 (1982): 73–85

________. "To Worship God in Spirit and in Truth: Reflections on John 4, 20–26." In *Standing Before God: Studies on Prayer in Scriptures and in Traditions with Essays in Honor of John M. Oesterreicher*, edited by A. Finkel and L. Frizzell, 53–72. New York: Ktav Publishing House Inc., 1981.

Billerbeck, P. *Kommentar zum Neuen Testament aus Talmud und Midrasch*. 4 vols. München: Beck, 1922–28.

Bishop J. "Encounters in the New Testament." In *Literary Interpretations of Biblical Narratives*, vol. 2, edited by L. Gros and R. R. Kenneth, 285–94. Nashville: Abingdon, 1982.

Bishop, E. F. F. "Constantly on the Road." *EvQ* 41 (1969): 14–18.

Black, M. *An Aramaic Approach to the Gospels and Acts*. Oxford: Clarendon Press, 1967.

Blank, J. *Krisis: Untersuchungen zur johanneischen Christologie und Eschatologie*. Freiburg: Lambertus, 1964.

Blass, F., and A. Debrunner. *A Greek Grammar of the New Testament*. Edited and translated by R. W. Funk. Chicago: Chicago University Press, 1961.

Blenkinsopp, J. "John 7:37–39: Another Note on a Notorious Crux." *NTS* 6 (1959–60): 95–98.

Bligh, J. "Jesus in Samaria." *HeyJ* 3 (1962): 329–46.

Bloch, R. "Midrash." In *Approaches to Ancient Judaism*, edited by W. S. Green, 29–50. Missoula, MT: Scholars Press, 1978.

Böcher, O. *Der johanneische Dualismus im Zusammenhang des nachbiblischen Judentums*. Gütersloh: Mohn, 1965.

________. "Wasser und Geist." In *Verborum Veritas. Festschrift für Gustav Stählin zum 70. Geburtstag*, edited by K. Haacker, 197–209. Wuppertal: Brockhaus, 1970.

Bodi, D. "Der altorientalische Hintergrund des Themas der 'Strome lebendigen Wassers' in Joh 7,38." In *Johannes-Studien*, edited by M. Rose, 137–58. Zürich: Theologischer Verlag, 1991.

Boers, H. "Discourse Structure and Macro-Structure in the Interpretation of Texts: John 4:1–41 as an Example." SBLSP 116 (1980): 159–82.

________. *Neither on This Mountain Nor in Jerusalem: A Study of John 4*. SBLMS 35. Atlanta: Scholars Press, 1988.

Bogart, J. "Review Article: Recent Johannine Studies." *ATR* 60 (1978): 80–87.

Boismard, M.-E. "De son ventre couleront des fleuves d'eau (Jo. 7,38)." *RB* 65 (1958): 423–546.

________. "L'évolution du thème eschatologique dans les traditions johanniques." *RB* 68 (1961): 507–24.

________. "Les traditions johanniques concernant le Baptiste." *RB* 70 (1963): 5–42.

Bonneau, N. R. "The Woman at the Well: John 4 and Genesis 24." *The Bible Today* 24 (1973): 1252–59.

Borgen, P. "Some Jewish Exegetical Traditions in the Fourth Gospel." In *L'Évangile de Jean: Sources, rédaction, théologie*, edited by M. de Jonge, 243–58. BETL 44. Leuven: Leuven University Press, 1977.

Born, J. B. "Literary Features in the Gospel of John." *Direction* 17, no. 2 (1988): 3–17.

Bornkamm, G. "Die Zeit des Geistes." In *Geschichte und Glaube, Gesammelte Aufsätze*, 3:90–103. München: Kaiser, 1968.

Botha, J. E. *Jesus and the Samaritan Woman: A Speech Act Reading of John 4:1–42*. NovTSup 65. Leiden: E. J. Brill, 1991.

________. "John 4:16: A Difficult Text Speech Act Theoretically Revisited." *Scriptura* 35 (1990): 1–9.

________. "Reader 'Entrapment' as Literary Device in John 4:1–41." *Neot* 24 (1990): 37–47.

Bowen, C. R. "The Fourth Gospel as Dramatic Material." *JBL* 49 (1930): 292–305.

Bowman, J. "Early Samaritan Eschatology." *JJS* 6 (1955): 63–72.

________. "The Fourth Gospel and the Samaritans." *BJRL* 40 (1958): 207–11.

________. *Samaritanische Probleme: Studien zum Verhältnis von Samaritanertum, Judentum und Urchristentum*. Stuttgart: W. Kohlhammer GmbH., 1967.

________. "Samaritan Studies." *BJRL* 40 (1958): 298–308.

Braun, F.-M. "Avoir soif et boire (Jn 4,10–14; 7,37–39)." In *Mélanges bibliques en hommage au R P Béda Rigaux*, edited by A. Descamps and A. Halleux, 247-58. Gembloux: Duculot, 1970

________. "L'eau et l'esprit." *RevThom* 49 (1949): 5–30.

________. *Jean le théologien: Les grandes traditions d' Israël et l' accord des écritures selon le quatrième évangile*. Paris: J. Gabalda, 1964.

Brodie, T. L. *The Gospel According to John: A Literary and Theological Commentary*. Oxford: Oxford University Press, 1993.

Brooke, A. E., ed. *The Commentary of Origen on St. John' s Gospel: The Text Revised with a Critical Introduction and Indices*. Cambridge: Cambridge University Press, 1896.

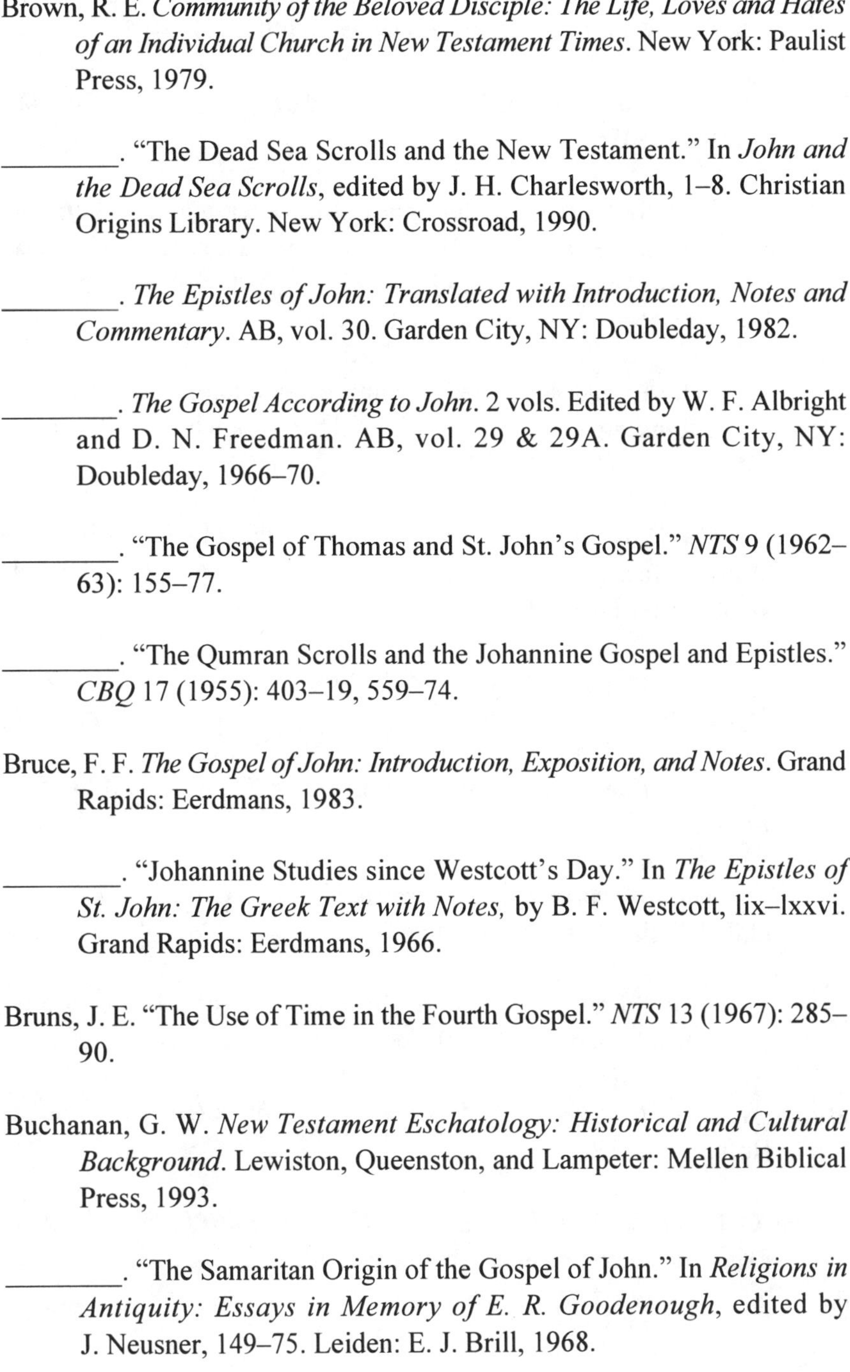

Brown, R. E. *Community of the Beloved Disciple: The Life, Loves and Hates of an Individual Church in New Testament Times*. New York: Paulist Press, 1979.

________. "The Dead Sea Scrolls and the New Testament." In *John and the Dead Sea Scrolls*, edited by J. H. Charlesworth, 1–8. Christian Origins Library. New York: Crossroad, 1990.

________. *The Epistles of John: Translated with Introduction, Notes and Commentary*. AB, vol. 30. Garden City, NY: Doubleday, 1982.

________. *The Gospel According to John*. 2 vols. Edited by W. F. Albright and D. N. Freedman. AB, vol. 29 & 29A. Garden City, NY: Doubleday, 1966–70.

________. "The Gospel of Thomas and St. John's Gospel." *NTS* 9 (1962–63): 155–77.

________. "The Qumran Scrolls and the Johannine Gospel and Epistles." *CBQ* 17 (1955): 403–19, 559–74.

Bruce, F. F. *The Gospel of John: Introduction, Exposition, and Notes*. Grand Rapids: Eerdmans, 1983.

________. "Johannine Studies since Westcott's Day." In *The Epistles of St. John: The Greek Text with Notes*, by B. F. Westcott, lix–lxxvi. Grand Rapids: Eerdmans, 1966.

Bruns, J. E. "The Use of Time in the Fourth Gospel." *NTS* 13 (1967): 285–90.

Buchanan, G. W. *New Testament Eschatology: Historical and Cultural Background*. Lewiston, Queenston, and Lampeter: Mellen Biblical Press, 1993.

________. "The Samaritan Origin of the Gospel of John." In *Religions in Antiquity: Essays in Memory of E. R. Goodenough*, edited by J. Neusner, 149–75. Leiden: E. J. Brill, 1968.

Büchner, W. "Über den Begriff der Eironeia." *Hermes: Zeitschrift für klassische Philologie - Einzelschriften* 76 (1941): 339–58.

Bull, R. J. "An Archaeological Context for Understanding John 4:20." *BA* 38 (1975): 54–59.

Bultmann, R. "Die Bedeutung der neuerschlossenen mandäischen und manischäischen Quellen für das Verständnis der Johannesevangeliums." *ZNW* 24 (1925): 100–46. Reprinted in *Exegesis*, 55–104. Tübingen: Mohr, 1967.

________. "Die Eschatologie des Johannesevangeliums." In *Faith and Understanding*, edited by R. W. Funk, translated by L. P. Smith, 165–83. London: SCM, 1969.

________. *The Gospel of John: A Commentary*. Edited by G. R. Beasley-Murray. Translated by R. W. N. Hoare and J. K. Riches. Philadelphia: Westminster Press, 1971.

________. "History and Eschatology in the New Testament." *NTS* 1 (1954–55): 5–16.

________. "The Interpretation of the Fourth Gospel." *NTS* 1 (1954–55): 77–91.

________. *The Johannine Epistles*. Translated by K. Grobel. Hermeneia. Philadelphia: Fortress, 1973.

________. *The Theology of the New Testament*. 2 vols. Translated by K. Grobel. London: SCM, 1955.

Burch, V. *The Structure and Message of St. John's Gospel*. London: Hopkinson, 1928.

Burge, G. M. *The Anointed Community: The Holy Spirit in the Johannine Tradition*. Grand Rapids: Eerdmans, 1987.

Cahill, P. J. "Narrative Art in John 4." *Religious Studies Bulletin* 2 (1982): 41–47.

Calvin, J. *Commentary on the Gospel According to John*. 2 vols. Translated by W. Pringle. Grand Rapids: Eerdmans, 1949.

Carroll, J. T. "Present and Future in Fourth Gospel." *BTB* 19 (1989): 63–69.

Carson, D. A. *The Gospel According to John*. Grand Rapids: Eerdmans, 1991.

________. "John and the Johannine Epistles." In *It is Written: Scripture Citing Scripture: Essays in Honour of Barnabas Lindars*, edited by D. A. Carson and H. G. M. Williamson, 145–64. Cambridge: Cambridge University Press, 1988.

________. "Spirit and Eschatology in the Gospel of John." Tyndale Fellowship Paper, Cambridge, England, 1975.

________. "Understanding Misunderstandings in the Fourth Gospel." *TynBul* 33 (1982): 59–91.

Cassirer, E. *An Essay on Man*. New Haven: Yale University Press, 1947.

Clavier, H. "L'ironie dans le quatrième évangile." *SE* 1 (1959): 261–76.

Coggins, R. J. *Samaritans and Jews*. Oxford: Blackwell, 1975.

Colwell, E. C., and E. L. Titus. *The Gospel of the Spirit: A Study in the Fourth Gospel*. New York: Harper & Row, 1953.

Connick, C. M. "The Dramatic Character of the Fourth Gospel." *JBL* 67 (1948): 159–69.

Conzelmann, H. "Eschatologie." In *Die Religion in Geschichte und Gegenwart*, 3:665–72. Tübingen: Mohr-Siebeck, 1959.

Cook, R. W. *The Theology of John*. Chicago: Moody, 1979.

Cortez, J. B. "Yet Another Look at John 7:37–38." *CBQ* 29 (1967): 75–86.

Cotterell, P., and M. Turner. *Linguistics and Biblical Interpretation*. Downers Grove, IL: IVP, 1989.

Craddock, F. B. "The Witness at the Well." *Christian Century* 107 (1990): 243.

Craig, C. T. "Sacramental Interest in the Fourth Gospel." *JBL* 58 (1939): 31–41.

Cross, F. L., ed. *Studies in the Fourth Gospel*. London: Mowbray, 1957.

Crown, A. D., ed. *The Samaritans*. Tübingen: Mohr, 1989.

Cullmann, O. *Baptism in the New Testament*. SBT 1/1. Translated by J. K. S. Reid. London: SCM, 1950.

________. *Christ and Time: The Primitive Christian Conception of Time and History*. Revised edition. Translated by F. V. Filson. Philadelphia: Westminster Press, 1964.

________. *Early Christian Worship*. London: SCM, 1953.

________. "Der johanneische Gebrauch doppeldeutiger Ausdrücke als Schlüssel zum Verständnis des vierten Evangeliums." *TZ* 4 (1948): 360–71.

________. *The Johannine Circle*. Translated by J. Bowden. London: SCM, 1975.

________. "A New Approach to the Interpretation of the Fourth Gospel." *ExpTim* 71 (1959): 8–12, 39–43.

________. "Samaria and the Origin of the Christian Mission." In *The Early Church*, edited by A. J. B. Higgin, translated by A. J. B. Higgins and

S. Godman, 185–92. London: SCM, 1956.

Culpepper, R. A. *Anatomy of the Fourth Gospel: A Study in Literary Design*. FFNT. Philadelphia: Fortress, 1983.

Daniélou, J. "Joh 7,37 et Ezéch 47,1–11." *SE* 2 (1964): 158–63.

Daube, D. "Jesus and the Samaritan Woman: The Meaning of συγχράομαι." *JBL* 69 (1950): 137–47.

Davies, M. *Rhetoric and Reference in the Fourth Gospel*. JSNTSup 69. Sheffield: JSOT, 1992.

de Boer, M. C. "John 4:27—Women (and Men) in the Gospel and Community of John." In *Women in the Biblical Tradition*, edited by G. J. Brooke, 208–30. Lewiston, NY: The Edwin Mellen Press, 1992.

Deeks, D. "The Structure of the Fourth Gospel." *NTS* 15 (1968–69): 107–28.

de Jonge, M. "Jewish Expectations About 'Messiah' According to the Fourth Gospel." *NTS* 19 (1973): 246–70.

________. "Nicodemus and Jesus: Some Observations on Misunderstanding and Understanding in the Fourth Gospel." *BJRL* 53 (1971): 337–59.

Derrett, J. D. M. "The Samaritan Woman's Purity."*EvQ* 60 (1988): 291–98.

Diel, P., and J. Solotareff. *Symbolism in the Gospel of John*. Translated by N. Marans. San Francisco: Harper & Row, 1988.

Dillistone, F. W. *Christianity and Symbolism*. London: Collins, 1955.

Dockery, D. S. "Reading John 4:1–45: Some Diverse Hermeneutical Perspectives." *Criswell Theological Review* 3 (1988): 127–40.

Dodd, C. H. *The Apostolic Preaching and Its Developments*. London: Hodder and Stoughton, 1963.

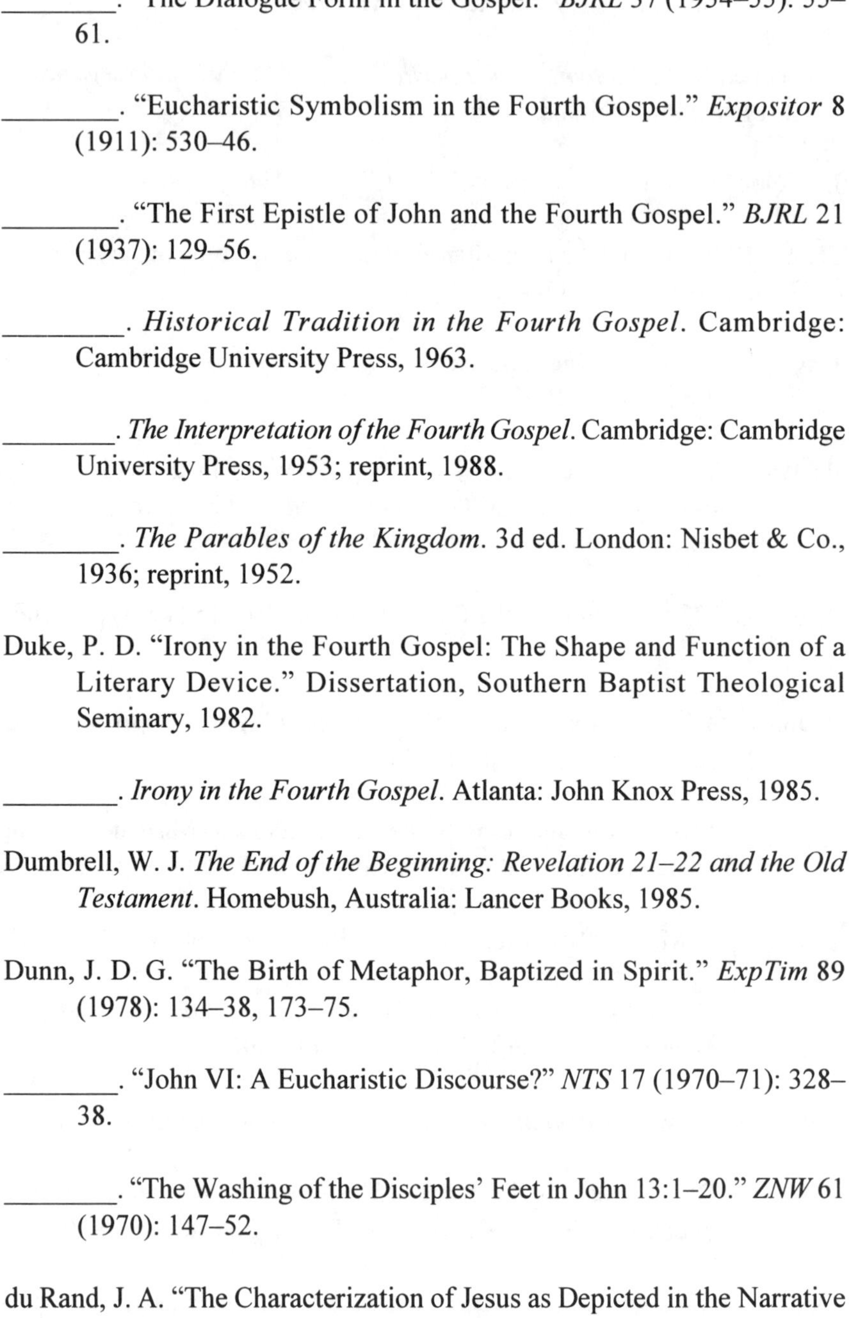

________. "The Dialogue Form in the Gospel." *BJRL* 37 (1954–55): 55–61.

________. "Eucharistic Symbolism in the Fourth Gospel." *Expositor* 8 (1911): 530–46.

________. "The First Epistle of John and the Fourth Gospel." *BJRL* 21 (1937): 129–56.

________. *Historical Tradition in the Fourth Gospel.* Cambridge: Cambridge University Press, 1963.

________. *The Interpretation of the Fourth Gospel.* Cambridge: Cambridge University Press, 1953; reprint, 1988.

________. *The Parables of the Kingdom.* 3d ed. London: Nisbet & Co., 1936; reprint, 1952.

Duke, P. D. "Irony in the Fourth Gospel: The Shape and Function of a Literary Device." Dissertation, Southern Baptist Theological Seminary, 1982.

________. *Irony in the Fourth Gospel.* Atlanta: John Knox Press, 1985.

Dumbrell, W. J. *The End of the Beginning: Revelation 21–22 and the Old Testament.* Homebush, Australia: Lancer Books, 1985.

Dunn, J. D. G. "The Birth of Metaphor, Baptized in Spirit." *ExpTim* 89 (1978): 134–38, 173–75.

________. "John VI: A Eucharistic Discourse?" *NTS* 17 (1970–71): 328–38.

________. "The Washing of the Disciples' Feet in John 13:1–20." *ZNW* 61 (1970): 147–52.

du Rand, J. A. "The Characterization of Jesus as Depicted in the Narrative of the Fourth Gospel." *Neot* 19 (1985): 18–36.

________. "Plot and Point of View in the Gospel of John." In *A South African Perspective on the New Testament: Essays by South African New Testament Scholars*, edited by J. H. Petzer and P. J. Hartin, 149–69. Leiden: E. J. Brill, 1986.

Edwards, A. D. "The Eschatology of the Fourth Gospel." Dissertation, London , External, 1974–76.

Edwards, M. "The World Could Not Contain the Books." In *The Bible as Rhetoric: Studies in Biblical Persuasion and Credibility*, edited by M. Warner, 178–94. London: Routledge, 1990.

Ellingworth, P. *The Epistle to the Hebrews: A Commentary on the Greek Text*. Grand Rapids: Eerdmans, 1993.

Ellis, E. E. *The World of St. John*. Grand Rapids: Eerdmans, 1984.

Ellis, P. F. *The Genius of John: A Composition-Critical Commentary on the Fourth Gospel*. Collegeville: Liturgical Press, 1984.

Enz, J. J. "The Book of Exodus as a Literary Type for the Gospel of John." *JBL* 76 (1957): 208–15.

Eslinger, L. "The Wooing of the Woman at the Well: Jesus, the Reader and Reader-response Criticism." *Literature and Theology* 1 (1987): 167–83.

Evans, C. A. "On the Quotation Formulas in the Fourth Gospel." *BZ* 26 (1982): 79–83.

Fawcett, T. *The Symbolic Language of Religion: An Introductory Study*. London: SCM, 1970.

Fee, G. "Once More, John 7:37–39." *ExpTim* 89 (1978): 116–18.

Fenton, J. C. *The Gospel According to St. John*. Oxford: Clarendon Press, 1970.

Feuillet, A. *Johannine Studies*. Translated by T. E. Crane. New York:

Alba, 1964.

________. "The Structure of First John: Comparison with the 4th Gospel, the Pattern of Christian Life." *BTB* 3 (1973): 194–216.

Filson, F. "The Gospel of Life: The Study of the Gospel of John." In *Current Issues in New Testament Interpretation: Essays in Honor of Otto A. Piper*, edited by W. Klassen and G. F. Snyder, 111–23. London: SCM, 1962.

Ford, J. M. "'Mingle Blood' from the Side of Christ (John 19:34)." *NTS* 15 (1968–69): 337–38.

Fortna, R. T. *The Gospel of Signs: A Reconstruction of the Narrative Source Underlying the Fourth Gospel*. SNTSMS 11. Cambridge: Cambridge University Press, 1970.

Fortna, R. T., and B. R. Gaventa. *The Conversation Continues: Studies in Paul and John: In Honor of J. Louis Martyn*. Nashville: Abingdon, 1990.

Freed, E. D. "Did John Write His Gospel Partly to Win Samaritan Converts?" *NovT* 12 (1970): 241–56.

________. "The Manner of Worship in John 4:23f." In *Search the Scriptures: NT Studies in Honor of R. T. Stamm*, edited by J. M. Meyers, O. Reimherr and H. N. Bream, 33–48. Leiden: E. J. Brill, 1969.

________. *Old Testament Quotations in the Gospel of John*. Leiden: E. J. Brill, 1965.

________. "Samaritan Influence in the Gospel of John." *CBQ* 30 (1968): 580–87.

________. "Variations in the Language and Thought of John." *ZNW* 55 (1964): 167–97.

Freedman, W. "The Literary Motif: A Definition and Evaluation." *Novel* 4

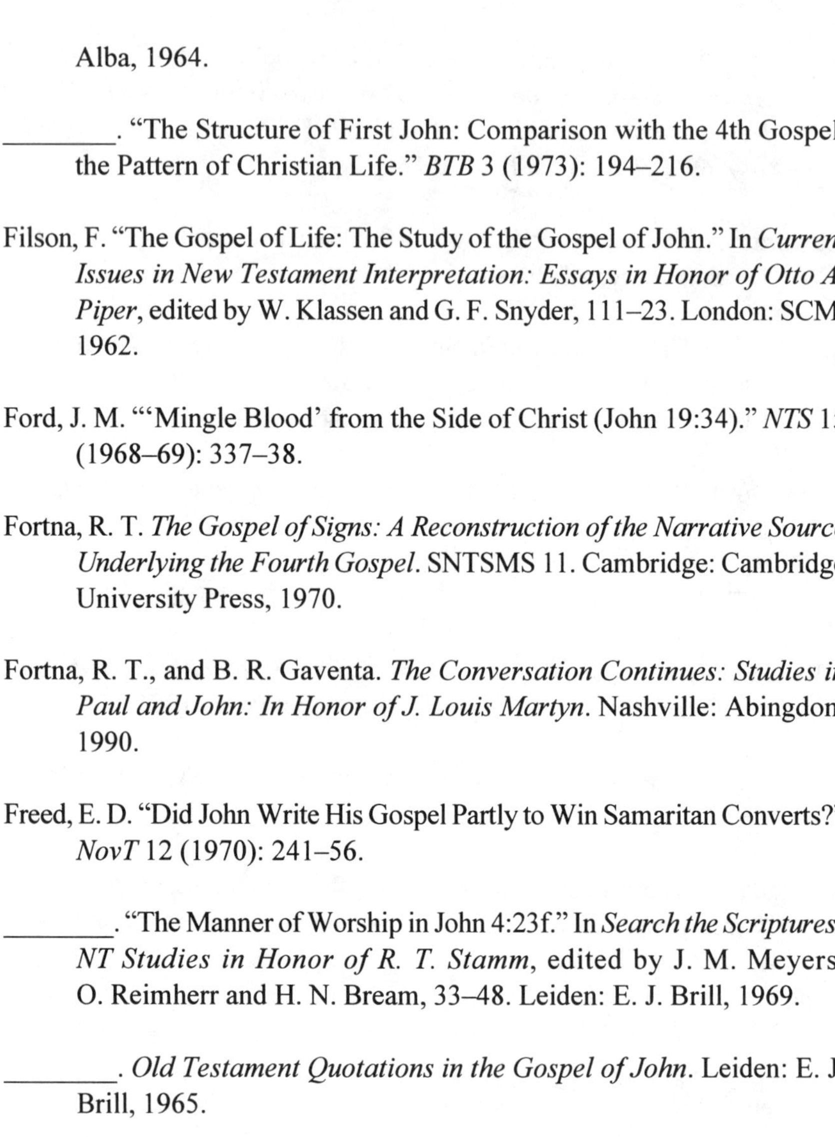

(1971): 123–31.

Friedman, N. *Form and Meaning in Fiction*. Athens: The University of Georgia Press, 1975.

Fuchs, E. "Die Sprache im Neuen Testament." In *Zur Frage nach dem historischen Jesus*, 258–79. Tübingen: Mohr, 1960.

Funk, R. W. *Language, Hermeneutic, and Word of God: The Problem of Language in the New Testament and Contemporary Theology*. New York: Harper & Row, 1966.

Gartner, B. *John 6 and the Jewish Passover*. Lund: Gleerup, 1959.

Gaster, M. *Samaritan Oral Law and Ancient Traditions*. London: The Search Publishing Co., 1932.

________. *The Samaritans: Their History, Doctrines and Literature*. London: Oxford University Press, 1925.

Gates, H. L. "A Comparative Study of Heaven in the Fourth Gospel and in the Apocalypse." Dissertation, Southwestern Baptist Theological Seminary, 1979.

Gerhard, J. "The Literary Unit of the Gospel of John." Dissertation, The Catholic University of America, 1975.

Giblin, C. H. "The Tripartite Narrative Structure of John's Gospel." *Bib* 71 (1990): 449–68.

Girard, M. "Jésus en Samarie (Jean 4:1–42): Analyse des structures stylistiques et du processus de symbolisation." *Église et Théologie* 17 (1986): 275–310.

Glasson, T. F. *Moses in the Fourth Gospel*. SBT 1/40. London: SCM, 1963.

Godet, F. L. *Commentary on John's Gospel*. New York: Funk and Wagnalls, 1886; reprint, Grand Rapids: Kregel Publications, 1978.

Goppelt, L. *Typos: The Typological Interpretation of the Old Testament in the New*. Translated by D. H. Madvig. Grand Rapids: Eerdmans, 1982.

Grayston, K. *The Gospel of John*. Narrative Commentaries. Philadelphia: Trinity Press International, 1990.

Grigsby, B. H. "If Any Man Thirst: Observations on the Rabbinic Background of John 7:37–39." *Bib* 67, no. 1 (1986): 101–8.

________. "Washing in the Pool of Siloam: A Thematic Anticipation of the Johannine Cross." *NovT* 27 (1985): 227–35.

Guilding, A. *The Fourth Gospel and Jewish Worship*. Oxford: Clarendon Press, 1960.

Haacker, K. "Gottesdienst ohne Gotteserkenntnis: Joh 4,22 vor dem Hintergrund der judisch-samaritanischen Auseinandersetzsungen." In *Wort und Wirklichkeit: Studien zur Afrikanistik u. Orientalistik: Eugen Ludwig Rapp zum 70. Geburtstag*, 2 vols., edited by B. Benzing, 1:110–26. Meisenheim am Glan: Hain, 1976–77.

Haenchen, E. *A Commentary on the Gospel of John Chapters 1–6*. Translated by R. W. Funk. Edited by R. W. Funk and U. Busse. Hermeneia. Philadelphia: Fortress, 1984.

Hahn, F. "Das Glaubensverständnis im Johannesevangelium." In *Glaube und Eschatologie: Festschrift für Werner Georg Kümmel zum 80. Geburtstag*, 51–69. Tübingen: Mohr, 1985.

________. "'Das Heil kommt von den Juden': Erwägungen zu Joh 4,22b." In *Wort und Wirklichkeit: Studien zur Afrikanistik u. Orientalistik: Eugen Ludwig Rapp zum 70. Geburtstag,* 2 vols., edited by B. Benzing, 1:67–84. Meisenheim am Glan: Hain, 1976–77.

Hall, D. R. "Meaning of *Synchraomai* in John 4:9." *ExpTim* 83 (1971): 56–57.

Hammer, P. L. "Baptism with Water and the Spirit." *Theology and Life* 8

(1965): 35–43.

Hanson, A. T. "John's Use of Scripture." In *The Gospels and the Scriptures of Israel*, edited by C. A. Evans and W. R. Stegner, 358–79. JSNTSup 104. Sheffield: Sheffield Academic Press, 1994.

________. *The Living Utterances of God: The New Testament Exegesis of the Old*. London: Darton, Longman and Todd, 1983.

________. *The New Testament Interpretation of Scripture*. London: SPCK, 1980.

________. *The Prophetic Gospel: A Study of John and the Old Testament*. Edinburgh: T. & T. Clark, 1991.

Harrington, W. J. *The Path of Biblical Theology*. Dublin: Gill and Macmillan, 1973.

Hatch, E., and H. A. Redpath. *A Concordance to the Septuagint*. 3 vols. Oxford: Clarendon Press, 1897–1906.

Hawthrone, G. F. "The Concept of Faith in the Fourth Gospel." *BSac* 116 (1959): 117–26.

Hendriksen, W. *An Exposition of the Gospel of John*. London: Banner of Truth, 1959.

Hengel, M. *The Johannine Question*. Translated by J. Bowden. London: SCM, 1989.

________. "The Old Testament in the Fourth Gospel." In *The Gospels and the Scriptures of Israel*, edited by C. A. Evans and W. R. Stegner, 380–95. JSNTSup 104. Sheffield: Sheffied Academic Press, 1994.

Hickling, C. J. A. "Attitudes to Judaism in the Fourth Gospel." In *L'Évangile de Jean: Sources, rédaction, théologie*, edited by M. de Jonge, 347–54. BETL 44. Leuven: Leuven University Press, 1977.

Hitchcock, F. R. M. "The Dramatic Development of the Fourth Gospel." *Expositor* 7 (1907): 266–79.

________. "Is the Fourth Gospel a Drama?" *Theology* 7 (1923): 307–17.

Hodges, Z. "Water and Spirit—John 3:5." *BSac* 135 (1978): 206–20.

Holwerda, D. E. *The Holy Spirit and Eschatology in the Gospel of John: A Critique of Rudolf Bultmann's Present Eschatology*. Kampen: Kok, 1959.

Hoskyns, E. C. *The Fourth Gospel*. Edited by F. N. Davey. 2d ed. London: Faber and Faber, 1954.

________. "Gen. 1–3 and St. John's Gospel." *JTS* 21 (1920): 210–28.

Howard, W. F. *Christianity According to St. John*. London: Duckworth, 1943.

________. "The Common Authorship of the Johannine Gospel and Epistles." *JTS* 48 (1947): 12–25.

________. "Symbolism and Allegory." In *The Fourth Gospel in Recent Criticism and Interpretation*, edited by C. K. Barrett, 179–94. London: Epworth, 1955.

Huges, H. D. "Salvation-History as Hermeneutic." *EvQ* 48 (1976): 79–89.

Hunter, A. M. *The Gospel According to John*. Cambridge: Cambridge University Press, 1965.

________. "Modern Trends in New Testament Theology." In *The New Testament in Historical and Contemporary Perspective: Essays in Memory of G. H. C. MacGregor*, edited by H. Anderson and W. Barclay, 133–48. Oxford: Basil Blackwell, 1965.

Jeremias, J. *The Eucharistic Words of Jesus*. Translated by N. Perrin. Philadelphia: Fortress, 1977.

Johnson, A. M. Jr. "The Cultural Context of the Gospel of John: A Structural Approach." Dissertation, University of Pittsburgh, 1978.

Johnston, G. "'Spirit' and 'Holy Spirit' in the Qumran Literature." In *New Testament Sidelights: Essays in Honor of A. C. Purdy*, edited by H. K. McArthur, 27–42. Hartford: Hartford Seminary Foundation, 1960.

Jones, L. P. *The Symbol of Water in the Gospel of John*. JSNTSup 145. Sheffield: Sheffield Academic Press, 1997.

Käsemann, E. *The Testament of Jesus, According to John 17* (Philadelphia: Fortress, 1968).

Kennedy, H. A. A. *Philo's Contribution to Religion*. London: Hodder & Stoughton, 1919.

Kieffer, R. "Different Levels in Johannine Imagery." In *Aspects on the Johannine Literature: Papers Presented at a Conference of Scandinavian New Testament Exegetes at Uppsala*, edited by L. Hartman and B. Olsson, 74–84. Coniectanea Biblica, New Testament Series 18. Uppsala: Almqvist & Wiksell, 1987.

Kilpatrick, G. D. "John 4:9." *JBL* 87 (1968): 327–28.

________. "The Punctuation of John 7:37–39." *JTS* 17 (1960): 340–42.

________. "The Religious Background of the Fourth Gospel." In *Studies in the Fourth Gospel*, edited by F. L. Cross, 36–44. London: Mowbray, 1957.

Kippenberg, H. G. *Gerizim und Synagoge: Traditionsgeschichtliche Untersuchungen zur samaritanischer Religion der aramäischen Periode*. Berlin: de Gruyter, 1971.

Kistemaker, S. J. *New Testament Commentary: Exposition of the Epistles of Peter and the Epistle of Jude*. Grand Rapids: Baker, 1987.

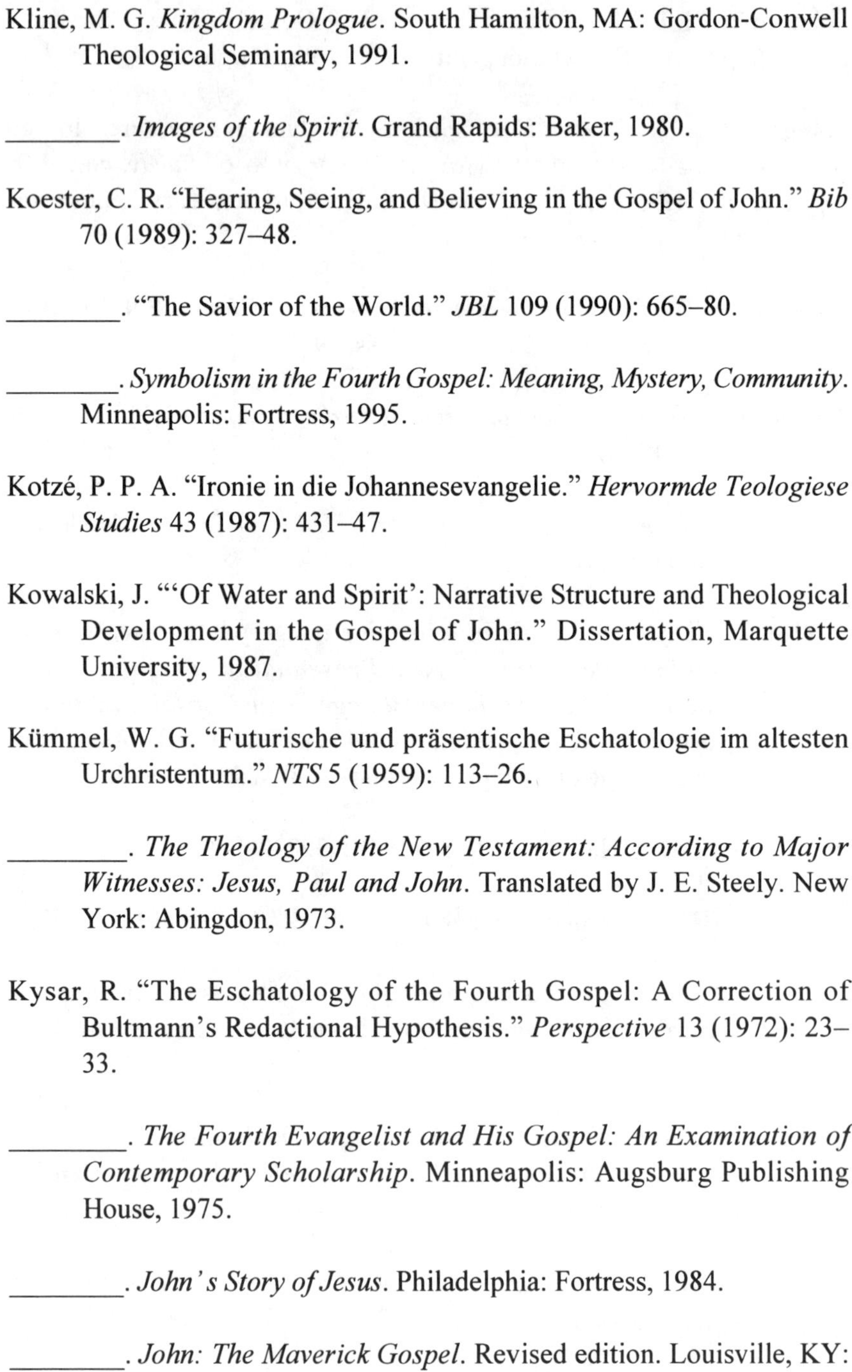

Kline, M. G. *Kingdom Prologue*. South Hamilton, MA: Gordon-Conwell Theological Seminary, 1991.

________. *Images of the Spirit*. Grand Rapids: Baker, 1980.

Koester, C. R. "Hearing, Seeing, and Believing in the Gospel of John." *Bib* 70 (1989): 327–48.

________. "The Savior of the World." *JBL* 109 (1990): 665–80.

________. *Symbolism in the Fourth Gospel: Meaning, Mystery, Community*. Minneapolis: Fortress, 1995.

Kotzé, P. P. A. "Ironie in die Johannesevangelie." *Hervormde Teologiese Studies* 43 (1987): 431–47.

Kowalski, J. "'Of Water and Spirit': Narrative Structure and Theological Development in the Gospel of John." Dissertation, Marquette University, 1987.

Kümmel, W. G. "Futurische und präsentische Eschatologie im altesten Urchristentum." *NTS* 5 (1959): 113–26.

________. *The Theology of the New Testament: According to Major Witnesses: Jesus, Paul and John*. Translated by J. E. Steely. New York: Abingdon, 1973.

Kysar, R. "The Eschatology of the Fourth Gospel: A Correction of Bultmann's Redactional Hypothesis." *Perspective* 13 (1972): 23–33.

________. *The Fourth Evangelist and His Gospel: An Examination of Contemporary Scholarship*. Minneapolis: Augsburg Publishing House, 1975.

________. *John's Story of Jesus*. Philadelphia: Fortress, 1984.

________. *John: The Maverick Gospel*. Revised edition. Louisville, KY:

Westminster / John Knox Press, 1993.

Ladd, G. E. "Eschatology and the Unity of New Testament Theology." *ExpTim* 68 (1956): 268–73.

________. *Jesus and the Kingdom: The Eschatology of Biblical Realism*. New York: Harper & Row, 1964.

________. "The Search for Perspective." *Int* 25 (1971): 41–62.

la Potterie, I. de. "Naître de l'eau et naître de l'Esprit. Le texte baptismal de Jn 3,5." In *La Vie selon l'Esprit, Condition du chrétien*, edited by I. de la Potterie and S. Lyonnet, 31–63. Unam Sanctam 55. Paris: Cerf, 1965.

Leal, J., S. J. "El simbolismo histórico del iv evangelio." *Estudios bíblicos* 19 (1960): 229–348.

Leaney, A. R. C. "The Johannine Paraclete and the Qumran Scrolls." In *John and the Dead Sea Scrolls*, edited by J. H. Charlesworth, 38–61. Christian Origins Library. New York: Crossroad, 1990.

Lee, D. A. *The Symbolic Narratives of the Fourth Gospel: The Interplay of Form and Meaning*. JSNTSup 95. Sheffield: JSOT, 1994.

Lee-Pollard, D. A. "The Symbolic Narratives of the Fourth Gospel: The Interplay of Form and Meaning." Thesis, University of Sydney, 1991.

Leidig, E. *Jesu Gespräch mit der Samaritanerin und weitere Gespräche im Johannesevangelium*. Band XV der theologischen Dissertationen, herausgegeben von B. Reicke. Basel: Friedrich Reinhardt Kommissionsverlag, 1979.

Léon-Dufour, X. "Towards a Symbolic Reading of the Fourth Gospel." *NTS* 27 (1981): 439–56.

Leroy, H. *Rätsel und Missverständnis: Ein Beitrag zur Formgeschichte des Johannesevangeliums*. Bonn Biblische Beitrage 30. Bonn: Peter

Hanstein, 1968.

Lightfoot, R. H. *St. John's Gospel: A Commentary with the Text of the Revised Version*. Edited by C. F. Evans. Oxford: Clarendon Press, 1956.

Lincoln, A. T. *Ephesians*. WBC, vol. 42. Dallas, TX: Word Books Publisher, 1990.

Lindars, B. *Behind the Fourth Gospel*. London: SPCK, 1971.

________. *The Gospel of John*. Edited by R. E. Clements and M. Black. New Century Bible. Grand Rapids: Eerdmans, 1981.

Lohmeyer, E. "Über Aufbau und Gliederung des vierten Evangeliums." *ZNW* 27 (1928): 11–36.

Longenecker, R. *The Christology of Early Jewish Christianity*. SBT 2/17. London: SCM, 1970.

Louw, J. P. "On Johannine Style." *Neot* 20 (1986): 5–12.

Louw, J. P., and E. A. Nida, eds. *Greek-English Lexicon of the New Testament Period: Based on Semantic Domains*. 2d ed. Vol. 2, *Introduction and Domains*. New York: UBS, 1989.

Macdonald, J. *Theology of the Samaritans*. Philadelphia: Westminster Press, 1964.

MacDonald, W. G. "Problems of Pneumatology in Christology: The Relationship of Christ and the Holy Spirit in Biblical Theology." Dissertation, Southern Baptist Theological Seminary, 1970.

Mack, B. L. *Rhetoric and the New Testament*. Philadelphia: Fortress, 1990.

MacRae, G. W., S. J. "Theology and Irony in the Fourth Gospel." In *The Word in the World: Essays in Honor of Frederick Moriarty*, edited by R. J. Clifford and G. W. MacRae, 83–96. Cambridge, MA: Weston

College Press, 1973.

Malatesta, E. *St. John's Gospel 1920–1965*. Rome: Biblical Institute Press, 1967.

Manns, F. *Le symbole eau-Esprit dans le Judaisme ancien*. Studium Biblicum Franciscanum Analecta 19. Jerusalem: Franciscan Printing Press, 1983.

Marshall, I. H. *The Epistles of John*.NICNT.Grand Rapids: Eerdmans,1978.

________. "The Problem of New Testament Exegesis [John 4]." *JETS* 17 (1974): 172–76.

Martyn, J. L. *History and Theology in the Fourth Gospel*. 2d ed. Nashville: Abingdon, 1979.

Mathiot, E. "Du Texte Au Sermon: Jean 4/42." *Etudes Théologiques et Religieuses* 48, no. 3 (1973): 265–73.

McCool, F. J. "Living Water in John." In *The Bible in Current Catholic Thought*, edited by J. L. McKenzie, 226–33. New York: Herder, 1962.

Meeks, W. A. "The Divine Agent and His Counterfeit in Philo and the Fourth Gospel." In *Aspects of Religious Propaganda in Judaism and Early Christianity*, edited by E. S. Fiorenza, 43–67. Notre Dame, IN: University of Notre Dame Press, 1976.

________. "Galilee and Judea in the Fourth Gospel." *JBL* 85 (1966): 159–69.

________. "Man from Heaven in Johannine Sectarianism." *JBL* 91 (1972): 44–72.

________. *The Prophet-King: Moses Traditions and the Johannine Christology*. Leiden: E. J. Brill, 1967.

Menken, M. J. J. *Numerical Literary Techniques in John: The Fourth*

Evangelist's Use of Numbers of Words and Syllables. NovTSup 55. Leiden: E. J. Brill, 1985.

Meyer, P. W. "The Eschatology of the Fourth Gospel: A Study in Early Christian Reinterpretation." Dissertation, Union Theological Seminary, 1955.

Meyers, C. L., and E. M. Meyers. *Zechariah 9–14: A New Translation with Introduction and Commentary*. AB, vol. 25c. Garden City, NY: Doubleday, 1993.

Michaels, J. R. *1 Peter*. WBC, vol. 49. Waco, TX: Word Books Publisher, 1988.

Milgrom, J. *Numbers: The Traditional Hebrew Text with the New JPS Translation*. The JPS Torah Commentary. Philadelphia: The Jewish Publication Society, 1990.

Minor, M. *Literary-Critical Approaches to the Bible: An Annotated Bibliography*. West Cornwall, CT: Locust Hill Press, 1992.

Mlakuzhyil, G. *The Christocentric Literary Structure of the Fourth Gospel*. AnBib 117. Rome: Pontifical Biblical Institute, 1987.

Montgomery, J. *The Samaritans: The Earliest Jewish Sect; Their History, Theology, and Literature*. Philadelphia: The John C. Winston Co., 1907.

Moo, D. J. *The Old Testament in the Gospel Passion Narratives*. Sheffield: The Almond Press, 1983.

Moore, R. R. "Soteriology and Structure: A Study of the Relation between the Soteriology and Present Literary Structure of the Fourth Gospel." Dissertation, Emory University, 1982.

Moore, S. D. *Literary Criticism and the Gospels: The Theoretical Challenge*. New Haven: Yale University Press, 1989.

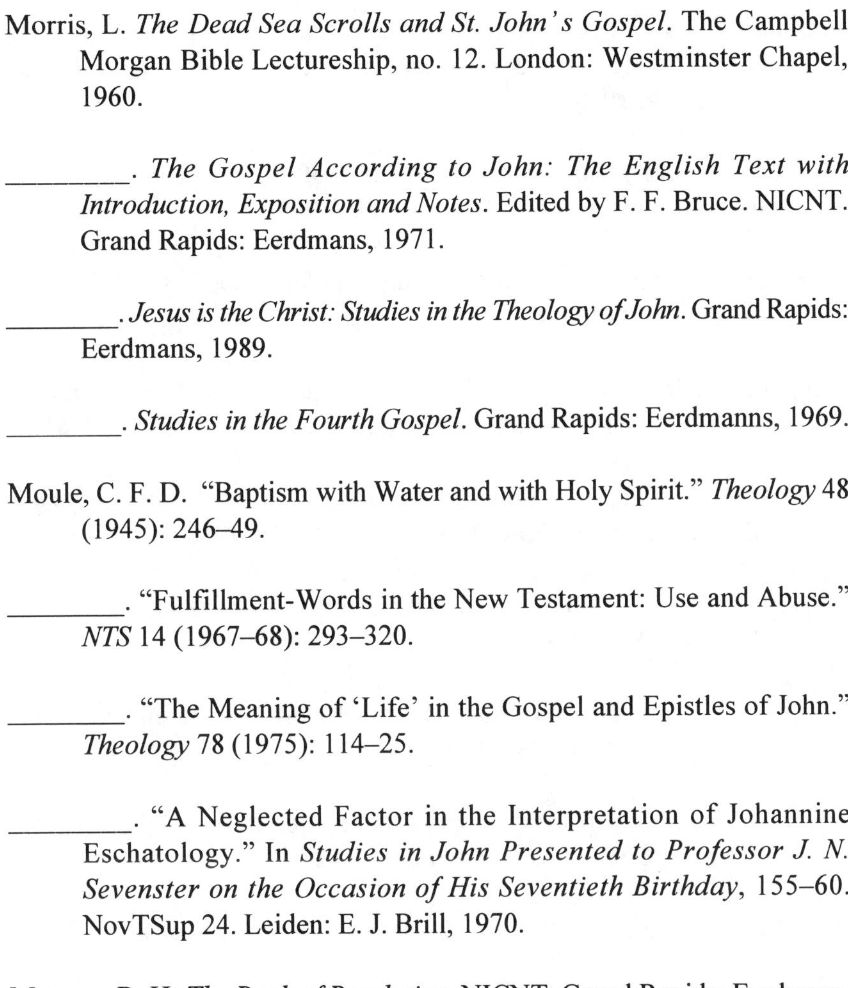

Morris, L. *The Dead Sea Scrolls and St. John's Gospel*. The Campbell Morgan Bible Lectureship, no. 12. London: Westminster Chapel, 1960.

________. *The Gospel According to John: The English Text with Introduction, Exposition and Notes*. Edited by F. F. Bruce. NICNT. Grand Rapids: Eerdmans, 1971.

________. *Jesus is the Christ: Studies in the Theology of John*. Grand Rapids: Eerdmans, 1989.

________. *Studies in the Fourth Gospel*. Grand Rapids: Eerdmanns, 1969.

Moule, C. F. D. "Baptism with Water and with Holy Spirit." *Theology* 48 (1945): 246–49.

________. "Fulfillment-Words in the New Testament: Use and Abuse." *NTS* 14 (1967–68): 293–320.

________. "The Meaning of 'Life' in the Gospel and Epistles of John." *Theology* 78 (1975): 114–25.

________. "A Neglected Factor in the Interpretation of Johannine Eschatology." In *Studies in John Presented to Professor J. N. Sevenster on the Occasion of His Seventieth Birthday*, 155–60. NovTSup 24. Leiden: E. J. Brill, 1970.

Mounce, R. H. *The Book of Revelation*. NICNT. Grand Rapids: Eerdmans, 1977.

Mowry, L. "The Dead Sea Scrolls and the Background for the Gospel of John." *BA* 17 (1954): 78–97.

Muecke, D. C. *Irony*. The Critical Idiom 13. London: Methuen & Co., 1970.

Muilenberg, J. "Literary Form in the Fourth Gospel." *JBL* 51 (1932): 40–53.

Mussner, F. "NT Theology: III Johannine Theology." In *Sacramentum Mundi*. 6 vols., edited by K. Rahner, 4:227–31. New York: Herder and Herder, 1969.

Myers, D. E. "Irony and Humor in the Gospel of John." *Occasional Papers in Translation and Text Linguistics* 2 (1988): 1–13.

Neirynck, F. "John 4: 46–51: Signs Source and/or Synoptic Gospels." *ETL* 60, no. 4 (1984): 367–75.

Neugebauer, Johannes von. "Die Textbezüge von Joh 4,1–42 und die Geschichte der johanneischen Gruppe," *ZNW* 84 (1993): 135-41.

Newman, B. M., and E. A. Nida. *A Translator's Handbook on the Gospel of John. Helps for Translators*. London: UBS, 1980.

Neyrey, J. H. "Jacob Traditions and the Interpretation of John 4:10–26." *CBQ* 41 (1979): 419–37.

________. "John 3—A Debate Over Johannine Epistemology and Christology." *NovT* 23 (1981): 115–27.

Ng, W. "Johannine Eschatology as Demonstrated in First John." Thesis, Westminster Theological Seminary, 1988.

Nicol, W. *The Semeia in the Fourth Gospel*. Leiden: E. J. Brill, 1972.

Niewalda, P. *Sakramentssymbolik im Johannesevangelium?* Limburg: Lahn, 1958.

O'Day, G. R. "Narrative Mode and Theological Claim: A Study in the Fourth Gospel." *JBL* 105 (1986): 657–68.

________. *Revelation in the Fourth Gospel: Narrative Mode and Theological Claim*. Philadelphia: Fortress, 1986.

________. *The Word Disclosed: John's Story and Narrative Preaching*. St. Louis, MO: CBP, 1987.

Odeberg, H. *The Fourth Gospel Interpreted in Its Relation to Contemporaneous Religious Currents in Palestine and the Hellenistic-Oriental World.* Uppsala: Almquist & Wiksell, 1929.

Okure, T. *The Johannine Approach to Mission: A Contextual Study of John 4:1–42*. WUNT 31. Tübingen: Mohr, 1988.

Olsson, B. *Structure and Meaning in the Fourth Gospel: A Text-Linguistic Analysis of John 2:1–11 and 2:1–42*. Translated by J. Gray. Coniectanea Biblica, New Testament 6. Lund: Gleerup, 1974.

O'Rourke, J. "John's Fulfillment Texts." *Sciences Ecclesiastiques* 19 (1967): 433–44.

Østenstad, G. "The Structure of the Fourth Gospel: Can It Be Defined Objectively." *ST* 45 (1991): 33–55.

Ousersluys, R. C. "Eschatology and the Holy Spirit." *RTR* 19 (1965): 3–12.

Owanga-Welo, J. "The Function and Meaning of the Footwashing in the Johannine Passion Narrative: A Structural Approach." Dissertation, Emory University, 1980.

Pagels, E. H. *The Johannine Gospel in Gnostic Exegesis*. Nashville: Abingdon, 1973.

Pahk, Sung Sang. "Structural Analysis of John VI:1–58: Meaning of the Symbol 'Bread of Life.'" Dissertation, Vanderbilt University, 1984.

Painter, J. "Eschatological Faith in the Gospel of John." In *Reconciliation and Hope: New Testament Essays on Atonement and Eschatology: Presented to L. L. Morris on His Sixtieth Birthday*, edited by R. Banks, 36–52. Exeter: Paternoster, 1974.

________. "John 9 and the Interpretation of the Fourth Gospel." *JSNT* 28 (1986): 31–61.

Pamment, M. “Eschatology and the Fourth Gospel.” *JSNT* 25 (1982): 81–85.

________. “Is There Convincing Evidence of Samaritan Influence on the Fourth Gospel?” *ZNW* 73 (1982): 121–30.

Parratt, J. K. “The Holy Spirit and Baptism.” *ExpTim* 82 (1971): 333–35.

Paschal, R. W. Jr. “Sacramental Symbolism and Physical Imagery in the Gospel of John.” *TynBul* (1981): 151–76.

Pascher, J. “Der Glauben als Mitteilung des Pneumas nach Jo 6,61–65.” *Tübingen Theologische Quartalschrift* 117 (1936): 301–21.

Pazdan, M. M. “Nicodemus and the Samaritan Woman: Contrasting Models of Discipleship.” *BTB* 17 (1987): 145–48.

Phillips, G. L. “Faith and Vision in the Fourth Gospel.” In *Studies in the Fourth Gospel*, edited by F. L. Cross, 83–96. London: Mowbray, 1957.

Plummer, A. *The Gospel According to St John: With Maps, Notes and Introduction*. Cambridge: Cambridge University Press, 1912.

Poffet, J. M. “La méthode exégétique d’Héracléon et d’Origène, Commentateurs de Jn 4: Jésus, la Samaritaine et les Samaritains.” *TLZ* 112, no. 2 (1987): 128–30.

Pollard, T. E. *Johannine Christology and the Early Church*. Cambridge: Cambridge University Press, 1970.

Porsch, F. *Pneuma und Wort: Ein exegetischer Beitrag zur Pneumatologie des Johannesevangeliums*. Frankfurter Theologische Studien, no. 16. Frankfurt: Knecht, 1974.

Porter, S. E. “Can Traditional Exegesis Enlighten Literary Analysis of the Fourth Gospel? An Examination of the Old Testament Fulfilment Motif and the Passover Theme.” In *The Gospels and the Scriptures of Israel*, edited by C. A. Evans and W. R. Stegner, 396–428. JSNTSup 104. Sheffield: Sheffield Academic Press, 1994.

Poythress, V. S. *The Shadow of Christ in the Law of Moses*. New Jersey: Presbyterian and Reformed Publishing Co., 1991.

Price, J. L. "Light from Qumran Upon Some Aspects of Johannine Theology." In *John and the Dead Sea Scrolls*, edited by J. H. Charlesworth, 9–37. Christian Origins Library. New York: Crossroad, 1990.

Purvis, J. D. "The Fourth Gospel and the Samaritans." *NovT* 17 (1975): 166–68.

Quispel, G. "Qumran, John, and Jewish Christianity." In *John and the Dead Sea Scrolls*, edited by J. H. Charlesworth, 137–55. Christian Origins Library. New York: Crossroad, 1990.

Ralinson, A. E. J. "In Spirit and in Truth: An Exposition of St. John 4:16–24." *ExpTim* 44 (1932): 12–14.

Reim, G. *Studien zum alttestamentlichen Hintergrund des Johannesevangelium*. SNTSMS 22. Cambridge: Cambridge University Press, 1974.

Rena, J. "Women in the Gospel of John." *Église et Théologie* 17 (1986): 131–47.

Rhees, R. "The Fourth Gospel." In *The Bible as Literature*, edited by L. Abbott, 281–97. New York: Thomas Y. Croell & Co., 1986.

Ricca, P. *Die Eschatologie des vierten Evangeliums*. Zürich: Gotthelf, 1966.

Richards, E. "Expressions of Double Meaning and Their Function in the Gospel of John." *NTS* 31 (1985): 96–112.

Richardson, A. *The Gospel According to St. John*. Torch Bible Commentary. London: SCM, 1959.

________. *An Introduction to the Theology of the New Testament*. New York: Harper & Row, 1958.

Richter, G. "Blut und Wasser aus der durchbohrten Seite Jesu (Joh 19,34b)." In *Studien Zum Johannesevangelium*, edited by J. Hainz, 120–42. Regensburg: Pustet, 1977.

Ricoeur, P. *Interpretation Theory: Discourse and the Surplus of Meaning*. Fort Worth: Texas Christian University Press, 1976.

________. *Le conflit des interprétations. Essais d'herméneutique*. Paris: Éditions du Seuil, 1969.

Ridderbos, H. *The Coming of the Kingdom*. Translated by H. de Jongste. Philadelphia: Presbyterian and Reformed Publishing Co., 1962.

________. *When the Time Had Fully Come*. Reprinted edition. Ontario: Paideia Press, 1982.

Ringe, S. H. "On the Gospel of John: The Gospel as Healing Word." *Quarterly Review* 6, no. 4 (1986): 75–103.

Ringgren, H. *The Faith of Qumran: Theology of the Dead Sea Scrolls*. Translated by E. T. Sanders. Philadelphia: Fortress, 1963.

Rissi, M. "Der Aufbau des vierten Evangeliums." *NTS* 29 (1983): 48–54.

Robertson, A. T. *A Grammar of the Greek New Testament in Light of Historical Research*. Nashville: Broadmann, 1934.

Robinson, D. W. B. "Born of Water and Spirit: Does John 3:5 Refer to Baptism?" *RTR* 25 (1966): 15–23.

Robinson, J. A. T. "The Baptism of John and the Qumran Community." *HTR* 50 (1957): 175–91.

________. "The Destination and Purpose of St. John's Gospel." *NTS* 6 (1959–60): 117–31.

________. "The Destination and Purpose of the Johannine Epistles." *NTS* 7 (1960–61): 56–65.

________. *Jesus and His Coming*. London: SCM, 1979.

________. "The Johannine Trajectory." In *Trajectories Through Early Christianity*, edited by J. M. Robinson and H. Koester, 232–52. Philadelphia: Fortress, 1971.

________. "The New Look on the Fourth Gospel." *SE* 1 (1959): 338–50.

________. "The 'Others' of John 4,38: A Test of Exegetical Method." *SE* 1 (1959): 510–15.

________. "Recent Research in the Fourth Gospel." *JBL* 78 (1959): 242–53.

________. "The Use of the Fourth Gospel in Christology Today." In *Christ and Spirit in the New Testament: Studies in Honour of C. F. D. Moule*, edited by B. Lindars and S. Smalley, 61–78. Cambridge: Cambridge University Press, 1973.

Rogers, T. F. "The Gospel of John as Literature." *Brigham Young University Studies* 28, no. 3 (1988): 67–80.

Rossow, F. C. "Dramatic Irony in the Bible—With a Difference." *Concordia Journal* 8 (1982): 48–52.

Roth, W. "Scriptural Coding in the Fourth Gospel." *BR* 32 (1987): 6–29.

Ruland, V. "Sign and Sacrament: John's Bread of Life Discourse." *Int* 18 (1964): 450–62.

Russell, E. A. "The Holy Spirit in the Fourth Gospel." *IBS* 2 (1980): 84–94.

Sahlin, H. *Zur Typologie des Johannesevangeliums*. Uppsala: Almquist & Wiksell, 1950.

Sanders, J. N. *The Fourth Gospel in the Early Church: Its Origin and Influence on Christian Theology up to Irenaeus*. Cambridge: Cambridge University Press, 1943.

Sanders, J. N., and B. A. Mastin. *A Commentary on the Gospel According to St. John*. Edited by H. Chadwick. Harper's New Testament Commentaries. New York: Harper & Row, 1968.

Sava, A. F. "The Wound in the Side of Christ." *CBQ* 19 (1957): 343–46.

Schlatter, A. *Der Evangelist Johannes*. 3 vols. Stuttgart: Calwer Verlag, 1960.

Schmid, L. "Die Komposition der Samaria-Szene John 4:1–42." *ZNW* 28 (1929): 148–58.

Schmidt, T. E., and M. Silva, eds. *To Tell the Mystery: Essays on New Testament Eschatology in Honor of Robert H. Gundry*. JSNTSup 100. Sheffield: JSOT, 1994.

Schnackenburg, R. "Die 'anbetung in Geist und Wahrheit' (Joh 4,23) im Licht von Qumran Texten." *BZ* 3 (1959): 88–94.

________. *God's Rule and Kingdom*. Translated by J. Murray. New York: Herder, 1963.

________. *The Gospel According to St John*. Vols. 1 & 2, translated by K. Smith et al. Herder's Theological Commentary on the New Testament. New York: Seabury, 1980.

________. *The Gospel According to St John*. Vol. 1, translated by D. Smith et al. Herder's Theological Commentary on the New Testament. New York: Crossroad, 1982.

________. *Die Johannesbriefe*. 3d ed. Herders theologischer Kommentar zum Neuen Testament. Freiburg: Herder, 1963.

________. *Present and Future: Modern Aspects of New Testament Theology*.

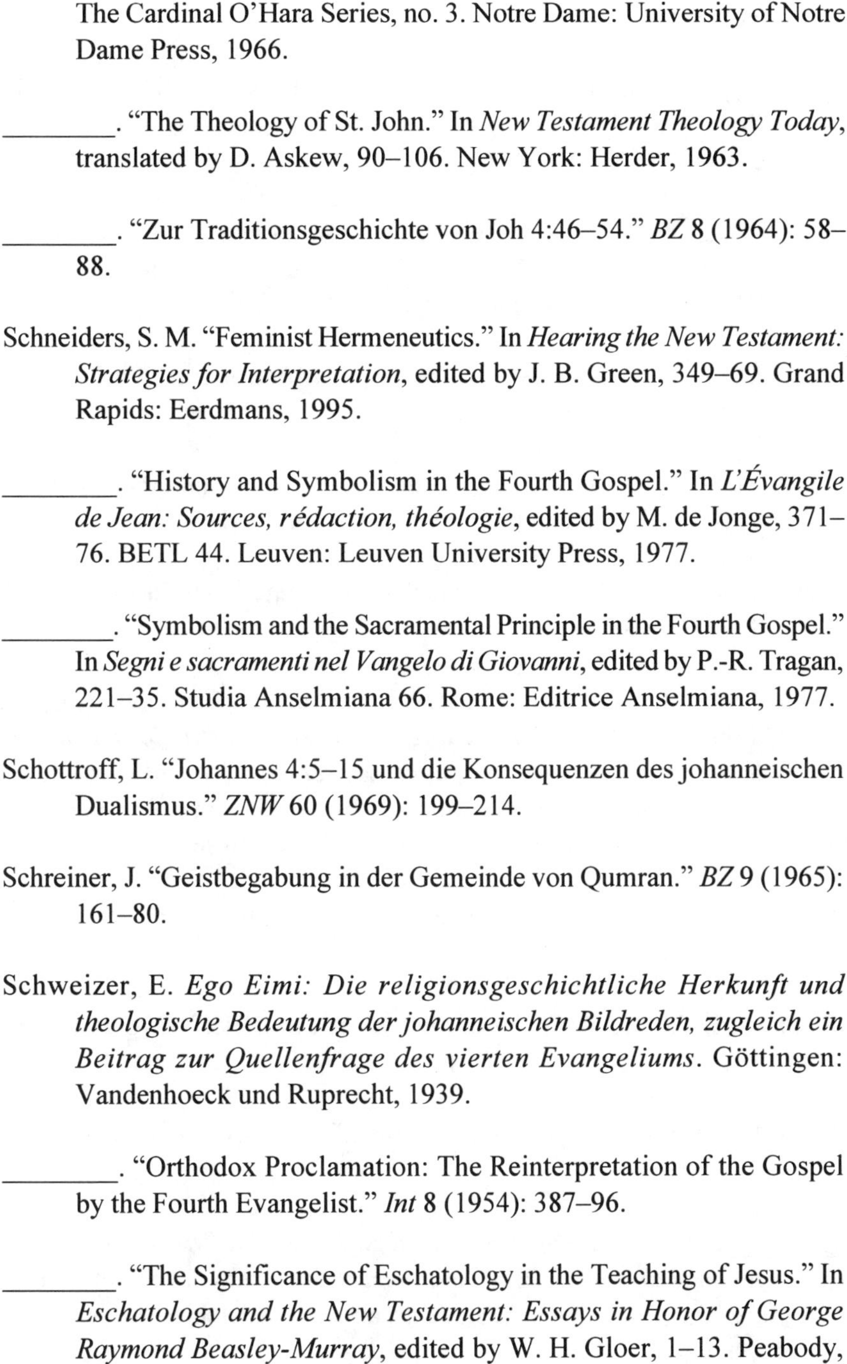

The Cardinal O'Hara Series, no. 3. Notre Dame: University of Notre Dame Press, 1966.

________. "The Theology of St. John." In *New Testament Theology Today*, translated by D. Askew, 90–106. New York: Herder, 1963.

________. "Zur Traditionsgeschichte von Joh 4:46–54." *BZ* 8 (1964): 58–88.

Schneiders, S. M. "Feminist Hermeneutics." In *Hearing the New Testament: Strategies for Interpretation*, edited by J. B. Green, 349–69. Grand Rapids: Eerdmans, 1995.

________. "History and Symbolism in the Fourth Gospel." In *L'Évangile de Jean: Sources, rédaction, théologie*, edited by M. de Jonge, 371–76. BETL 44. Leuven: Leuven University Press, 1977.

________. "Symbolism and the Sacramental Principle in the Fourth Gospel." In *Segni e sacramenti nel Vangelo di Giovanni*, edited by P.-R. Tragan, 221–35. Studia Anselmiana 66. Rome: Editrice Anselmiana, 1977.

Schottroff, L. "Johannes 4:5–15 und die Konsequenzen des johanneischen Dualismus." *ZNW* 60 (1969): 199–214.

Schreiner, J. "Geistbegabung in der Gemeinde von Qumran." *BZ* 9 (1965): 161–80.

Schweizer, E. *Ego Eimi: Die religionsgeschichtliche Herkunft und theologische Bedeutung der johanneischen Bildreden, zugleich ein Beitrag zur Quellenfrage des vierten Evangeliums*. Göttingen: Vandenhoeck und Ruprecht, 1939.

________. "Orthodox Proclamation: The Reinterpretation of the Gospel by the Fourth Evangelist." *Int* 8 (1954): 387–96.

________. "The Significance of Eschatology in the Teaching of Jesus." In *Eschatology and the New Testament: Essays in Honor of George Raymond Beasley-Murray*, edited by W. H. Gloer, 1–13. Peabody,

MA: Hendrickson, 1988.

________. "The Spirit of Power: The Uniformity and Diversity of the Concept of the Holy Spirit in the New Testament." *Int* 6 (1952): 259–78.

Sciberras, L. "Water in the Gospel of St. John According to the Greek Fathers and Writers of the Church." Thesis for the licentiate, Studium Biblicum Franciscanum, Jerusalem, 1974–75.

Scobie, C. H. H. "The Origins and Development of Samaritan Christianity." *NTS* 19 (1972–73): 390–414.

Scott, M. V. "The Eschatology of the Fourth Gospel and the Johannine Epistles." Dissertation, Edinburgh University, 1953.

Scroggs, R. "The Eschatology of the Spirit by Some Early Christians." *JBL* 84 (1965): 359–73.

Seim, T. K. "Roles of Women in the Gospel of John." In *Aspects on the Johannine Literature: Papers Presented at a Conference of Scandinavian New Testament Exegetes at Uppsala*, edited by L. Hartman and B. Olsson, 56–73. Coniectanea biblica, New Testament Series 18. Uppsala: Almqvist & Wiksell, 1987.

Shorter, M. "The Position of Chapter 6 in the Fourth Gospel." *ExpTim* 84 (1973): 181–83.

Siegman, E. F. "St John's Use of the Synoptic Material." *CBQ* 30 (1968): 182–98.

Silva, M. "Approaching the Fourth Gospel." *Criswell Theological Review* 3 (1988): 17–29.

________. "The Present State of Johannine Studies." In *The Gospels Today: A Guide to Some Recent Developments*, edited by J. H. Skilton, 114–22. The New Testament Students, no. 6. Philadelphia: Skilton House, 1990.

Simon, U. E. "Eternal Life in the Fourth Gospel." In *Studies in the Fourth Gospel*, edited by F. L. Cross, 97–109. London: Mowbray, 1957.

Smalley, S. S. "Diversity and Development in John." *NTS* 17 (1970–71): 276–92.

________. *John: Evangelist and Interpreter*. Nashville: Thomas Nelson, 1983.

________. "New Light on the Fourth Gospel." *TynBul* 17 (1966): 35–62.

________. *1, 2, 3 John*. WBC, vol. 51. Waco, TX: Word Books Publisher, 1984.

Smith, D. M. *The Composition and Order of the Fourth Gospel—Bultmann's Literary Theory*. New Haven: Yale University Press, 1965.

________. "The Presentation of Jesus in the Fourth Gospel." *Int* 31 (1977): 367–78.

Smith, R. H. "Exodus Typology in the Fourth Gospel." *JBL* 81 (1962): 329–42.

Snaith, H. H. "The Spirit of God in Jewish Thought." In *The Doctrine of the Holy Spirit*, 9–38. Headingly Lectures, 1937. London: Epworth, 1937.

Sparks, H. F. D. *The Johannine Synopsis of the Gospels*. New York: Harper & Row, 1974.

Spriggs, D. G. "Meaning of Water in John 3:5." *ExpTim* 85 (1974): 149–50.

Stagg, F. "Orthodoxy and Orthopraxy in the Johannine Epistles." *RevExp* 67 (1970): 423–32.

Stählin, G. "Zum Problem der johanneischen Eschatologie." *ZNW* 33 (1934): 225–59.

Staley, J. “The Structure of John’s Prologue: Its Implication for the Gospel’s Narrative Structure.” *CBQ* 48 (1986): 241–64.

Staley, J. L. “The Print’s First Kiss: A Rhetorical Investigation of the Implied Reader in the Fourth Gospel.” SBLDS 82. Atlanta: Scholars Press, 1988.

Stanley, D. M. “From His Heart Will Flow Rivers of Living Water (John 7:38).” In *Cor Jesu I*, 509–42. Commentationes in Litteras Encyclicas, “Haurietis Aguas.” Roma: Herder, 1959.

Stemberger, G. *La symbolique du bien et du mal selon saint Jean*. Parole de Dieu. Paris: Éditions du Seuil, 1970.

Stewart, J. S. “On a Neglected Emphasis in New Testament Theology.” *SJT* 4 (1951): 292–301.

Stibbe, M. W. G. *John as Storyteller: Narrative Criticism and the Fourth Gospel*. SNTSMS 73. Cambridge: Cambridge University Press, 1992.

________. *John’s Gospel*. London: Routledge, 1994.

________, ed. *The Gospel of John as Literature: An Anthology of Twentieth-Century Perspectives*. Leiden: E. J. Brill, 1993.

Stöger, A. “Sinnerfülltes Leben: Joh 4.” In *Verbum caro factum est*, edited by H. Schurmann and J. Marbock, 39–43. Vienna, Austria: Niederösterreichisches Pressehaus, 1984.

Strachan, R. H. *The Fourth Gospel: Its Significance and Environment*. 3d ed. London: SCM, 1947.

Strack, H. L., and P. Billerbeck. *Kommentar zum Neuen Testament aus Talmud und Midrasch*. 3d ed. München: Beck, 1961.

Summers, R. “The Johannine View of the Future Life.” *RevExp* 58 (1961): 331–47.

Swain, L. *The Gospel According to John for Spiritual Reading*. London: Sheed and Ward, 1978.

Swete, H. B. *Commentary on Revelation: The Greek Text with Introduction, Notes and Indexes*. 3d ed. London: Macmillan, 1911; reprint, Grand Rapids: Kregel Publications, 1977.

Tasker, R. V. G. *The Gospel According to St. John: An Introduction and Commentary*. The Tyndale New Testament Commentaries. Grand Rapids: Eerdmans, 1960.

________. "Qumran and the Origin of the Fourth Gospel." *NovT* 4 (1960): 6–25.

Temple, S. *The Core of the Fourth Gospel*. London: Mowbray, 1975.

Temple, W. *Readings in St. John's Gospel*. London: Macmillan, 1959.

Terry, F. "Jesus and the Era of the Spirit." *HeyJ* 51 (1952–53): 10–15.

Thomas, R. L. *Revelation 8–22: An Exegetical Commentary*. Chicago: Moody, 1995.

Thompson, J. D. "An Analysis of Present and Future in the Eschatology of the Fourth Gospel, and An Examination of the Theological Relationship between the Two." Dissertation, Emory University, 1967.

Thyen, H. "Aus der Literatur zum Johannesevangelium." *TRu* 39 (1974–75): 1–69, 222–52, 289–330; 43 (1978): 328–59; 44 (1979): 97–134.

Töpel, L. J. "A note on Methodology of Structural Analysis in John 2:23–3:21." *CBQ* 33 (1971):211–20.

Turner, M. M. B. "The Concept of Receiving the Spirit in John's Gospel." *Vox Evangelica* 10 (1976): 24–42.

Turner, N. *A Grammar of New Testament Greek*. Vols. 3 and 4 of Moulton

Series. Edinburgh: T. & T. Clark, 1963–76.

Turner, W. "Believing and Everlasting Life; A Johannine Inquiry." *ExpTim* 64 (1952): 50–52.

Van Aarde, A. G. "Narrative Criticism Applied to John 4:43–54." In *Text and Interpretation: New Approaches in the Criticism of the New Testament*, edited by P. J. Hartin and J. H. Petzer, 101–28. Leiden: E. J. Brill, 1991.

Van Belle, G. *Johannine Bibliography 1966–1985: A Cumulative Bibliography on the Fourth Gospel*. BETL 82. Leuven: Leuven University Press, 1988.

________. "Johannine Style Characteristics." Appendix 2 in *The Sign Source in the Fourth Gospel: Historical Survey and Critical Evaluation of the Semeia Hypothesis*. BETL 116. Leuven: Leuven University Press, 1994.

Vanderlip, D. G. *Christianity According to John*. Philadelphia: Westminster Press, 1975.

________. *John: The Gospel of Life*. Valley Forge, PA: Judson, 1979.

Van der Waal, C. "The Gospel According to John and the Old Testament." *Neot* 6 (1972): 28–47.

Van Hartingsveld, L. *Die Eschatologie des Johannesevangeliums: Eine Auseinandersetzung mit Rudolf Bultmann*. Assen: Van Gorcum, 1962.

Van Tilborg, S. "The Gospel of John: Communicative Processes in a Narrative Text." *Neot* 23 (1989): 19–31.

Van Unnik, W. C. "A Greek Characteristic of Prophecy in the Fourth Gospel." In *Text and Interpretation: Studies in the New Testament Presented to Matthew Black*, edited by E. Best and R. McL. Wilson, 211–29. Cambridge: Cambridge University Press, 1979.

Vawter, B. "Ezekiel and John." *CBQ* 26 (1964): 450–58.

________. "John's Doctrine of the Spirit: A Summary of His Eschatology." In *A Companion to John*, edited by M. J. Taylor, 177–85. New York: Alba, 1977.

________. "Some Recent Developments in Johannine Theology." *BTB* 1 (1970): 30–58.

Verhoef, P. A. "Some Thoughts on the Present-Day Situation in Biblical Theology." *WTJ* 33 (1970–71): 1–19.

Volz, P. *Die Eschatologie der jüdischen Gemeinde im neutestamentlichen Zeitalter nach den Quellen der rabbinischen apokalyptischen und apokryphen Literatur*. 2d ed. Tübingen: Mohr-Siebeck, 1934.

Vorster, W. S. "The Gospel of John as Language." *Neot* 6 (1972): 19–27.

Vos, G. *Biblical Theology: Old and New Testaments*. Grand Rapids: Eerdmans, 1948.

Wallace, D. B. "The Semantics and Exegetical Significance of the Object-complement Construction in the New Testament." *Grace Theological Journal* 6, no. 1 (1985): 91–112.

Warner, M. "The Fourth Gospel's Art of Rational Persuasion." In *The Bible as Rhetoric: Studies in Biblical Persuasion and Credibility*, edited by M. Warner, 153–77. London: Routledge, 1990.

Watson, W. G. E. "Antecedents of a New Testament Proverb." *VT* 20 (1970): 368–70.

Watts, D. J. "Eschatology in the Johannine Community: A Study of Diversity." Dissertation, University of Edinburgh, 1980.

Wead, D. W. "The Johannine Double Meaning." *ResQ* 2 (1970): 106–20.

________. "Johannine Irony as a Key to the Author-Audience Relationship in John's Gospel." In *American Academy of Religion Biblical Literature: 1974*, compiled by F. O. Francis, 33–50. Missoula, MT: Scholars Press, 1974.

________. *The Literary Devices in John's Gospel.* Theologischen Dissertation no. 4. Basel: Fredrich Reinhardt Kommissionsverlag, 1970.

Webster, E. C. "Pattern in the Fourth Gospel." In *Art and Meaning: Rhetoric in Biblical Literature*, edited by D. J. Clines, D. M. Gunn, and A. J. Hauser, 230–57. Sheffield: JSOT, 1982.

Weisengoff, J. P. "Light and Its Relation to Life in St. John." *CBQ* 8 (1946): 448–51.

Wenham, D. "Spirit and Life: Some Reflections on Johannine Theology." *Themelios* 6 (1980): 4–8.

Westcott, B. F. *The Gospel According to St. John: The Authorized Version with Introduction and Notes*. Grand Rapids: Eerdmans, 1908; reprint, 1973.

Wheelwright, P. E. *The Burning Fountain*. Bloomington, IN: Indiana University Press, 1954.

________. *Metaphor and Reality*. Bloomington, IN: Indiana University Press, 1962.

Wilckens, U. "Der eucharistische Abschnitt der johanneischen Rede vom Lebensbrot (Joh 6,51c–58)." In *Neues Testament und Kirche. Für Rudolf Schnackenburg*, edited by J. Gnilka, 220–48. Freiburg: Herder, 1974.

Wilder, A. N. *The Language of the Gospel: Early Christian Rhetoric*. New York: Harper & Row, 1964.

Wiles, M. F. *The Spiritual Gospel: The Interpretation of the Fourth Gospel in the Early Church.* Cambridge: Cambridge University Press, 1960.

Wilson, W. G. "An Examination of the Linguistic Evidence Adduced Against the Unity of Authorship of the First Epistle of John and the Fourth Gospel." *JTS* 49 (1948): 147–56.

Windisch, H. "Jesus und der Geist im Johannesevangelium." In *Amicitiae Corolla: A Volume of Essays Presented to Dr. James Rendel Harris on His 80th Birthday*, edited by H. G. Wood, 303–18. London: University of London Press, 1933.

________. "Der Johanneische Erzählungsstil." In EYXAPISTHPION: Studien zur Religion und Literatur des Alten und Neuen Testaments, Hermann Gunkel zum 60. Geburtstags, edited by H. Schmidt, 174–213. Göttingen: Vandenhoeck & Ruprecht, 1923.

Witherington, B. III. "The Waters of Birth: John 3:5 and 1 John 5:6–8." *NTS* 35 (1989): 155–60.

Woodhouse, H. F. "The Spirit Was Not Yet Given." *Theology* 67 (1965): 310–12.

Woods, M. W. "The Use of the Old Testament in the Fourth Gospel: The Hermeneutical Method Employed in the Semeia and Its Significance for Contemporary Biblical Interpretation." Dissertation, Southwestern Baptist Theological Seminary, 1980.

Wyller, E. A. "In Solomon's Porch: A Henological Analysis of the Architectonic of the Fourth Gospel." *ST* 42 (1988): 151–67.

Yates, J. E. *The Spirit and the Kingdom*. London: SPCK, 1963.

Young, F. W. "A Study of the Relation of Isaiah to the Fourth Gospel." *ZNW* 46 (1955): 215–33.

Ziener, G. "Weisheitsbuck und Johannesevangelium." *Bib* 38 (1957): 329–42, 396–416.

INDEX OF AUTHORS

P

R

S

T

V

W

Z

Studies in Biblical Literature

This series invites manuscripts from scholars in any area of biblical literature. Both established and innovative methodologies, covering general and particular areas in biblical study, are welcome. The series seeks to make available studies that will make a significant contribution to the ongoing biblical discourse. Scholars who have interests in gender and sociocultural hermeneutics are particularly encouraged to consider this series.

For further information about the series and for the submission of manuscripts, contact:

Hemchand Gossai
Department of Religion
Muhlenberg College
2400 Chew Street
Allentown, PA 18104-5586

To order other books in this series, please contact our Customer Service Department:

(800) 770-LANG (within the U.S.)
(212) 647-7706 (outside the U.S.)
(212) 647-7707 FAX

or browse online by series at:

WWW.PETERLANG.COM